Frank L. Smiley

Professor Huntley has published over sixty articles on seventeenth-century English literature, and is particularly well known for his studies of Sir Thomas Browne. Among his books are *On Dryden's Essay of Dramatic Poesy* (1951), *Sir Thomas Browne: A Biographical and Critical Study* (1962), and *Jeremy Taylor and the Great Rebellion: a Study of his Mind and Temper in Controversy* (1970).

BISHOP JOSEPH HALL

1574–1656

A biographical and critical study

FRANK LIVINGSTONE HUNTLEY

D. S. Brewer Ltd · Cambridge

© 1979 Frank Livingstone Huntley

Published by D. S. Brewer Ltd.,
240 Hills Road, Cambridge and P. O. Box 24, Ipswich IP1 1JJ

First published 1979

British Library Cataloguing in Publication Data
Huntley, Frank Livingstone
Bishop Joseph Hall, 1574–1656.
1. Hall, Joseph 2. Church of England–Biography
283′.092′4   BX5199.H25

ISBN 0-85991-035-0

Photoset in Great Britain at the Benham Press
by William Clowes & Sons Limited, Colchester and Beccles

Printed and bound in Great Britain by
REDWOOD BURN LIMITED
Trowbridge & Esher

In memory of Jesse F. Mack,
who at Oberlin College in
Ohio first taught me to love
literature not merely for
its own sake

Contents

Preface

Joseph Hall was a part of England's seventeenth century – sharing its passionate concern for religion; the excitement of its politics; the rigour of its scholarship; its skill in rhetoric; and its distinction in literature.

Fascination with England in the seventeenth century transcends space and time. On a Fulbright lectureship many years ago I finished writing a book on Sir Thomas Browne in a comfortable Japanese room overlooking the Imperial Palace Gardens of the ancient and beautiful city of Kyoto. The present study was completed in Heidelberg, Germany, where as visitor to the university I was teaching the metaphysical poets. What a pleasure to work amidst stimulating colleagues and warm friends beside the Neckar River in the shadow of the great castle where Elizabeth, daughter of James I, lived with her Elector Palatine! Almost daily I walked past the Church of the Holy Spirit, where, in 1619, John Donne preached to her and her courtly retinue.

Most of my debts, I hope, are acknowledged in the notes, although I must be echoing throughout the wisdom and even the diction of un-identifiable scholar-friends. In this place I particularly want to thank the University of Michigan's Rackham School of Graduate Studies for the subvention with which to publish; three distinguished Fellows of Emmanuel College, Cambridge – Derek Brewer, Gordon Rupp, and Frank Stubbings; my former chairman and loyal friend, Russell Fraser; and my dear, charming, brave and witty wife of fifty years, 'Trink'.

The writing of every book involves some egotism. In attempting to reassess Joseph Hall, the man and his work and the times he lived in, I have been sustained by the words of another Anglican parson of the following century, the Reverend Lawrence Sterne:

The learned Bishop Hall, I mean the famous Dr Joseph Hall, who was Bishop of Exeter in King James the First's reign, tells us in one of his *Decads*, at the end of his divine art of meditation, . . . 'That it is an abominable thing for a man to commend himself;' – and I really think it is so.

And yet, on the other hand, when a thing is executed in a masterly kind of fashion, which thing is not likely to be found out; – I think it is full as abominable, that a man should lose the honour of it, and go out of the world with the conceit of it rotting in his head.

This is precisely my situation.

[*Tristram Shandy*, Book I, chapter 22]

Ann Arbor, Michigan
November 1976

1. *Beginnings*

Joseph Hall, an Anglican clergyman with moderate 'Puritan' leanings, contributed to a wide variety of literary and para-literary genres that flourished in England's seventeenth century. These include satire, meditation, character-writing, essays, sermons, casuistry, controversy, epistles and autobiography. The last named, under the title of 'Observations of Some Specialities in the Life of Joseph Hall, Bishop of Norwich, Written with his Own Hand' (it was written in prison),makes possible a fairly accurate outline for a biography of him. It has been the basis for the lives by John Jones (1826), George Lewis (1886), Canon Perry in the *Dictionary of National Biography*, Arnold Davenport in the introduction to his edition of Hall's poems (1949), and T. F. Kinloch (1951).[1]

He was born of humble parentage on 1 July 1574, at Bristow Park, just east of Ashby-de-la-Zouch in Leicestershire. The settlement was founded by the Danes. From the city of Leicester one drives over rolling countryside up Broadgates Hill and then down, through the village of Coalville, towards the stark ruined tower of Ashby Castle. This was once so much the centre of the town's lively history that Sir Walter Scott made it the scene of the climactic tournament in *Ivanhoe*.

Given by William the Conqueror to one of his nobles, the manor of Ashby subsequently passed by marriage to a family named Zouch, whose ancestors had come from Brittany. Edward IV, after the Wars of the Roses, granted it to his Lord Chamberlain, William Lord Hastings, who built the castle but was executed for treason in 1483 by Richard III. His son, Edward Lord Hastings, avenged his father's death on nearby Bosworth field and won the estates back at the hand of Henry VIII. The grandson of the first Lord Hastings in 1529 was made the first Earl of Huntingdon. His son, the second earl, married the niece of Cardinal Pole, and died in 1561. In Ashby's St Helen's Church stands their magnificent tomb, with the two recumbent figures.

All this leads up to their son, the third Earl of Huntingdon, President of the North and the employer of Joseph Hall's father. It was on this estate that Joseph was born, and he could not help imbibing much of its history. Also, the third Earl of Huntingdon played an important part in the lad's education, by founding the famous Ashby Grammar School and helping in the creation of the new 'Puritan settlement' of Emmanuel College at Cambridge. For a short time the third Earl was the official guardian of Mary Queen of Scots, so that the boy inherited, so to speak, a suspicion of the Roman Catholic queen and a sympathy for her Calvinistic Protestant son, James VI of Scotland. On their way from Scotland in 1603 to attend the coronation of husband and father, Queen Anne (James's Danish wife) and young Prince Henry were entertained at Ashby Castle, and James was a guest there on three separate occasions.

The great Huntingdon manor house has long since disappeared, but one can visit the remains of the castle, its tall Hastings tower still looking very much as it did in 1850 for Turner's painting. Near by are the old grammar school, now a bustling 'comprehensive', and St Helen's Church, the three buildings forming a single unit with the church appropriately in the centre.[2]

Joseph speaks of his father, a steward on the Huntingdon estate, only in terms of the difficulties he had educating twleve children and his general interest in their welfare. But early in his autobiography he spends two pages on his mother. Her influence upon the boy must have been so profound, and he describes her with such skill and feeling, that part of what he says about her should be transcribed:

> My mother Winifride, of the house of Bambridges, was a woman of that rare sanctity, that, were it not for my interest in nature, I durst say that neither Aleth [the mother of St Bernard] nor Monica [the mother of St Augustine], nor any other of those pious matrons anciently famous for devotion, need to disdain her admittance to comparison. She was continually exercised with the affliction of a weak body, and oft of a wounded spirit, the agonies whereof, as she would oft recount with much passion, professing that the greatest bodily sicknesses were but flea-bites to those scorpions; so from them all at last she found an happy and comfortable deliverance . . .

Here he tells how during her physical sufferings she dreamed that she was about to die and go to heaven. On waking, she was disappointed not to have that joy, but her pastor convinced her that both the premonition and the recovery of her health were surely gifts from God.

> What with the trial of both these hands of God [Joseph continues], so had she profited in the school of Christ that it was hard for any friend to come

from her discourse no whit holier. How often have I blessed the memory of those divine passages of experimental divinity which I have heard from her mouth! What day did she pass without a large task of private devotion? whence she would still come forth, with a countenance of undissembled mortification. Never any lips have read to me such feeling lectures of piety; neither have I known any soul that more accurately practised them than her own. Temptations, desertions, and spiritual comforts, were her usual theme. Shortly, for I can hardly take off my pen from so exemplary a subject, her life and death were saint-like. [Wynter, I, xx–xxi][3]

The bishop was sixty-eight years old when he penned this tribute to his mother.

Her spiritual counsellor, the Reverend Anthony Gilby, rector of St Helen's, was a preacher of extreme Calvinistic beliefs and a prime reorganizer of the school's curriculum. During Queen Mary's reign, Gilby had fled to Frankfurt-am-Main, and there had translated some of the treatises of Beza as well as lending his knowledge of Hebrew to the translators of the Geneva Bible. After thirty-five years of arguing against presbytery, Joseph Hall remembers this zealous teacher with little enthusiasm:

For me, although I have not age enough to have known the father of this discipline [Calvin], yet one of the godfathers of it I did know; who, after his peregrination in Germany at Geneva, undertook for this newborn infant at our English font; under whose ministry my younger years were spent: the author of that bitter dialogue betwixt Miles Monopodius and Bernard Blinkard, one of the hottest and busiest sticklers in these quarrels at Frankfort. So young is this form of government, being until that day unheard of in the Christian world. [IX, 272–3]

Thus both at home and at school the young Joseph Hall, already singled out by his parents for the ministry, became 'Puritan' in his theology but never Presbyterian in ecclesiastical polity.

In 1589, when Joseph Hall was fifteen, he and two promising classmates, Hugh Cholmley and William Bradshaw, left Ashby Grammar School for Emmanuel College, Cambridge. Hall was convinced he got there by the grace of God. The Reverend Mr Pelset, a powerful persuader by his learning and oratory, had lately come as a visiting preacher to St Helen's Church. Noticing the brightness of young Joseph Hall, he offered to take the boy home with him and in seven years train him to become a minister with the same degree of accuracy in languages and divinity as any college could. The elder Hall, economically hard-pressed, gladly agreed. It so happened that one of Joseph's brothers on a trip to Cambridge called upon Mr Gilby's son

Nathaniel, then a Fellow at Emmanuel College. Upon hearing of the plan for Joseph's private education, Nathaniel pleaded that the boy might be allowed instead to acquire a university experience. The moment Joseph's father relented and gave his permission, a messenger arrived from Mr Pelset with the indentures ready to be signed – too late. 'O God', cries Joseph in his autobiography, 'how was I then taken up with a thankful acknowledgement and joyful admiration of thy gracious providence over me!' [I, xxiii]

After two exciting years at Emmanuel under the tutorship of Nathaniel Gilby, evidently more liberal than his father, Joseph was called home. The elder Hall could no longer support him and advised him to take the offer of a teaching position (at the age of seventeen) in Ashby Grammar School. Again providentially, an uncle by marriage, Mr Edmund Sleigh of Derby, offered to furnish half of Joseph's expenses at Cambridge through the MA degree. Joyfully Hall returned to Cambridge and became a Fellow at Emmanuel, again not without some extraordinary arrangements made for him in heaven.

Emmanuel College was founded in 1584 by Sir Walter Mildmay, who a decade or so previously had given a Greek lectureship, six scholarships and a preacher to his own college, Christ's.[4] The older colleges were still training statesmen from among the gentry, but Mildmay's new college had inscribed over the doorway SACRAE THEOLOGIAE STUDIOSIS POSUIT GUALTERIUS MILD-MAIUS A° DN. 1584. Into its statutes Sir Walter wrote: 'Therefore let fellows and scholars who obtrude into the college with any other design than to devote themselves to sacred theology and eventually to labour in preaching the Word, know that they are frustrating my hope and occupying the place of a scholar contrary to my ordinance.' An unusual provision forbade any Fellow to linger, as many relaxed students did at Oxford and Cambridge, more than ten years after the MA and one year after the doctorate in divinity.[5] Many years later, William Bedell, close friend of Joseph Hall at Emmanuel, after serving in Venice with Sir Henry Wotton, wrote the same provision into the statutes of Trinity College Dublin when he was Master there, and for that received from Charles I the bishopric of Kilmore.[6] At an early point in Emmanuel's history, Queen Elizabeth is reported to have said, 'Sir Walter, I hear you have erected a puritan foundation.' Mildmay replied that he had done nothing against the laws of the realm, but, 'I have set an acorn, which, when it becomes an oak, God alone knows what will be the fruit thereof.' Out of the 132 English university graduates who emigrated to New England in the seventeenth century, 100 were graduates of Cambridge; and of these Cambridge men, 35 were from Emmanuel.[7] An acorn to Sir Walter's liking would be the

4

new college in Cambridge, Massachusetts, named in 1639 after John Harvard of Emmanuel.

Emmanuel College's first Master, and still the head when Joseph Hall enrolled, was Dr Lawrence Chaderton, a 'Puritan' delegate in 1604 to King James's Hampton Court Conference and one of the translators of the new Bible proposed at that conference by the Puritan Dr Rainolds.[8] Revered by Anglicans for having saved the life of Richard Bancroft in a town–gown riot, Dr Chaderton married the sister of the wife of Dr William Whitaker, Master of St John's; and perhaps for that reason there was a close alliance between St John's, more populous and fashionable, and Emmanuel – small, new and 'Puritan'. The only other college founded under Queen Elizabeth at Cambridge was likewise Puritan, Sidney Sussex, whose Master for thirty-three years was Dr Samuel Ward, once a Fellow at Emmanuel. Oliver Cromwell attended Sidney Sussex. Meanwhile, in Roman Catholic Ireland, the Queen saw to it that young men could receive a Protestant training at Trinity College Dublin.

Most of the older men responsible for these new colleges were humanists trained in the traditional classical curriculum. Nor did they introduce much that was new, except perhaps increased biblical study and the rhetoric and logic of Peter Ramus. Besides the famous three laws – of justice, truth and wisdom – Ramism depends greatly on the disjunctive syllogism: 'The specimen must be either a fish or a reptile; it is not a reptile; therefore it must be a fish.' Embraced by continental reformed theologians, the method was brought to Glasgow University by the great Scottish Calvinist Andrew Melville, and later was taught at Cambridge, particularly at Emmanuel.[9]

Moreover, the teachers were not rabidly 'Puritanical'. Emmanuel College was still Anglican, though leaning heavily towards the theology of Geneva, and in churchmanship 'free' rather than 'low'. The teachers and students, for example, made their communion sitting down, because, it was explained by Dr Chaderton, the pews were so badly arranged as to leave no room for kneeling. The original chapel, today a part of Emmanuel's library, faced north. Noting this in 1615 during his visit to Cambridge, King James said, 'God will not turn away his face from the prayers of any holy and pious man, to what-soever region of heaven he directs his eyes. So, doctor, I beg you to pray for me.'[10] Emmanuel's reputation for sobriety was caught in the following verse of a poem by Richard Corbett of Christ Church, Oxford, sung to the tune of 'Bonny Nell':

> But the pure house of Emanuel
> Would not be like proud Iezebel,
> Nor show her selfe before the King

An Hypocrite, or painted thing:
But, that the wayes might prove all faire,
Conceiv'd a tedious mile of Prayer.[11]

During that visit, King James was particularly pleased with the clever argument in Latin by a young John Preston of King's that dogs could indeed make syllogisms. A great hunter himself, how the king must have roared at the Ramistic proof that went something like this: 'The dog says, "The hare went either in that direction or in this; he did not go in this direction; therefore he went in *that*." And away the dog follows with open jaws.' No one knew then that the young orator would become first a Fellow at Emmanuel, and then, as a Puritan divine, would succeed Dr Chaderton as Master of Emmanuel College.

Warned of the dangers to the church from without and within, the boys at the Protestant foundation of Emmanuel paid strict attention to their studies. In James's reign, three chaplains were needed for three important royal embassies abroad, and all three were Emmanuel men: William Bedell with Sir Henry Wotton to Venice, James Wadsworth to Madrid, and Joseph Hall with Lord Doncaster to France. As Izaac Walton said, they were 'all bred in one University, all of one Colledge, all Benefic'd in one diocese, and all most dear and intire Friends'.[12] But Wadsworth, to everyone's consternation, 'perverted' to Rome almost as soon as he arrived in Spain, and became tutor to Henrietta Maria. Joseph Hall appealed to his friend in vain by reminding him of the pride they had taken together in their training at Emmanuel. This letter was so important that he placed it first among his epistles published in 1608. 'Was not your youth,' he wrote, 'spent in a society of such comely order, strict government, wise laws, religious care (it was ours, yet, let me praise it, to your shame), as may justly challenge, after all the brags, either Rhemes or Doway; or, if your Jesuits have any other den, more cleanly, and more worthy of ostentation' (VI, 130)?

In Lambeth Palace lies a manuscript entitled 'Statuta Dni. Gualter. Mildmaii Militis quae pro administratione Coll. Emmanuelis ab eo fundat'. It includes the annual recitation of 'the worthy names of our ever Honour'd Benefactors'.

Sr. Walter Mildmay Knt. Chancellor of the Excheqr. & privy Councellr. to Queene Elizabeth, out of his pious care for the advancet. of learning, & for the maintenance of the true protestant religion against popery and all other heresies whatsoever, did in the year 1584 found this College to be a nursery of Divines, endowing it forth a considerable yearly revenue ... and constituting one Master, 3 Fellows & 4 Scholars besides inferior Officers. Which has been much increased by the pious bounty & beneficence of many Nobles & worthy persons, our deservedly honour'd Benefactors, and first of all Queen Elizabeth of famous memory besides her patents and licence of Mortmain gave out of her Exchecqr. a perpetual anmity of £ 10, 13s, 4d. The Rt. Honble Henry Hastings Earl of Huntingdon gave the perpetual patronage of the Rectories of Loughbowry, Allerton, & North Cadbury.

The list continues: 'Thomas Hobs Esqr. gave abt. 8£ p. annum for 2 exhibitions', and 'Benj. Whichcot D.D. sometimes Fellow of this College in execution of the Will of John Larkin citizen of London gave 1000 £'. Among the givers to Emmanuel's library: 'The Rt. Reverd. Wm. Bedel Ld Bp. of Kilmore in the Kingdome of Ireland gave this College . . . a manuscript Hebrew Bible in 3 volumes of great value.'[13]

In that library's 'Order Book' occur the signatures of the Master and Fellows (1595, p. 11), headed by Lawrence Chaderton and including Joseph Hall. For 1598, again, Hall is there along with Bedell, Cudworth, Cholmley and Braithwaite; and finally in 1600. The library, besides Bedell's Hebrew Bible, possesses a Coverdale of 1535; a 1588 Geneva Bible in French presented by the church in Geneva to Sir Walter Mildmay; and a Latin Bible once belonging to Edward VI, prefaced with a fascinating illustrated 'Chronology' that shows, among other biblical events, Jesus Christ born in the year '3962 Mundi', '2305 Deluvii'.

Pre-eminent in every part of the curriculum, Joseph Hall was also the poet of Emmanuel College. When he was twenty-one he contributed his first published poem to the book commemorating the death in 1595 of Dr William Whitaker, Regius Professor of Divinity, a champion of Calvinistic theology in the Anglican church, and brother-in-law through marriage of Emmanuel's Master. The poem, called 'Hermae', cannot compare, of course, with a later threnody entitled 'Lycidas'. Consisting of seventeen six-line stanzas, its Spenserian lilt combines some wit with deep feeling. The best stanza, I think, is the fifteenth:

> *Open ye golden gates of Paradise,*
> Open ye wide vnto a welcome Ghost:
> Enter, O Soule, into thy *Boure* of *Blisse,*
> Through all the throne of *Heauens* hoast:
>   Which shall with *Triumph* gard thee as thou go'st
>   With *Psalmes* of *Conquest* and with crownes of cost.[14]

The word 'ghost' at the end of the second line is a welcome change from 'guest'.

'He passed all his degrees with great applause,' wrote Thomas Fuller; 'First noted in the University, for his ingenuous maintaining, (be it *truth* or *paradox*) that *Mundus senescit, The world groweth old.* Yet, in some sort, his position confuteth his position, the wit and quickness whereof did argue an increase, rather than a decay of parts in the latter age.'[15] Rhetoric at Emmanuel the knowledge very useful and necessary', was based not merely on Ramus but on the best of Cicero, Quintilian, and later, on Consinus' *De Eloquentia Sacra et Humana.* [16] So good was Joseph Hall at spoken rhetoric that, for two years in succession, he was elected to teach it. He himself records one disputation which brought him and his opponent fame, the one with the brilliant blind student of Trinity, Ambrose Fisher:

> There was one in my time, very eminent in the University of Cambridge, whom I had occasion to dispute with for his degrees, of great skill both in tongue and arts, and of singular acuteness of judgement ... Sure, I may say boldly of our Fisher, that he was more dexterous in picking the locks of difficult authors, and fetching forth the treasures of their hidden senses, than those that had the sharpest eyes about him: insomuch as it was noted, those were singular proficients which employed themselves in reading to him. If they read books to him, he read lectures the while to them: and still taught more than he learned. [VII, 76–7]

This debate took place in 1597–8, when Joseph Hall, still a Fellow at Emmanuel, was publishing his two volumes of satires written in imitation of Martial, Persius and Juvenal. He received the MA in 1596, the BD in 1603, and the DD in 1610. In 1598 he was incorporated at Oxford.

Hall's own nephew, John Brinsley, was made head of Ashby Grammar School in 1601, and in 1612 secured a place in the history of English education by the publication of *Ludus Literarius.* Dedicated to the two princes, Henry and Charles (there is no doubt that permission for this was achieved by Joseph Hall, by that time in good grace at court), the book is designed to make learning fun. It has a four-page 'Commendatory Preface' by a former graduate of Ashby Grammar School, signing himself 'Ios. Hall, Dr. of Divin.'.

> Arts are the only helpe towards humane perfection, and hence God has recorded the names of the first makers of shepherds' tents, ironworks, musical instruments and golden ornaments. Language and literature are humane arts. Our grandfathers studied these arts till their beards grew as long as their pens, but this book makes such study easier and more delightful.
> The Iesuits have won much of their reputation, and stollen many hearts with their diligence in this kinde. How happie shall it be for the Church and vs, if we excite our selves at least to imitate this their forwardnesse? We may out-strip them ... Behold here, not feete, but wings offered to vs.'[17]

Divinity was important at Emmanuel College, but so were construing texts in Hebrew, Latin and Greek; using wit and eloquence in the spoken word; and finding accuracy and grace in the writing of English prose and poetry.

2. The Satirist in English Verse and Latin Prose

Joseph Hall and John Donne (two years older) were writing verse-satires at the same time, and shortly after they were both taken under the wing of Sir Robert Drury; later, they both accompanied embassies abroad, and both became famous churchmen. While there is no doubt that Donne is the greater lyric and religious poet, his five satires were only passed around in manuscript. Hall, while still a Fellow at Cambridge, published two volumes of satires called *Virgidemiarum Six Bookes* in 1597–8, and he wrote in Latin prose a satirical novel entitled *Mundus Alter et Idem* (Another World Yet the Same), which was published anonymously in 1605. His initial claim to be included in the history of English literature, therefore, lies in the field of satire.[1]

Alexander Pope, anxious to 'improve' his predecessors, wished he had come across Hall's satires before he tackled Donne's;[2] but criticism begins with Thomas Warton's *History of English Poetry* (1774–81). These 'nervous and elegant satires', wrote Warton,

... are marked with a classical precision, to which English poetry had yet rarely attained. They are replete with animation of style and sentiment. The indignation of the satirist is always the result of good sense. Nor are the thorns of severe invective unmixed with the flowers of pure poetry. The characters are delineated in a strong and lively colouring, and their discriminations are touched with the masterly traces of genuine humour. The versification is equally energetic and elegant, and the fabric of the couplets approaches to the modern standard ... His chief fault is obscurity, arising from a remote phraseology, constrained combinations, unfamiliar allusions, elliptical apostrophes, and abruptness of expression. Perhaps some will think that his manner betrays too much of the laborious exactness and pedantic anxiety of the scholar and the student. Ariosto in Italian and Regnier in French, were now almost the only writers of satires ... But Hall's acknowledged patterns are Juvenal and Persius, not without some touches of the urbanity of Horace. His parodies of these poets, or rather his adaptations of ancient to modern manners . . . discover great facility and dexterity of invention. The moral gravity and censorial declamation of Juvenal, he frequently enlivens with a train of more refined reflection, or adorns with a novelty and variety of images.[3]

Except for Warton's animadversions on Hall's 'obscurity', I agree with this evaluation. Hall's satires are obscure, but so purposeful a characteristic can hardly be called a fault. And rather than bemoan, as some have after Warton, the early confusion between 'satyr' and 'satire', perhaps it is better, if we are to appreciate the poems, to attempt to discover the reasons for that obscurity and Hall's literary means of attaining it. That they were immediately successful is shown by the fact that, in 1598, Francis Meres included among England's foremost satirists 'Hall of Imanuel Colledge in Cambridge'.[4]

Hall begins his prologue with these oft-quoted words:

> I first aduenture, with fool-hardie might
> To tread the steps of perilous despight:
> I first aduenture: follow me who list,
> And be the second English Satyrist.[5]

But he himself mentions 'angry *Skeltons* breath-lesse rimes' (VI, i, 76), and he had certainly read Lodge's *A Fig for Momus* (1593). He must have been aware, also, that John Marston was writing scurrilous verses about him.

One way to prove Hall's boast is to weigh his achievement within the bounds of his stated definition and philosophy of satire. Hall is using the word 'satire' in its double sense: that of a collection, mixture, *olla podrida*, on the one hand; and on the other, that of a poetic corrective in 'rough' style to bad poetry, manners and morals. Perhaps B. L. Ullman most succinctly gives us the history of the term: '*Satura* was first used to mean a collection of miscellaneous poems. In Horace's time it came to be used of a collection of satirical poems and of the genus satire. Finally in the time of Juvenal it began to be applied to a single poem of satirical nature.'[6] Well read in classical literature, Joseph Hall was familiar with his Roman predecessors. He divides his 'collection' of 'satires' into two parts: poems of a mild character into three books of one volume called *Toothless Satyres*, and his harsher poems into three books called *Byting Satyres*. The milder, more urbane poems of Volume One are based on Horace; Volume Two on Juvenal; and the whole 'imitates' stylistically the purposefully rough-hewn quality of 'crabbed Persius' (V, i, 10). The ancient association of *satura* with satyr and goat, mistaken though it may have been, established a tradition for a rough, shaggy style of writing. The early Lucilian satire was 'rude' in the cradle of history, but later Roman satirists were 'rude' by design. So Hall opened his first volume with a poem called 'Defiance to Envy':

> That Enuy should accost my Muse and mee,
> For this so rude, and recklesse Poesie.
>
> [lines 29–30]

This does not mean that other poets will 'envy' Hall's poetic skill. Rather, it means that though Hall by deliberate obscurity will hide the identity of his victims, nevertheless he will dare draw unto himself their ill will for discovering their faults. 'Envy' is malice, odium, like that which Antonio accuses Shylock of harboring: 'No lawful means can carry me/Out of his envy's reach' (*Merchant of Venice*, IV, i, 10). That Hall succeeded in satire thus defined is shown not only by his own boast and Meres's compliment, but also by Marston's double reaction of personal hatred for Joseph Hall and admiration of Hall's stylistic involution:

> Helpe to vnmaske the Satyres secresie,
> Delphick *Apollo*, ayde me to vnrip,
> These darke Enigmaes, and strange ridling sense.[7]

Hence the first ingredient of Hall's definition of satire is obscurity, and that obscurity is largely linguistic.[8] For example, take a single couplet:

> O times! since euer Rome did kings create.
> Brasse Gentlemen, and Caesars Laureate.
>
> [IV, ii, end]

Hall means: 'The times are out of joint when the Papacy can crown kings, money can make aristocrats, and the powerful decide who is and who is not a poet.' Though differing in tone and degree of obscurity, stylistically both volumes portray the 'crabbed' style of Persius in strange, unexpected circumlocutions, parentheses, recondite allusions, omitted grammatical connections and a diction that freely mixes neologisms and archaisms, bold images and clichés, vulgarisms and pietistic simperings. There are shocking oppositions, like the jump from the stacks of wasted paper in a literary controversy to the microscopic writing that can preserve the whole *Iliad* on a walnut shell (II, i, 38). Witty parables abound, like the one of the client as a poor sheep and the sharp lawyer as the briar: during the storm the sheep seeks shelter under the bush, which in no time at all has scratched every bit of fleece off the unsuspecting animal (II, iii). There are witty, veiled and almost blasphemous parodies of Scripture, such as the echo of 'In my Father's house' that Hall brings into his account of the various 'mansions' (named after popular Cambridge pubs) that the lover may inhabit in the mock-astrological table (II, vii, 27ff.). There is a hint of St Paul's metaphor of the union of the various parts of the human body in the description of the over-dressed but hungry man whose belly grumbles at the richness of cloth upon the back (III, vii, 55ff.). Often, especially in the second volume, an effect of harshness and obscurity is attained through an unannounced shift in speaker. For example, in V, i, 89, 'a smiling Land-lord' is introduced; at line 101, without quotation marks, he starts speaking; then at line 107, Hall's voice is heard again. All these stylistic mannerisms take time and trouble for the reader to 'puzzle' out.

In diction, Hall's neologisms must have been a special source of puzzlement to his readers, despite his mock scowl in:

> Fie on the forged mint that did create
> New coyne of words neuer articulate.
>
> [I, vi, 17–18]

Among the many new words are 'hedge-creeping' for clandestine (IV, i, 160), and 'salt' in the sense of lecherous (IV, i, 160), both of which are cited by the *Oxford English Dictionary* with reference to Hall's satires. Among his words which the Oxford dictionary cites for initial occurrence in our language, perhaps the most significant is the word 'plagiary', which he uses for the first time in English[9] as he transfers Virgil's famous 'Hos ego' verse to Petrarch; he cannot stand

> ... a Catch-pols fist vnto a Bankrupts sleeue;
> Or an, *Hos ego*, from old *Petrarchs* spright
> Vnto a Plagiarie sonnet-wright.
>
> [IV, ii, 82–4]

Among Hall's other brand-new words are the following: 'Autumnitie', for the must of autumn wine (III, i, 61); 'ding-thrift' as an adjective to mean careless with money (IV, v, 59); 'minerall' for mine (VI, i, *148); 'rife' meaning trivial *(IV, i, 162);* and 'yeomanrie', peasant dress (III, i, 75). Finally, though the *Oxford English Dictionary* fails to record the following words as appearing as early as 1597–8, they actually occur in Hall's *Virgidemiae*: 'appurtenance', an ironic use of the word as a personal dependant (V, ii, 89); 'galled', that is, scuffed or scraped, a transference from an animate context (horse) to a tree (IV, v, 33); and 'shak't', meaning reduced in a rough manner (IV, i, 34). Joseph Hall's deliberate coining of new words and stretching the meaning of old ones is part of the obscurity and roughness he believed to be characteristic of the genre of satire.

As an experiment we are going to dismiss the witty rimes, changes in metre and some of the strong language in order to see for ourselves, by avoiding the built-in obscurity just described, what one of Hall's satires is like. Perhaps this can be accomplished through the medium of modern prose, despite the fact that to paraphrase any poem is to violate its fundamental being. For this exercise there is no less a precedent than Thomas Warton. For example, in Satire I, i, 25–32, Hall had written:

> Nor need I craue the muses mid-wifry,
> To bring to light so worth-lesse Poetry:
> Or if mee list, what baser Muse can bide,
> To sit and sing by *Grantaes* naked side.
> They haunt the tyded *Thames* and salt *Medway*,
> Ere since the fame of their late Bridall day.
> Nought haue we here but willow-shaded shore,
> To tell our *Grant* his banks are left forelore.

Warton comments:

> But had I, says the poet, been inclined to invoke the assistance of a Muse, what Muse, even of a lower order, is thére now to be found, who would condescend to sit and sing on the desolate margin of the Cam? The muses frequent other rivers, ever since Spenser celebrated the nuptials of Thames and Medway (*F. Q.*, IV, xi, 8 seq.). Cam has now nothing on his banks but willows, the types of desertion.

But the satires of the first volume are fairly comprehensible without Mr Warton's aid. In the Prologue to Book III, Hall confessed that they were blamed for not being 'dark' enough: 'Not ridle-like obscuring their intent:/But packe-staffe plaine vttering what thing they ment.'

The *Byting Satyres* are a different matter. In commenting on the confession just quoted, C. S. Lewis adds: 'His pains were successful and IV, i, is, in places, a mere puzzle.'[10] This is true. But instead of giving up, let us try, in prose, to discover what Hall is saying in this 'puzzle', and why his style should be so 'dark and riddling'. The satire, on sexual irregularities, is long (175 lines), but so densely packed that only with difficulty have we omitted parts of it from our paraphrase:

Satire IV, i – 'Whoso wishes to jest, let him' – Ariosto

(1)   Who dares accuse my frank satires of transparency by comparing them with blindfold Juvenal's, subtle Horace's, or rough-hewn Scaliger's in either his antique or modern vein? Whoever reads me has to rub his brow and puzzle over the intent of each line, scoring the margin with hundreds of blazing asterisks and interlinear squiggles, like a shopkeeper's account-book when a delinquent customer's house is finally sold for debt . . .

(29) When you have pored over my crabbed satires as often as Philip II has been rumoured to be dead and prayed to the furies to haunt each peevish line that has racked your eyes worse than the books of anagrams and riddles so popular these days, should I heed your curses? No living person is intended in my rhymes. Look, when I whip Willy for being so atrocious a poet, he laughs. Why? Because I take such pains to conceal his identity. Even if he had a conscience to be pricked, he doesn't care about my blows so long as he is thus protected against them. Like a crafty squid when he feels himself detected, he envelopes himself in a thick cloud of his own vomit for further concealment. And who can complain of libel when he can turn my barbs so easily towards another person's head? . . . Each points his finger at his friend, and no one sees himself well enough to say, 'That's me' – as Socrates stood up at the performance of *The Clouds* to let the audience identify the original of Aristophanes' caricature.

(53) But just try saying flat and plain that you, coy Alice, are a whore; or you, false Jack, choked your wealthy guest while he lay asleep and had his body hauled away in a dung-cart; or you, proud Peter, for all your strutting actually wear third-hand suits and eat nothing but leftovers; or you, Professor G., had no place to sleep until you married that dying rich widow and now, for the price of one night's discomfiture, have kept your job, inherited her mansion, and married a pretty young graduate student. Without giving their names, I can make fireflakes blaze from their eyes; their cheeks puff out like a swollen toad bitten by a spider; their mouth shrink sideways like a fish's to take the place of ungrateful ears; and their ears droop like a sow's dugs to seek advice from their grieving eyes. So, I laugh out loud at the pleasing pastime of my satires. It's more fun than the bear-pit, or the puppet-play, or Mimo whistling to his tambourine for a plate of cold meat. Go on, then, my sacred satires, and please me the more you displease others . . .

(92) Do you think George's skin will laugh at the purple welts on the backs of others? Not if he were as near to my satire as the brothels (so they say) are to the tennis courts. While thousands envy him his sexy wife, George neighs after fresh maidenhead. His slavish wife doesn't dare frown on such imperious rivalry, even though she sees her wedding ring reset for some strumpet's finger or has to rent a night's lodging for her husband's con-cubine. Whether his twilight torch calls him to a lecherous music-hall, or a midnight play, or a tavern for new wine, hie, you white aprons, to the

landlord's sign where everyone except old men and babes is summoned to the court of venery.

(110) Who wants out when wives hire snot-nosed youths for gigolos and feed them eggs and oysters as horse-breeders do their stallions at studding time? O goddess of childbirth, Lizzie gives her husband an heir after a dozen years of barren marriage and bribes the midwife to swear that the little bastard looks exactly like him ...

(132) If the River Trent runs dry or the River Lee empty, hence, you hot lechers, to the cathouse for a cooling. Tiber, you infamous sink of Christendom, turn into Thames, and Thames, run towards Rome – what other streams could quench George's lusting liver's heat? Your double draught may bring down his temperature with some stale whore or obsequious boy whom the wrinkled madam advertises as wares in front of the house she keeps. Or does he prefer some veiled matron's face, or young apprentice trading there?

(144) The secret adulteress, when her name (and price) is called, comes crawling from her husband's lukewarm bed, her carrion skin bedawbed with perfume, groping down the backstairs on bare feet. Now, whoever wishes, play the satirist – St Valentine himself or someone as chaste as he. In vain she wishes this night would last three times as long, cursing the too hasty dawn. As the cruel star of Venus rises in the morning sky, she seeks her third bout on silent toes, smirched with the loathsome smoke of lust and polluted like Acheron's streams. Yet all day long she chastely simpers in her parlour-chair like a saint in her niche. Meanwhile her husband wallows in the brothel with a swollen head and drained carcass until his salty bowels flare with venereal fire, a second Hercules in the poisoned shirt of Nessus. O Aesculapius, how fallen the art of medicine when every barber who owns a brass basin professes to cure all comers of the pox, at ten groats a shot!

(166) All these and more deserve my blood-drawn lines. Even my biting satires are far too easy on 'em. But some sniffing pedant will say that my couplets smell of the classroom, beaten out by one whose deepest skill has construed a Latin poem three times and recited it back to teacher. Must I wait until my beard is white before I become a really fierce satirist? No. I would rather be blamed for the indignation of hot-blooded youth than for the doting that may come in the coldness of my old age.

Finis

Hall was youthfully proud of this satire; in the 'Postscript to the Reader' that accompanied both the 1598 and 1599 editions, he singled it out as one that 'doth somewhat resemble the soure and crabbed face of Iuuenals' (p. 99). Now, add to this Juvenalian anger an amazing inventiveness of heroic couplet that prefigures Dryden and Pope, in six books comprising no less than thirty-five separate satires, and we may well agree with the young student of classics and theology at Cambridge that nothing like this had ever appeared in English before.

For the studied obscurity in style and moral indignation in spirit that characterized the burst of satirical poetry during Elizabeth's declining years, there existed philosophical, political and personal reasons. A satirist appeals to a norm of behaviour from which, he feels, present society is departing. In 'the good old days' men were men and women were women; poets wrote on noble subjects (*The Faerie Queene* appeared four years before Hall's satires); people were generous, kind and good. But there is change, and for this reason satirists – 'Muttring what censures their distracted minde,/Of brain-sicke Paradoxes deeply hath defined:/... of darke *Heraclite*' (II, ii, 51–3) – often recall Heraclitus, the philosopher of change and also noted for stylistic obscurity. Politically the satirist is in danger of running counter to the establishment of his day that has allowed such change to take place, and as we shall see, Marston, Davies, Hall and other satirists and epigrammatists were proscribed by one of Queen Elizabeth's watchful committees. From a personal point of view, the satirist had to be obscure in order to escape libel suits, scurrilous attacks from fellow-poets or such non-literary retaliation as was later visited upon John Dryden by hired cudgels in Rose Alley.

Hall's very title for his complete satires must have raised many an inquiring eyebrow: *Virgidemiarum, Sixe Bookes*. The Latin word is rare, meaning a bundle of rods, its plural genitive case governed by the English that follows. Hence the intent becomes 'six *virgidemiae* or sheaves of rods now bundled together to form a scourge for the correction of the evils I see around me'. The *virgidemiae* are obviously whips. The satirist's function is to correct, and throughout Hall emphasizes this purpose:

> *Nay, no despight: but angry* Nemesis,
> *Whose scourge doth follow all that done amisse:*
> *That scourge I beare, albe in ruder fist,*
> *And wound, and strike, and pardon whom she list.*
>
> [Prologue, Bk II]

Again, he concludes the first volume with:

> *Hold out ye guiltie, and ye galled hides,*
> *And meet my far-fetch'd stripes with waiting sides.*
>
> [p. 43]

By 1601, the title had inspired several 'Whipper'-pamphlets, such as *The Whipping of the Satyre* by William Ingram (?), Guilpin's *The Whipper of the Satyre his penance in a white sheete*, and Breton's (?) *No Whippinge nor trippinge: but a kinde friendly Snippinge*. In those days public thrashing was a corporal and literary form of punishment.

Hall's canes for whipping, it would appear, are made of willow. Every English schoolboy was well acquainted with the willow-switch held in the hand of the master: it is lean, long and pliable; makes a whistling noise as it swings through the air; and it can cut. But Hall's willow metaphor is more complicated than that. Through the centuries poets have celebrated trees, and have identified places with particular trees: the cedars of Lebanon, the palms of Palmyra, the great oaks of Dodona, the pines of Ida. Cambridge and the Cam, Hall says plaintively, have only the humble willow (I, i, 31–2). But Hall can at least make some use of his willow trees: he can cut their branches for his whipping-withes, and, as other poets have worn laurel, he can crown his own poetic head with willow as a sign of lament for the recently departed spirit of decency in poetry and morals. Du Bartas of France and Ariosto of Italy may yield the laurel to the English Spenser, Hall says, but –

> ... let all others willow weare with mee,
> Or let their vnderseruing *Temples* Bared bee.
>
> [I, iv, 27–8]

Hall's description of the waning golden age in the final years of Elizabeth (III, i) reveals his longing for that time when Englishmen received a fair day's wages for an honest day's work; wore English clothes, not Italian; and ate 'thrifty leeks' and 'manly garlic' instead of rich viands imported from around the globe:

> Then farewell fayrest age, the worlds best daies,
> Thriuing in ill, as it in age decaies.
>
> [III, i, 40–41]

In college, as we have seen, he had won declamatory fame for arguing that *mundus senescit*. This Stoic primitivism makes the willows on the banks of the Cam symbols of mourning as well as the means for punitive attack and a poetic crown. Since Hall, finally, is recalling the great poets of ancient Rome, it may well be that his image of a bundle of rods suggests, finally, the Roman *fasces* – 'the Lordly *Fasces* borne of old' (IV, vii, 17) – symbol of authority and threatened punishment.

18

The surrounding rods could be used for flogging; and within, the axe, its edge facing outwards, for cutting.

Under the general rubric of 'six books of willow-withes for whipping', it would seem that very early Hall had decided to make of them two volumes and to divide his satires into two oppositional categories of three books each. For one thing, his most contemporary precedent, J. C. Scaliger, whom he is following to no small degree, divides his satires (1581) into 'Mild' and 'harsh': 'Unum genus est quod dividitur . . . Sic aut atroces aut ridiculi.'[11] Given Hall's Ramistic turn of mind, trained as he was in logic and rhetoric by Dr Chaderton of Emmanuel, it is no wonder that he adopts a disjunction. Fairly innocuous faults of society come in the first three books, accompanied, in manner, by a much milder attack. The more heinous 'crimes' come in the last three books, where the style must be harsh. Bad poetry is scored in the first three books, whereas greed, adultery and 'Papisticall' religion are thrashed in the next three. These offences against man and God are Hall's major concern; these, as was shown by our paraphrase of their introductory poem, are the more spirited; and it is these, I believe, which he first named 'biting satires'. In contradistinction, he then named the first three books, despite the mixed metaphor with *Virgidemiarum*, 'toothless satires', meaning, of course, satires which do not, and do not need to, 'bite' quite so much. Milton, much later, quibbled on this sub-title. The grand architect of metaphor could be quite literal when the occasion suited. But if a willow-switch can 'bite' into the miscreant's flesh were he to deserve a severe punishment, so could the same willow-switch render a milder punishment for a less opprobrious deviation from rectitude, like the affectation of expensive wigs (III, v). The adjective 'toothless' in opposition to 'biting' is a joke.

Bad poetry, we said, is an important 'mild' subject of Volume One. Hall introduces his theme in the two disjunctive pictures of the Muses (I, ii), the whole redolent of his favourite Spenser. In the first picture, the Muses are quietly reading poetry by a beautiful stream; in the second, rough satyrs attack them, the water is muddied, the pastoral quite ruined. Among those responsible for thus creating bad poetry are the drunken playwrights who thunder in the ears of the penny-benchers; the writers of so-called epic who strain credulity by their departures from nature; millenarian mourners who dolefully indite the end of everything; the sonneteers who write of their ladies as they would of the Virgin Mary; 'religious' poets who sing of the Virgin Mary as though she were a beauty-queen; and worst of all, bawdy poets. Hall trounces Stanyhurst's attempting English dactylic hexameters in 'Mánhoŏd & gárboĭls Ĭ cháunt' for 'Arma virumque cano (I, vi). He scolds prolixity and, most vehemently, pornography.

'Labeo', a name used seven times in *Virgidemiae*, is the typical bad poet, no matter what his poetic crime may be; and, as we shall see when we discuss Hall's use of fictitious names, the type looms more importantly than individual contemporaries who may be targets. What engages the modern reader is not whether Hall is scolding Nashe or Lodge or Drayton, but a literary criticism in which decorum, a classical virtue, is the leading criterion.

Following Book I on bad poets, Books II and III of 'toothless satires' include such social and moral deviants from civilized behaviour as gourmandizers and drunkards (who are also spanked in the Latin *Mundus*). One Rabelaisian poem (III, vi) tells how Gullion drinks so much that when he becomes Charon's passenger he imbibes even the River Styx so dry that the boat rests on mud, yet the cargo of souls ('Tendebantque manus ripae ulterioris amore') patiently wait until Gullion relieves himself and floats their ship again. Among other victims of Hall's 'toothless satires' are grasping lawyers, doctors who overcharge the rich and let the poor die, lords and ladies who pay their chaplains starvation wages, and astrologers who gull the public. None of these escape whipping, but no blood is drawn.

The second volume, *Byting Satyres*, overlaps in subjects at times, but by contrast is far more obscure and angry. Hall bites with his whiplash into the vanity of pedigrees, the effeminacy of Elizabethan youth, the decay of hospitality – all matters more serious than those treated in the first volume. His most scathing attack is on the Roman Catholic church (IV, vii). Here he includes all the well-known prejudices of the Puritan Anglican, such as costly ostentation, unchristian pride, deliberate falsification of history, moral laxity and even 'Pope Joan' (lines 67–9).

Less biased than Hall's views on the Papacy are his serious and biting attacks in the second volume upon England's contemporary economic ills. From his own experience, and that of his fellow students at Cambridge, he had complained in Volume One of the poor pay granted to those in the academic profession (though he would not change for the world – IV, vi, 83ff.):

> What needs me care for any bookish skill,
> To blot white papers with my restless quill:
> Or poare on painted leaues: or beate my braine
> With far-fetcht thoughts: or to consume in vaine
> In later Euen, or mids of winter nights,
> Ill smelling oyles, or some still-watching lights?
>
> [II, ii, 19–24]

And for what? Ten pounds a year, and no extra for baby-sitting.

In the second volume he says farewell to 'smooth Horace' (V, i, 10) in order to invoke Juvenal's indignation against the greed of landlords. A field used to be rented to a deserving farmer, who worked it for 'a summer's snowball, or a winter-rose', but now for a price that condemns most of England's farm-tenants to a lifetime of penury. Enclosure was keeping poor farmers from their once-held 'common' land:

> And so our Grandsires were in ages past,
> That let their lands lye all so widely wast,
> That nothing was in pale or hedge yspent
> Within some prouince or whole shires extent:
> As Nature made the earth, so did it lie,
> Saue for the furrows of their husbandrie:
> When as the neighbour-lands so couched layne,
> That all bore show of one fayre Champian.
>
> [V, iii, 34–41]

But 'Plato is dead' (line 28), and so is his ideal of communalism. 'Koina philon' from the *Phaedrus*, meaning the common bonds of friends, is Hall's epigraph for this seething satire on agricultural conditions in England at the end of the sixteenth century.[12] Hall's poem sounds in neo-classical accents the Christian and medieval 'ethos of complaint'.[13] and in the very year it was published, 1598, the 'New Poor Law' was enacted.

The opposition between 'toothless' and 'biting' satires is enhanced by several built-in devices that would seem to tax Hall's inventiveness in disjunction. For one thing, the second volume is far more concentrated: Volume One, consisting of 930 lines, has in it twenty-three satires; whereas Volume Two, exceeding in bulk by a three-to-two ratio, has in it only twelve separate poems. Volume One's three books are more separated one from the other by the sub-titles prefixed – '1. Poeticall. 2. Academicall. 3. Morall.'; Volume Two has no sub-titles. In Volume One, again, there are very few exceptions to straight heroic couplets; in fact, the only exceptions consist of one half-line (III, i, 7) and two Alexandrines together (III, vii, 20–21). The satires of Volume Two, however, are cluttered with irregularities that range from extremes of length (from 305 lines in VI, i, down to only 22 lines in V, iv) to the inclusion of six sets of triplets, several short lines and several off-rimes (for example, IV, vi, 76–7 rimes 'Grasshopper' with 'enquire'). Whether by Hall's device or by the printer's is not certain, but the first volume is numbered in Roman numerals whereas the second is numbered in Arabic. Volume One has no epigraphs, whereas each satire in the second volume is headed with a quotation or saying in Latin, French, Greek or Italian as if to universalize the subject-matter. Hall distinguishes between his 'biting' and 'toothless' satires by further metaphors: the first volume is like a 'smooth cedar tree' whereas the second is a 'crabbed oak' (conclusion of III); again, Volume One is the summer lightning, whereas Volume Two is the crash of thunder (IV, i, 9). The poems in Volume One came out almost by accident, he says; the implication being that those of Volume Two are more by design. The first volume's satires, we have seen, are inadvertently too clear; apparently those of Volume Two are satisfactorily obscure. As for the victims of Hall's lash, there may be another disjunctive in the epigram which Marston said Hall had written and pasted into every copy of Marston's poems lying in the Cambridge book-stalls. Punning on Marston's pseudonym of Kinsayder (from 'kinsing', the act of cropping dogs' tails), Hall may be dividing his victims into two classes:

> The dog was best cured by cutting & kinsing,
> The Asse must be kindly whipped for winsing.
> [p. 101]

That is, the asses are merely stupid and can be gently whipped as they are in the 'toothless' satires, where the money-grubber, for example, is 'a lave-ear'd Asse' (II, ii, 64). The mad dogs, on the other hand, are so dangerous as to require cutting with Hall's lash. The humorous disjunction strengthens, I believe, the assumption that this squib on Marston is by Hall.

Another part of the tradition and of Hall's contribution to it is the clever use of fictitious names for the victims of his lash. Early critics of Hall engaged in the game of trying to identify in Hall's poetry contemporary living persons, quite overlooking, first, Hall's repeated insistence that it is his own skill that, without his naming them, makes them feel guilty; secondly, the tradition in Roman satire of the same technique; and thirdly, the more important dramatic function of the character within the poem. Too often critic-scholars have substituted the discipline of history for that of literature.[14] In addition to the custom of Horace, Martial and Juvenal, Hall had before him his beloved English Spenser saying in *The Teares of the Muses*:

> For better farre it were to hide their names
> Than telling them to blazon out their blames.
> [lines 101–2]

Thus, when Hall writes that composing his satires is more fun than listening to 'Mimo whistling to his tambourine' (IV, i, 78), Warton suggested that he meant the actor William Kemp, and Singer was equally certain that Hall meant Richard Tarleton, I think that Hall meant 'Mimo'. Again, for Fortunio (IV, iii, 28), Mr S. M. Atkins suggests Captain Lawrence Kemys, who went to Guiana for gold in 1596. And yet John Marston, reflecting contemporaneously on this passage in his 'Reactio' (lines 111–14), takes 'Fortunio' only in a typical, and probably correct, sense. Despite Warton, again, 'some drunken rimer' (IV, vi, 50) does not have to be William Elderton, notorious as he was; many poets drank too much sack.

The most extensive attempts to identify characters in Hall's satires have concerned themselves with two names: 'Labeo' and 'Valentine'. As for the first, Warton argued that 'the bad poet' was Chapman; Singer, Drayton; Salyer, Nashe; Parsons, Shakespeare; and Dent, Bacon.[15] 'Labeo' could not possibly be all of these, and even as he appears in various satires he is not one poet but a convenient name like 'Tigellius' for any bad poet, whether windy, flaccid, dishonest or salacious. 'Valentine' has been identified with Nashe, whose long-drawn-out controversy with Gabriel Harvey was still echoing in Cambridge. This connection was first made by Schultz in his 1910 edition of Hall's satires, and was carried further by Salyer and Davenport. Their most important argument for the identification is the suggestion of two of Nashe's titles in a context of licentious poetry, particularly in two of Hall's couplets:

> Now play the *Satyre* who so list for mee,
> *Valentine* selfe, or some as chast as he,
> > [IV, i, 149–50]

and:

> Nay let the Diuell, and Saint *Valentine*,
> Be gossips to those ribald rymes of thine.
> > [I, ix, 35–6]

It must be admitted that, in an age when 14 February was celebrated less innocently than it is today, these couplets seem to echo Nashe's *Pierce Penilesse his Supplication to the Deuell* and *The Choice of Valen-*

tines, the latter a much-read contribution to the Elizabethan literature on the dildo. And yet, Joseph Hall of Emmanuel College is enough of a Christian to detest the sin rather than the sinner, and usually too sure of his well-studied methodology of satire to allow so easy a personal application of his lines.

Such bookish skill in concealing the actual identity of his victims emerges in the commonplace fact that most of the fictional names in his satires are justified either by their etymology or by their literary-historical source. 'Fortunio' (IV, iii, 28), for example, is well named, as he sells his farm and goes to the new world for gold. 'Sartorio' (IV, ii, 64) is a flashy dresser whose sleeve with an inadvertent needle stuck into it identifies his trade. Other names come from ancient history or refer to characters in Horace, Martial, Terence and other Latin writers. So 'Gellia' (VI, i, 115), who wears a patch on her temples, is a woman of excessive make-up in Martial. And 'Caenis' (IV, vi, 6), of ambivalent sex in myth and in Ovid (*Metamorphoses*, XII, 189), appears in Hall as one who cannot make up his mind whether to act like a man or a woman. Joseph Hall would say that if any living person thinks he is intended by one of these or any other self-declaratory name, let him.

We may conclude that by the use of fictitious names, with the possible exception of an allusion to the literary quarrel between Nashe and Harvey, Joseph Hall fulfilled his boast that, like their Roman model, his satires keep well hidden the actual identity of the persons attacked. It is part of the built-in obscurity demanded of the genre of which he felt, in 1596, his satires were the first full-scale demonstration in English.

The ingenious handling of this quality by Hall in his satires, finally, must account, I believe, for the strange event of their being condemned and then immediately reprieved. On 1 June 1599 an order went out from Archbishop John Whitgift of Canterbury and Bishop Richard Bancroft of London to have certain books 'called in' and thereafter proscribed.[16] The order has attracted a great deal of attention from scholars, for its real purpose is not clear and the list of books is peculiar. If the condemnation were intended to bring an end to political satire, it would have had to include many stage-plays. Or, if the bishops wished to 'punish' eroticism, why did they omit *Venus and Adonis* and *Hero and Leander*? The list is as follows: Joseph Hall's *Virgidemiarum Six Books* (1599); John Marston's *Pygmalion* and *The Scourge of Villanie* (1598); Edward Guilpin's *Skialethia* (1598); Sir John Davies's *Epigrammes* and [Christopher Marlowe's] *Elegies* (1599); Thomas Middleton's (?) *Micro-Cynicon Six Snarling Satyres* (1599); all of the pamphlets comprising the quarrel between Gabriel Harvey and

Thomas Nashe; *Willobie his Avisa* (1594); 'The booke against woemen viz. of marriage and wyvinge' (probably the early sixteenth-century *Complainte of the soon married* and the *Complainte of the too late married*); *The Fifteen Joyes of Marriage* (anonymously issued from de Worde's press in 1509 and surviving only in French); and Thomas Cutwode's *Caltha Poetarum* (1599).

A few days later, on 4 June 1599, 'thereupon were burnt in the [Stationers'] hall' Marston's two books, as well as *Skialethia*, the *Epigrammes and Elegies, Micro-Cynicon* and the books that reflect on the sanctity of marriage. How the order disposed of *Willobie* and the Harvey–Nashe pamphlets we do not know, for no further mention is made of them.

Cutwode's *Caltha* and Hall's *Satires*, however, alone were singled out 'to be staied', that is, not burnt. As for *Caltha Poetarum, or the Bumble Bee*, in a commendatory poem one 'G. S.' says of its author:

> Without offense or fault, by Flower, Plant, or Tree,
> Persons of good worth are meant, conceale thus doth hee.

Some thought the poem defended Sir Walter Raleigh's friends against the Essex–Southampton group,[17] but a sillier, more fantastic, and more veiled botanical allegory has never been written. In 187 seven line stanzas riming ABABBCC, Cutwode tells the story of Woodbyne courting Marygold. As Cupid shoots his arrow, a bee lands on Marygold and gets wounded by the arrow. Venus scolds her son for being a rotten shot. The Bee, 'All his britches from his buttocks torne, was from his body wasted and quight worne.' He receives first-aid from Marygold, falls in love with her (as who hasn't with his nurse?). He builds a chapel of wax called *La Santa Caltha*, in which with his fellow bees to worship her. But Venus and Cupid harry the heretic 'Calthanists', and capture their leader the Bee. He escapes. Then Caltha the Marygold is metamorphosed into a lovely naked lady, flees from the lascivious coils of a mandrake root, and marries a nice boy named Musaeus, who makes his first entrance on the last page. I assume that the bishops decided rather quickly that this poem was not worth a public burning.

The same authorities were worried about the increase in personal scurrility and 'dangerous' comment by satirists on social problems. Everyone knew that Marston had been attacking Joseph Hall with all the vocabulary of defamation he was master of. Joseph Hall had complained of bad times and had eloquently inveighed against enclosure. Also, in view of the Marprelate pamphlets, it might have been thought that his sweeping attack on Roman Catholicism (IV, vii) smacked of

Martinism. The only way to account for Hall's reprieve on 4 June 1599 is that a second reading by the censors found his satires to be free of libellous personal attack (even against John Marston), dangerous thoughts and ecclesiastical *lèse majesté*. His satires were so cleverly written that they escaped the public punishment. In 1599 and 1602, they went into new editions; and beginning with W. Thompson in 1753, they have been reprinted in their entirety sixteen times.

So much for Hall's verse satires, which brought him literary fame when he was only twenty-three years of age – a fame based primarily on their literary excellence and secondarily on their open criticism of social ills and veiled attack on contemporary writing.

Joseph Hall's *Mundus Alter et Idem* (Another World Yet the Same), the satirical *voyage imaginaire* in Latin prose, stems from a different tradition, not that of the classical Roman poets but that of Brandt's *Ship of Fools* and Rabelais' *Pantagruel*. It is narrative and fictional, its setting far away and its time long ago. The genre has its own peculiar means of persuading its audience and of exculpating its author from libel; hence no one has charged *Mundus Alter et Idem* with obscurity. Using various accounts of explorers and maps by Ortelius and Mercator of Terra Australis, 'Mercurius Britannicus', the hidden author, pretends like an early Gulliver to visit four different countries, all south of Tierra del Fuego: Tenterbelly, where everyone eats and drinks too much; Shee-landt, an oppressive gynaecocracy; Fooliana, where only fools can survive; and Thievengen, inhabited by cozeners, cheaters and plagiarists. Two of the so-called sins are natural, being born female or foolish; and two are acquired, gluttony and dishonesty – a kind of neo-classical *discordia concors*.

Mundus was published without authorial consent in 1605 by Emmanuel College's William Knight. On the title-page, 'Franckfort' may well have been chosen by the author rather than the publisher to cast some opprobrium on the Calvinistic extremists responsible for the notorious 'troubles at Frankfort' in the 1550s; the many German-sounding names throughout the novel support the supposition. In 1609, John Healy translated, or rather adapted, the book in rollicking Elizabethan English under the title of *The Discovery of a New World*.

Questions have been raised concerning its authorship and the time of its composition, since it was published anonymously when Hall was a fully fledged Anglican priest. It has been argued that Alberigo Gentili was the author,[18] and some bibliographies still carry the notation 'probably by Hall' or 'attributed to Hall'. The original preface by Knight, however, seems to point towards Hall: 'But the author who explored this unknown world, having long ago bid farewell to the Muses, to whom he had paid court with applause, and being wholly departed from them, could never be tempted by no reward to allow his verses and other inventions of his, all most worthy of praise, to be put before the public gaze.'[19] John Healy addressed his translation to Joseph Hall: 'I. H. the translator, unto I. H. the Author.' In the preface to a second issue of his translation in 1613–14, Healy, again clearly referring to Joseph Hall as 'that Reuerend man', says: 'There was indeed a little booke some 8. or 9. yeares agoe that came from Franckford, which some few . . . affirmed to haue passed the file of his muse, which if it be true, it can be no way in the world either preiudiciall to his learning . . . nor to his grauity or profession seeing it was a birth of his youth' (p. 146).

Mundus is a funny, semi-bawdy, mock-scholarly and biting prose-satire. Its main contemporary thrust was a fierce anti-Catholicism, for it was published during the negotiations surrounding the interdiction of the Republic of Venice by Pope Paul V. By 1605–6, Frankfurt had become the 'Reformation City' and a publisher's paradise for anti-Roman propaganda. Hall writes to his friend William Bedell in Venice:

> Perhaps you complain of the inundations of Frankfort. How many have been discouraged from benefiting of the world by this conceit of multitude! Indeed, we all write; and, while we write, we cry out of number. How well might many be spared, even of those that complain of too many! Whose importunate babbling cloys the world, without use. [VI, 151]

Hall's 1608 publication of this letter (Decade I, epistle vii), which he himself edited, ends here. In the modern editions of Peter Hall, Pratt and Wynter, however, the letter continues from that point with:

> My suspicion gives me, that some may perhaps reflect this censure upon myself. I am content to put it to hazard; and, if needs be, bear it. But certainly, methinks, of profitable writings store is an easy fault. No man is bound to read; and he that will spend his time and eyes where no sensible profit draws him on, is worthy to lose his labour.

Thus in a letter written to a close friend who would know about *Mundus Alter et Idem* and its editor William Knight from college days, Hall mentions Frankfurt and his own writings in a single breath, very near the time when the great scholar Sarpi was resisting the incursions of the Roman church into civil affairs at Venice, all this to an English friend in Venice. Hall expunged this portion of his letter when he published it in 1608. That Joseph Hall wrote the satirical novel published in 1605, supposedly from Frankfurt, is witnessed later by John Milton, who had no doubt that Hall was its author.

It would seem equally certain that *Mundus* was written at about the same time as the verse satires, while Hall was still at Cambridge. Again, William Knight in 1605 says, 'Marry, he did use to say, as it were to excuse himself, that he had composed certain pieces in this kind in his young days and leisure at the University for his own instruction and delight . . .' (p. 143). We have had Healy's assertion of early composition. There is evidence that once Hall left Cambridge to take up his first duties in December 1601, as chaplain on the estate of Sir Robert Drury at Hawsted, Suffolk, he began to address his energies to becoming a churchman and a serious writer. S. M. Salyer argued unconvincingly that at least part of *Mundus* was written after Hall had arrived at Hawsted, on the ground that certain of his images appear in architectural iconography at the Drury mansion.[20] For example, Hall describes a banquet-room in Tenterbelly where a statue of Cupid stands holding a huge bowl for wine; when the bowl is filled the statue spews wine simultaneously from his mouth and from his urinary passage. Two initiates at once, attaching themselves to either spigot, must drink until the tun is empty. At Hawsted, writes Salyer, there used to be a fountain-statue of Hercules with a club on his shoulder and water flowing from his penis. But Salyer overlooks the fact that Cupid is not Hercules, and that many a Renaissance painting contains a *putto pisciatore*; also, few Englishman who visited Brussels failed to be impressed by 'le plus ancien bourgeois de la ville'.

There appears to be every reason, then, for thinking that *Mundus* was written by Joseph Hall and that it was written close in time to Hall's satires in verse. *Mundus* satirizes many of the same things that Hall attacks in poetry: it scores with possibly Puritan bias luxurious spending on clothes, food, tobacco and wine; it deplores the disregard for 'nature' that allows men to act like women and women to rule over men; and it is unmercifully anti-Roman Catholic.[21] Above all, it is engaging, witty and uproarious in its wilfully hyperbolical pictures of the 'seamier side' of Elizabethan society.

Virgidemiarum Six Books and *Mundus Alter et Idem* established Joseph Hall as a writer of the first rank.

3. The Cambridge Parnassus Plays, John Marston, and Hawstead, Suffolk

There is a strong probability that, in addition to writing satirical prose in Latin and satires in English verse, Joseph Hall while at college also tried his hand at drama. As part of their Christmas festivities in 1598, 1599 and 1602, the boys of St John's, Cambridge, presumably aided by any other collegians they could draft, produced the three so-called 'Parnassus plays'. The plays have aroused interest because of their anonymity, topical value and sheer fun.[1]

The first play, *The Pilgrimage to Parnassus*, describes two students on their way to the B.A. degree: the theologically inclined Studioso and the classicist-poet Philomusus. Passing through the 'countries' of Logic, Rhetoric and Philosophy, they successfully resist their tempters: the ministerial Studioso rejects a Ramistic Puritan, and Philomusus the poet turns his back on a drunken Aretine. Both of them, however, are attracted to Amoretto, reading Ovid, despite Ingenioso's warning that Hobson makes more money renting twelve nags than they could writing two hundred books.

The next two plays together are *The Returne from Parnassus*. In the first of these, having attained their degrees, the boys are set adrift in the real world, where, soon discovering that nobody seems willing either to buy their poetry or pay them living wages as schoolmaster or chaplain, they threaten to accept the bribe for 'perverting' to Rome. The second part of *The Returne*, subtitled, 'The Scourage of Simony', opens with the boys reading Bodenham's newly published *Belevedere or the Muses' Garden* (1600), and lampooning every contemporary poet in it except 'Mr Shakespeare', whose *Venus and Adonis* they think very good. As many as seventeen new characters are added (not counting 'Fiddlers'), each one remarkably differentiated. The comic turns of plot are more complex, and the dialogue wittier. While waiting for a benefice, which the patron sells to an ignoramus for £100, the boys try to live by pretending to be a French physician and his man, then as actors with two bedraggled characters named Burbage and Kempe, and finally as wandering fiddlers. After firing off a few initial shots in 'the war of the theatres' and complaining of this unappreciative world, they retire to the Arcadian simplicity of a shepherd's life in Kent.

This, the second part of *The Returne from Parnassus*, was the only one of the three plays that was printed (twice in 1606). It stood alone until the Rev W. D. Macray, Bodley's librarian, discovered in Thomas Hearne's collection the manuscripts of *The Pilgrimage to Parnassus* and the first part of *The Returne from Parnassus*. In 1886 he published the first edition of the comic trilogy.[2]

Almost immediately speculation on their authorship began, conjectures based on the charade-like hints in the prologues of the last two plays.[3] Of the author of *The Pilgrimage* the prologue of the first *Returne* says:

> Surelie it made our poet a staide man,
> Kepte his proude necke from baser lambskins weare,
> Had like to have made him senior sophister,
> He was faine to take his course by Germanie
> Ere he coulde get a silie poore degree.
> Hee neuer since durst name a peece of cheese,
> Thoughe Chesshire seems to priuiledge his name.[4]

So it has been argued that William Dodd, the only Cheshire name at St John's College at the time, was the author. Again, John Day, who sometimes spelled his name 'Dey', which means dairyman or a maker of cheese, has been named as the author. It has been proposed that by 'Germany' is meant 'Holland'; and consequently that William Holland must have written the first play. One might build a better argument for John Weever of Queen's. He was well known as a witty poet; he greatly admired Shakespeare's erotic verse; and his famous epigram on Gullio is actually quoted in the first *Returne from Parnassus* (1, 959, p. 182). He may well have given his friends fears that he would never graduate because of his drinking (Germany was notorious for its lack of sobriety). And since the Weaver is the principal river in the county of Cheshire, 'Cheshire seems to privilege his name' – John Weever.[5]

Slightly less obscure hints, this time of a possibly different author, appear in the prose and poetic prologues of the second part of *The Returne from Parnassus*. This 'is the last time that the Authors wit wil turne vpon the toe in this vaine' (p. 222) is what the manuscript version says, but the 1606 printed play has: 'that is both the first & the last time', which would make the author of the last play a different man from the author of the *Pilgrimage* and from the author of the first *Returne*. The poetic prologue to the final play tells us:

> In Scholers fortunes twise forlorne and dead
> Twise hath our weary pen earst laboured,
> Making them Pilgrims to *Pernassus* hill,
> Then penning their returne with ruder quill.
> Now we present vnto each pittying eye
> The schollers progresse in their miserye.
> [p. 224]

In his summary of the problem of authorship, Leishman (p. 31) concludes that there are two authors: one for the *Pilgrimage* and the other for both the *Returnes*. The prologue just quoted, however, clearly breaks the trilogy between the first two plays and the third with the words 'Now' and 'schollers progresse'. The last play shows a marked increase in satirical acerbity, and an artistic superiority in plot, character and wit. Could Joseph Hall have been its author?

Inevitably, where external proof of authorship is lacking, the literary scholar must argue by probability. He makes a hypothesis to stand or fall not by a chain of reasoning (which breaks at its weakest link), but rather by explaining more historical facts and literary traits than any other. The hypothesis, furthermore, is made attractive by its solving other problems that hang upon the solution of this particular one.

In this chapter I shall argue, then, that Joseph Hall may have had a hand in all three plays and was the major author of the last one, that is, the second part of *The Returne from Parnassus*. And I shall arrange the evidence to support my case in three major propositions ranging from fact to reasonable inference, as follows: (1) that certain facts, such as the verbal parallels in the Parnassan plays to Hall's published work and the absence in Hall's satires of direct attack on Marston, coupled with Marston's hatred of Hall, demand an explanation; (2) that in view of the satire on Marston in the second *Returne from Parnassus*, the origin of Marston's hitherto unexplained attack on Hall may be his conviction that Hall was mainly responsible for it; and (3) that several other pieces of evidence, quite apart from Marston's crucial testimony, point towards Hall's being the real author.

Obviously indisputable is that the Parnassan plays are filled with parallels to Hall's *Virgidemiae*. McCray, the first editor of all three plays, wrote: 'A comparison with Bishop Hall's *Satires* brings to view a great similarity alike in subjects and in language. The second book of

Satires deals, in fact, with many of the abuses of which our unknown author treats'—namely, poverty of scholars, charlatan lawyers, quack doctors, simony, hiring a well-educated tutor at starvation wages. Many of the personae are similar, too; Ingenioso's description of Amoretto is almost exactly like Hall's description of Gallio, both of whom are sonneteers. Also, most of the Parnassan wits admire Spenser, as does Hall.[6] Not a single passage in the plays reflects sarcastically upon the writing of Joseph Hall.

Dozens of verbal parallels have already been documented by scholars. Most of the parallels link Hall's *Virgidemiae* to the second part of *The Returne from Parnassus*, the only one of the three plays, as if to reflect superior authorship, that was printed. For example:

1 (a) Hall, I, 1, 8–9, p. 12:[7]
> Nor can I bide to pen some hungry Scene
> For *thick-skin eares*, and vndiscerning eyne.
(b) *Parnassus, 2nd Returne*, IV, 1340–41, p. 305:
> The [servile] current of my slyding verse
> Gently shal runne into his *thick-skind eares*.

2 (a) Hall I, ii, 25–6, p. 13:
> And where they wont sip of the simple floud,
> Now tosse they *Bowles of Bacchus boyling blood*.
(b) *Parnassus, 2nd Returne*, I, vi, 503, p. 257:
> There quaffing *Bowles of Bacchus blood* ful nimbly.

3 (a) Hall, II, ii, 15–16, p. 24:
> Scorne ye the world before it do complaine,
> And *scorne the world that scorneth you againe*.
(b) *Parnassus, 2nd Returne*, I, iv, 399, p. 251:
> Ile *scorne the world that scorneth me againe*.

4 (a) Hall, II, iii, 23–4, p. 26:
> Each home-bred science percheth in the *chaire*,
> Whiles sacred arts *grouell on the ground*sell bare.

(b) *Parnassus, 2nd Returne*, II, i, 557–9, pp. 261–2:
> Oh how it greeues my vexed soule to see
> Each painted asse in *Chayre* of dignitye;
> And yet we *grouell on the ground* alone.

5 (a) Hall, II, iv, 11–12, p. 27, on the medical fashion of uroscopy:
> And spie out maruels in each Vrinall,

And *tumble vp the filths that from them fall.*
(b) *Parnassus, 2nd Returne,* I, ii, 143–6, p. 228:
... like a needy Phisitian to stand whole yeares
tooting *and tumbling the filth that falleth.*

6 (a) Hall, IV, i, 72, p. 51 :
His Eares hang lauing like a new-lug'd swine.
(b) *Parnassus, 2nd Returne,* V, iv, 2195, p. 365:
Like a great *swine,* by his long *laue-eard lugges.*

7 (a) Hall, V, iv, 14, p. 86:
To drag his *Tumbrell* through the *staring Cheape.*
(b) *Parnassus, 2nd Returne,* I, i, 110–13, p. 226:
Nor can it 'mongst our gallants prayses reape,
Unlesse it be [y]done in *staring Cheape,*
In a sinne-guilty *Coach.*

Indeed, the parallels between these witty but still anonymous plays, especially the second *Returne,* and Hall's published satires are so numerous and so telling as to have brought the late editor of Hall's *Collected Poems,* Professor A. Davenport of Liverpool, to the very verge of my thesis: 'I would not positively affirm that Hall had a share in the writing of the Parnassus Plays, but it is demonstrable that the writer,whoever he was, knew *Virgidemiae* with suspicious intimacy and shared Hall's critical views.'[8]

Equally indisputable is that Marston launched a bitter attack on Hall in his *Certayne Satires,* published with *The Metamorphosis of Pygmalion's Image* (1598). These attacks Marston continued in *The Scourge of Villanie* of 1598, reissued twice in 1599. To explain Marston's hatred of Hall, Grosart and Bullen conjectured that Hall had seen a manuscript version of *Pygmalion's Image* before he wrote his three books of *Byting Satyres* (1598).[9]

But more recent scholarship does not find the cause in Hall's known published work. Ford E. Curtis, in his 1932 Cornell dissertation, concluded that 'there is in Hall no unmistakeable reference to Marston'. And though Davenport links the attack to the earlier Harvey–Nashe controversy, even he comes to this negative conclusion: 'Of the quarrel between Marston and Hall no completely satisfactory account can be given.'[10] Anthony Caputi, in *John Marston, Satirist,* thinks that the only item that might have been the ground for the attack is the epigram on 'Kinsayder' which Marston said Hall pasted into copies of Marston's book as they lay in the stalls at Cambridge.[11] Arnold Stein, R. M. Alden, K. Schultz and Morse Allen all feel that the epigram is not by Hall.[12] Acknowledging its poetic inferiority, Davenport nevertheless includes it in Hall's canon (p. 101) as possibly Hall's 'reactio' to Marston. I think it is by Hall, but if so it is an effect and not a cause. How personally Marston took some of Hall's general crticism of contemporary poetry in *Virgidemiae* we do not know. The fact is that Hall's published satires do not directly name Marston or his poetry, or even throw a particularizing glance in Marston's direction.

On the other hand, the Parnassan plays, especially the second *Returne*, are filled with libellous slurs on John Marston. The character Furor Poeticus in the final play, actually referred to as 'Kinsayder', Marston's chosen pseudonym, is a merciless lampoon. When Ingenioso reads the name 'John Marston' from *Belvedere*, Judicio cries: 'What *Monsieur Kinsayder*, lifting vp your legge and pissing against the world? Put vp man, put vp for shame' (2nd *Returne*, I, ii, 267–8, p. 241). The name 'Kinsayder' is connected to 'Kinsing', the act of docking dogs' tails, and the parody bristles with Marstonian dog-images. A perusal of Leishman's parallels and allusions to Marston's poems (pp. 82–92) and of the index (under 'Parnassus') to Davenport's edition of Marston's poems make argument unnecessary, but a few quotations from the two texts will illustrate the mocking 'Parnassan' tone:

1 (a) Marston, *Certaine Satyres*, V, 49–50, p. 88:
   In strength of lust and *Venus* surquedry
   Rob'd fifty wenches of virginity.[13]

 (b) *Parnassus, Pilgrimage*, IV, 479–90, p. 120:
   Theile freelie give what ere youre luste shall craue
   And make you melte in Venus surque[d]rie.

2 (a) Marston, *Scourge*, VIII, 143–4, p. 154:
   I am not saplesse, old, or rumatick,
   No *Hipponax* mishapen stigmatick . . .

 (b) *Parnassus, Pilgrimage*, II, 210, 215, pp. 105–6: the phrase 'old Stigmaticke' occurs in a speech that also mentions 'Kinsaders Satyres'.

3 (a) Marston, *Scourge*, 'To Detraction', 11, 7–12, p. 95:
   Know that the *Genius*, which attendeth on,
   And guides my powers intellectuall,
   Holds in all vile repute *Detraction*,
   My soule an essence metaphisicall,
   That in the basest sort scornes *Critickes* rage,
   Because he knowes his sacred parentage.

(b) *Parnassus, 2nd Returne*, III, iv, 1301–4, p. 303 (Furor Poeticus):
By that caelestiall fier within my brayne
That giues a liuing genius to my lines:
How ere my dulled intellectuall
Capres lesse nimbly than it did a fore.

4 (a) Marston, *Certaine Satyres*, V, 169, p. 92:
The subject is too sharp for my dull quill.

(b) *Parnassus, 2nd Returne*, I, vi, 471, p. 256 (Furor Poeticus):
Who's that runs headlong on my quills sharpe poynt?

So far there has been no room for argument. We have known for a long time that Hall's *Virgidemiae* are liberally quoted in the Parnassan plays; that despite Hall's abstention from particularizing Marston in his satires, Furor Poeticus in the second *Returne from Parnassus* is a scathing portrait of Marston; and that Marston published vitriolic assaults upon Joseph Hall for reasons that have never been determined.

Since there is less certitude about my second point, it must be put in the form of a question. Why did Marston attack Hall? Was he jealous? Both poets had joined the new school of young satirists, but Hall had preceded Marston by a whole year. And yet no poet as proud as Marston would attack a fellow-poet on grounds of jealousy alone lest he confess his own poems to be inferior. Could the jibes against Marston in the second *Returne from Parnassus* have been the seeds of Marston's anger? Another way of asking the same question is this: why, in his published work, does Marston so often combine his attacks on Hall with his quite justified resentment of the parody of his poetic style and person in *The Returne from Parnassus*?

That he does do this may be demonstrated by documenting passages of Marston's vilification of Joseph Hall that contain within themselves 'reactio's' to the St John's College Parnassan plays. Some examples follow.

In *The Scourge of Villanie* (XI, 104–6, p. 170), Marston uses against Hall the names of 'honest Phylo' and 'judiciall Musus', which combine by accident or design to form Philomusus, the main character in all three Parnassan plays.

In *The Scourge* (III, 11–18, pp. 114–15), Marston writes: 'What Academick starued Satyrist/Would once a thrice-turn'd bone-pick'd subject gnaw/When swarmes of Mountebancks, & Bandeti . . .' The 'thrice-turn'd bone', another dog-metaphor, may allude to the Parnassan trilogy,[14] while the term 'mountebanks' suggests actors on a stage.

In Satire IX, the repeated word 'apes' in the plural, as though Marston had more than merely Joseph Hall in mind, refers to poetic imitators, but it could also suggest the 'apish imitation' of the mimic stage:

> Come downe yee Apes, or I will strip you quite,
> Baring your bald tayles to the peoples sight.
>
> [IX, 11–12, p. 158]

'Athens apes' (line 21) means Cambridge students, and Marston's phrase 'furr'd with beard' and 'cas'd in a Satin sute' (line 15) may well glance at college boys costumed in a play. In the same satire Marston says of Hall:

> O senceless prose, iudiciall poesie,
> How ill you'r link'd. This affectation,
> To speake beyond mens apprehension
> How Apish tis. When all in fusten sute
> Is cloth'd a huge *nothing*, all for repute
> Of profound knowledge, when profoundness knowes
> There's nought contain, but only seeming showes.
>
> [IX, 65–71, p. 160]

The target of Satire IX is Hall, and yet 'O how on tiptoes proudly mounts my Muse' (line 5) had been mocked in *Parnassus*: 'Endite a tiptoe-strouting poesy' (2nd *Returne*, I, v, 503, p. 258), and 'my high tiptoe-strowting poesye' (ibid., III, v, 1345, p. 305). The 'fusten sute', of course, refers to style, but with 'showes' it may allude to a stage production. The 'Athens ape' that 'yaule[s] *auditores humanissimi*' merely makes fun of collegians by using a stock Latin phrase from a typical undergraduate prolusion. Hall was famous for his prolusions, and the phrase had been used as a nickname for an academic in *The Pilgrimage to Parnassus* (V, 622, p. 127). Most importantly, since Hall's published satires are all poetry, Marston's disparaging poetry and prose 'ill-linked' in this strike against Hall can refer only to the *Parnassus* plays, which actually do combine prose and poetry.

In Satire VIII of the first book of *Virgidemiarum*, Hall had written:

> Hence ye profane: mell not with holy things
> That *Sion* muse from *Palestina* brings.
> *Parnassus* is transform'd to Sion hill,
> And *Iu'ry-palmes* her steep ascents done fill.[15]
> Now good Saint *Peter* weeps pure Helicon,
> And both *Maries* make a Musick mone:

Yea and the Prophet of Heauenly Lyre,
Great *Salomon,* sings in the English Quire,
And is become a newfound Sonetist,
Singing his loue, the holy spouse of Christ:
Like as she were some light-skirts of the rest
In mightiest Ink-hornismes he can thither wrest.
                    [I, viii, 1–12, p. 19]

Marston is certainly answering this poem by Hall in 'Reactio':

Ye *Granta's* white Nymphs, come & with you bring
Some sillibub, whilst he doth sweetly sing
Gainst *Peters* teares, and *Maries* mouing moane,
And like a fierce enraged Boare doth foame
At sacred Sonnets, O daring hardiment,
At *Bartas* Sweet Semaines, raile impudent
At *Hopkins,. Sternhold,* and the *Scottish* King.
                    [lines 25–31, p. 82]

Hall's and Marston's references seem to tally well so far as they concern Southwell's sacred poetry, Gervase Markham's *The Peom of Poems or Sion's Muse,* and perhaps Lodge's *The Teares of Marie Mother of God.* But though Hall merely bids du Bartas of France and Ariosto of Italy to yield to the English Spenser (I, iv, 25–8), where does he 'raile impudent' against du Bartas, Hopkins, Sternhold and the Scottish king? A passage from the second *Returne from Parnassus* supplies the key, and convicts Marston of attempting to foist a charge of *lèse majesté* upon Joseph Hall. When, in that play, the names of Henry Lok (Locke) and Thomas Hudson are read out from *Belvedere,* Judicio says: '*Locke* and *Hudson,* sleep you quiet shauers, among the shauings of the presse, and let your bookes lie in some old nooke amongst old bootes and shooes, so you may [happ to] auoyd my censure' (p. 241). Henry Lok in 1591 had contributed a sonnet to the *Essayes of a Prentice* by James of Scotland. Lok's *Christian Passions* (1593) contained a hundred sonnets, and his *Ecclesiasticus* (1597) – from Solomon, 'abridged and also periphrastically dilated in English Poesie' – added 306 sonnets as well as 'Sundry Psalms of David translated into Verse' (reminding one of Hopkins and Sternhold, inveterate Psalm-versifiers). Lok's partner in Parnassan crime, Thomas Hudson, had dedicated his translation of du Bartas as *The History of Judith in forme of a Poeme* (Edinburgh, 1594) to His Majesty James VI of Scotland, and its frontal matter contains a royal sonnet. It is clear, then, that Marston got Hall railing impudently at du Bartas and the King of Scotland not from *Virgidemiae,* I, viii, but from the second *Returne from Parnassus,* for the very next poet for Parnassan condemnation, after Lok and Hudson, is John Marston as Monsieur Kinsayder lifting up his leg 'to piss against the world' (p. 241).

A similar proof comes in Marston's 'Reactio' (*Certaine Satyres*, IV, 81–2, p. 83), where Marston asks:

> What, shall not *Rosamond*, or *Gaueston*,
> Ope their sweet lips without detraction?

These are obvious references to Daniel's *The Complaint of Rosamund* (1592) and Drayton's *The Legend of Piers Gaveston* (1594). Marston is responding to Hall's *Virgidemiae*, I, v; but Professor Davenport confesses (*Marston*, p. 245) that he can see no clear trace in Hall's poem of criticism of these two pieces; he had made the same confession in 1949 in his commentary on Hall (pp. xlix and 168). Davenport's dilemma, however, is resolved by seeking background for Marston's 'reactio', not in Hall's *Virgidemiae* but in the second *Returne from Parnassus*. There the college wits say:

> Sweete hony dropping *Daniell* may wage
> Warre with the proudest big Italian
> That melts his heart in sugred sonetting:
> Onely let him more sparingly make vse
> Of others wit, and vse his owne the more.
>
> [I, ii, 235–9, pp. 238–9]

Without break there follows immediately a censure of the author of *The Legend of Piers Gaveston*:

> *Drayton's* sweete muse is like a sanguine dy,
> Able to rauish the rash gazers eye.
>
> [ll. 240–1]

Only, the boys continue, Drayton lacks one true mark of a poet of our times, that is, 'hee cannot swagger it well in a Tauerne'. Marston's attack on Hall's Satire I, v, of *Virgidemiae*, then, embraces a criticism expressed in *Parnassus* as if one man, Joseph hall, were responsible for them both.

In *The Scourge*, XI (110 ff., p. 170), Marston writes of 'judiciall Musus', who is Hall:

> ... Wilt thou credite me
> He neuer writ one line in poesy,
> But once at Athens in a theame did frame
> A paradox in prayse of Vertues name.

I suggest that this refers to the poetic speech spoken by Consiliodorus near the beginning of *The Pilgrimage to Parnassus*. One of the longest speeches in the whole trilogy (seventy-six lines), it is actually a theme in praise of virtue. As the young pilgrims start on their journey, Consiliodorus, a Dametas-like figure, advises them to beware of flatterers, carousers and lecherers; he counsels academic youth not to hope for this world's goods, but instead to be diligent 'to make the vallies heare with admiration/Those songs which youre refined tounge shall singe' (I, i, 101–2, p. 99). And yet, in view of the 'frame' in which the speech occurs – that is, the two plays of satire that follow it – to Marston it may very well be a paradox. It seems as though he refers to the same Parnassan speech in 'Reactio', which is a vehement denunciation of Joseph Hall:

> . . . thus it is when pitty Priscians
> Will needs step up to be Censorians.
> When once they can in true skan's verses frame
> *A braue* Encomium *of good Vertues name.*
> Why thus it is, when Mimick Apes will striue
> With Iron wedge the truncks of Oakes to riue
>
> [*Certaine Satyres*, IV, 103–8, p. 84]

A peculiarity of this long speech in praise of virtue is that it is in blank verse, a fact which may lie behind Marston's phrase, 'true skan'd verses' as opposed to rimed.

Still smarting at the picture of himself in the St John's College play, Marston seems to be convinced that the author is a Puritan, perhaps a member of Emmanuel College.[16] Marston (II, 56, p. 73) speaks of Hall as that 'deuote meale-mouth'd Precisean'. Similarly, the whole of 'Satyra Nova', added to the second edition of his book and dedicated to Edward Guilpin, once of Emmanuel College, is an attack on Hall. In it Marston says:

> Cryes beard-graue *Dromus*, when alas, God knowes,
> His toothles gums nere chew but outward showes.
> Poore Budgeface, bowcase sleeue, but let him passe,
> *Once fur and beard shall priuledge an Asse.*
>
> [lines 23–6, pp. 163–4]

This is the poem in which Marston quotes the epigram on Kinsayder which he accuses Hall of having pasted in the copies of his book. The 'toothles gums' are Hall's 'Toothless Satyres', and though Dromio is a slave in Terence, he is also a clown in *The Pilgrimage to Parnassus*. Again, the 'fur and beard' bespeaks an actor; and as for 'Budgeface', referring to an academic hood trimmed with white lamb's wool, Davenport comments: 'If so, Dromus will be a Fellow, perhaps of Emmanuel' (p. 353).

Moreover, in the ninth satire of *The Scourge*, entirely devoted to assailing Joseph Hall, Marston writes:

> Why lookes neate *Curus* all so simperingly?
> Why babbles thou of deepe Diuinitie?
> And of that sacred testimoniall?
> Liuing voluptuous like a *Bacchanall*?
> Good hath thy tongue : but thou ranke Puritan,
> I'll make an Ape as good a Christian.
> I'le force him chatter, turning vp his eye
> Looke sad, goe graue, Demure ciuilite
> Shall seeme to say, *Good brother, sister deere . . .*
> Disguised *Messaline,*
> I'le teare thy maske, and bare thee to the eyne
> Of hissing boyes, if to the Theaters
> I finde thee once more come for lecherers
> To satiate.
>
> [lines 105–25, pp. 161–2]

If the inspiration for this anger were the *Virgidemiae*, there would be no need to tear off a mask since Hall is speaking there in his own person. Rather, Marston places the snivelling Puritan, Joseph Hall, in a theatre, evidently disguised in a costume, acting in a stage piece whose audience is made up of boys: 'I'll teare thy maske, and bare thee to the eyne/Of hissing boyes, if to the Theaters/I finde thee once more come'.

And what about the minor problem of Joseph Hall's so-called 'lost Pastorals'?[17] In his most savage attack on Hall, Marston asks, with obvious sarcasm, 'Will not his Pastorals indure for euer?' ('Reactio', line 148, p. 85). The term could not possibly apply to the satires *Virgidemiarum*, in whose context it appears. In 'The King's Prophecy' of 1603, Hall refers to an early work of his own, a translation of Virgil's fourth eclogue in which (so he says) he had hailed the birth of Henry the prince, first son of James VI of Scotland (stanza 17, p. 112). There is no other record of this 'eclogue', which may have been a college exercise, since Henry was born in 1593. In 1598, Marston could not have been referring to Hall's 1603 notation of it; and if he knew about it, he would have used the singular, not the plural: 'Will not his Pastoralls indure foruer?' The Parnassan plays, on the other hand, show great admiration for the pastorals of Spenser, and the main characters actually become shepherds. As when Marston asked Hall to 'show vs the true forme of Dametas face' (*Certaine Satyres*, I, 120, p. 70), he seems to be wishing here that Hall had left the Parnassan plays all pastoral and not have added the satire. They *are* pastoral; at the end of the trilogy, Philomusus says:

> Perhaps some happy wit, with feeling hand,
> Hereafter may recorde the pastorall
> Of the two schollers of *Pernassus* hill,
> And then our scene may end and haue content.
>   [p. 366].

Hall had ended his introductory poem to *Virgidemiae*, 'Defiance to Envy', which Marston is savagely parodying in 'Reactio', with an idyllic view of pastoral verse. 'Speake ye attentiue swaynes that heard me late,' he says, and vows hereafter to write not pastoral but only satire: 'At Colins feete I throw my yeelding reed.' Are the Parnassan plays Hall's 'pastorals' that the Cambridge swains had 'lately heard', and is Marston wishing that his enemy had kept to the pastoral strain of innocent pilgrims to Parnassus? We shall never know for certain.

Meanwhile, however, the best way to account for Marston's associating his hatred of Joseph Hall with his resentment of the Cambridge players is to grant that, in 1598 and 1599, Marston believed Joseph Hall to be the main author of the second *Returne from Parnassus*. Although its first performance is recorded as having taken place in December 1601, whereas Marston published his reaction in 1598 and 1599, we do not know how long before its first performance the play was actually written. Its prologue says: 'What is presented here, is an old musty showe, that hath laine this twelfe-moneth in the bottome of a coale-house' (p. 220). That Marston actually uses lines from the play must show either that the play had received an earlier performance than the ones recorded, or that Marston had seen a manuscript version.

Other evidence, finally, a bit farther afield, strengthens the hypothesis that indeed Hall is the author. The entitling of Hall's second three books as *Byting Satyres* whereas the first three were 'Toothless' may bear some relationship to the fact that *The Returne from Parnassus* differs from *The Pilgrimage* as the harshness of the economic and literary world differs from the joys and temptations of academic life. It is even 'ruder' than the 'rude quill' of the prologue to the second play. In the opening of his 1597 publication of satires, Hall himself had said: 'The ruder Satyre should goe rag'd and bare:/And show his rougher and his hairy hide' (*His Defiance to Enuie*, lines 76–7). Thus the satire of the last play, like that of the *Virgidemiae*, shifts from the decorum of Horace to Juvenalian wrath heaped upon simony and philistinism, arch-sins of altar and pen. As the curtain rises, enter 'Ingenioso, with Iuvenall in his hand', whom Judicio greets with,

41

'What, Ingenioso, carrying a Vinegar bottle about thee?' The boys of St John's College needed a Joseph Hall to complete the Christmas satires they had begun.

But Hall was in Emmanuel, and these are St John's College plays. While a student at Cambridge, Hall is known to have been so popular for his wit and oratory as to have joined with friends from other colleges in their display. In 1597, for example, he took part in the university festivities that welcomed the Earl of Essex. George Coke, in a Latin letter to his brother John, who was staying with his friend Fulke Greville at Essex House in the Strand, describes the occasion. Among those taking part, Coke says, were Sutton of King's, Stanton of St John's, Sharton of Trinity, and Braithwaite and Joseph Hall of Emmanuel.[18] This was the year Hall published his first volume of satires. That he was even previously called upon as a poet by St John's is shown by his contribution (as we have seen) to the volume of *carmen funèbre* published in 1596 to mark the death of St John's famous theologian, Dr William Whitaker.

The Parnassan device of a *voyage imaginaire*, moreover, is shared by Hall's early 'novel', *Mundus Alter et Idem*, discussed in the preceding chapter. In the introduction to that book, William Knight, referrring to Hall, speaks of 'his verses and other inventions of his' and asserts that '[Hall] did use to say ... that he had composed certain pieces in this kind in his young days and leisure at the University for his own instruction and delight'. Surely Knight in 1605 is not thinking of Hall's satires: the 1599 edition had on the title page 'By I.H.', and everybody knew the satires were by Joseph Hall. By 'other inventions' could he mean 'dramatic'? In the same breath he asserts that these 'other inventions' were similar to the satirical, semi-bawdy and 'journeying' *Mundus Alter et Idem*. Surely he is pointing to the dramatic satires called 'the Parnassan plays'. Hall's own introduction to *Mundus* is signed 'Peregrinus quondam Academicus', in Healy's translation 'The Cambridge Pilgrim', a phrase that echoes the prologue of the last Parnassus play. 'Making them Pilgrims to *Pernassus* hill.'

Why was the second *Returne from Parnassus* the only one of the three plays printed, twice in 1606? Obviously because it mentions Shakespeare, Jonson and the 'warriors of the theatres'. It is also the best of the three plays. Could its publisher have received the manuscript from one of Hall's friends, Owen Gwynne of St John's, perhaps, to whom the Stationers' Register assigns it,[19] on condition that he respect Hall's wish to remain anonymous now that he was serving as rector in the parish of Sir Robert Drury and had just been asked by Lady Drury's brother, Sir Edmund Bacon, to acompany him on a mission to the continent? Cantabrigians must have known that just the year before, William Knight, possessing the manuscript of *Mundus*, had risked Hall's displeasure by publishing it without Hall's permission.

Later in the century, as we shall see, John Milton in *An Apology against a Pamphlet* lashed out against an opponent of his *Animadversions* whom he took to be Bishop Joseph Hall. Making fun of the youthful *Mundus Alter et Idem*, Milton wrote: 'Let him go now and brand another man injuriously with the name of *Mime*, being himselfe the loosest and most extravagant *Mime*, that hath been heard of; whom no lesse than almost halfe the world could serve for stage roome to play the *Mime* in.'[20] In his own day at Cambridge, Milton had seen with disgust divinity students play-acting in false beards and costumes. He almost puts himself back several college generations in order to watch the young Joseph Hall of Emmanuel:

> ... that Playes must have bin seene, what difficulty was there in that? When in the Colleges so many of the young Divines, and those in next aptitude to Divinity have bin seene so oft upon the Stage writhing and unboning their Clergie limmes to all the antick and dishonest gestures of Trinculo's, Buffons, and Bawds ... Judge now whether so many good text men were not sufficient to instruct me of false beards and vizards without more expositors; ...[21]

Forty years after the event, Milton is angry with this Anglican bishop for writing satires and a semi-bawdy *voyage imaginaire*, but also for something even worse, which Milton had evidently been told about: actually taking part at Cambridge in stage-performance. One might expect such behaviour in a St John's or Peterhouse man, but not in a Fellow at Emmanuel.

We can only argue, not *prove*, that Joseph Hall was the author of *The Second Returne from Parnassus*. If there were documentary proof, of course, there would be no need of a hypothesis. But if these facts and the suggested relations between them can convince us that Hall did write the play, then several other problems will fall into place: (1) why there are so many verbal parallels between the play and Hall's satires; (2) why Marston attacked Hall so vehemently; (3) what Hall's 'other inventions' cited in 1605 as springing from his college days were; (4) a correction to Davenport's assertion that '[Hall] had written and circulated in manuscript, but apparently not published, Pastorals which have not survived'; (5) why Hall so resolutely turned his back on his literary beginnings; and (6) why Milton in 1642 used theatrical images against Hall while defending the five Puritan co-authors.

In the very month that the second part of *The Returne from Parnassus* was performed, December 1601, Hall accepted the benefice from the Drury family at Hawstead, Suffolk, four miles from Bury St Edmunds, where his Emmanuel friend William Bedell was rector. He could have stayed on at Emmanuel, according to its provisions, for four more years. But he had been at Cambridge for twelve years, and Uncle Edmund's financial help had been exhausted for five. Like the characters in the play, he had to descend from Parnassus to the plains of reality, an aged 'student' of twenty-seven.

Today Hawstead is a village of not more than eight or nine houses. Beyond the little church of All Saints lies the meadow where once stood the 'Great Hall' of Sir Robert Drury. The church – Norman and later, the tower Perpendicular, hammerbeams and angles decorating the nave – still stands. It contains tombs of the illustrious Bacon family dating from the thirteenth century, and among the coats of arms in the porch is that of Drury. Here and in the chapel of the Drury household, Joseph Hall preached three times a week. Here he gave religious counselling to Elizabeth Drury from the age of seven; when she died in 1610 she was immortalized by Donne's *Anniversaries*, to which Hall provided introductory verses. At Hawstead he was dissatisfied with the pay he was getting, which seemed to make true the witty complaints he had published in his satires; he was also put to the expense of making his house habitable,[22] and he was gravelled in his religious duties by 'Mr Lily', a spy for Sir Robert's continental interests, whom Hall calls an 'atheist'.

In 1603 Hall married Elizabeth Wynniff of Brettenham, Suffolk, and in the same year he published a 384-line poem called *The Kings Prophecie: or Weeping Ioy*, in which he mourns the death of Queen Elizabeth and welcomes the accession of James I. Thus four events in the year 1603, two public and two private, seem to mark a change in his literary career: the end of one reign and the beginning of another, on the one hand; and, on the other, his marriage and the Bachelor of Divinity degree from Cambridge. In 1603, entering upon his thirtieth year, he decided with a great precedent before him just where his real ministry would lie. Henceforth he will put behind him the 'harsh verse' and 'rude satire' of his youth. Not only did he choose to pursue an ecclesiatical career within the new establishment, but he would become a serious writer and this more in prose than in poetry.

As a Christian, he wanted to do something closer to men's consciences, so he wrote one of the earliest English books of *Meditations* (1606). After taking the negative view common to scolding, he wanted to write something positive; hence the first of its genre in England, his *Characters of Vertues and Vices* (1608). He felt the necessity, as even John

Marston did, to separate the satirical condemnation of vice from that of the religious zealot by adopting a more moderate, humble and honest stance; hence the volumes of his own *Epistles* (1608–11). The moral position of the satirist is also that of the Stoic, above the pettiness of small minds; hence Hall's decision to become 'the English Seneca'.[23] Instead of indulging in poetamachias, finally, henceforth he would dedicate his skill in rhetoric to more important ends. He had barely escaped official condemnation for his *Satires*; after leaving Cambridge he had a great deal more at stake.

These are some of the reasons why Joseph Hall, among the candidates for authorship, should remain anonymous before and after the second *Returne from Parnassus* was twice acted, in 1601 and 1602, and twice printed, in 1606.

4. *Waltham, King James as Solomon, and* Characters of Vertues and Vices

In addition to his ordinary duties at Hawstead, Joseph Hall tells us, he had to write books in order to purchase books, since his salary was so small. In the spring of 1605, however, he took a leave of absence to accompany as chaplain Lady Drury's brother on an embassy abroad. Details of that trip and of the two meditational works he composed at Hawstead must wait, with slight chronological dislodgement, until a later chapter; it was during that trip upon the continent that Hall was inspired to write on Protestant meditation. Returning from the Lowlands, he continued at Hawstead for another two years, preaching three times a week, chafing under Mr Lily's taunts and his patron's refusal to pay him the £10 more a year he had promised, and writing books.

One of them, as though his discontents had prompted the pious wish, was entitled *Heauen vpon Earth* (1606). Professor Rudolf Kirk's edition joins it to the *Characters of Vertues and Vices* on the ground that both works display a classical strain.[1] 'Theophrastus and Seneca,' writes Kirk in his introduction 'supplied the classical models which Hall followed in developing (i) the form, and (ii) the style and the philosophy of his character sketchès' (p. 5). Hall's Neostoicism, however, in the earlier work, like that of Lipsius, de Mornay and du Vair, is more Christian than Senecan; and his Ramistic method of opposing pairs can hardly be called classical.

In his dedication of *Heauen vpon Earth*, Hall says: 'I haue undertaken a great taske ... wherein I have followed Seneca, and gone beyond him; followed him as a Philosopher, gone beyond him as a Christian, as a Divine.' Seneca's goal is tranquility of mind, but 'true peace of mind' is Hall's. That phrase on his title-page added to the word 'tranquillity' echoes John 14:27: 'Peace I leaue with you: my peace I giue vnto you: not as the worlde giueth, giue I vnto you' (Geneva version).

So at the end Hall says: 'I have chalked out the way of Peace: What remaineth, but that we walke along in it?' (p. 137).

Disturbers of this peace are two: the evil we have suffered, which we call 'crosses'; and the evil we have done, which we call 'sins'. The crosses we must learn to bear; but the sins are removed only by reconciliation, which is gained by remission, which can be brought about only by satisfaction – hardly a Stoical thesis. The whole of Section V is a paean of thanksgiving for Christ's sacrifice. And not classical but Christian is the idea that man is inadequate without God: 'Not out of the confidence of our owne power; impotant men, who are we, that we should either vow or performe?' (p. 127). Hall shows how ineffectual 'humane wisdom' is (Section III), how 'nature' teaches us all the rules but cannot teach us to abide by them. A marginal caveat at this point reads: 'Senacaes rules rejected as insufficient' (p. 89). Thus Hall's *Heauen vpon Earth* admits classical Stoicism as far as it goes, but the main thrust, like Sir Thomas Browne's *Christian Morals*, is to persuade the reader into becoming an 'Epictetus of the Mount'.[2]

Not only is the content of *Heauen vpon Earth* more Christian than Stoical, but its method of bifurcation is more Ramistic then Aristotelian. Hall's two antithetical 'disturbers of true peace' furnish the initial clue. The crowd of printer's braces in the frontal 'analysis' promises the reader that the whole treatise will be carried forward by a series of disjunctive dichotomies. Hall begins (a) negatively by rejecting 'the precepts of the Heathen' in order (b) positively to teach that which is Christian; the rest of the book concerns (b). This is divided next into (a) what Christian teaching is and (b) how it is attained; what follows largely concerns (b). This (b) is then divided into (a) the enemies of peace and (b) how these enemies can be subdued – and so on. One is reminded of the chart for a tennis-tournament, which must proceed by a series of either/or's.

Bearing his 'crosses' at Hawstead as best he could by thus creating a 'heaven upon earth', in the early summer of 1607 Hall finally went to London to have it out with Sir Robert at Drury House. He met with the same rebuffs, but God's providence was still waiting on him. Baron Edward Denny of Waltham, later Earl of Norwich, had read *Meditations and Vowes* and had heard commendations of Hall as a preacher. Denny thereupon invited Hall to become chaplain to his household at Waltham and rector of the abbey church of Waltham Holy Cross at a salary ten times that of Hawstead. Simultaneously, Mr Gurrey, tutor to the Earl of Essex, called on Hall to tell him that young Prince Henry was so pleased with the *Meditations and Vowes* that he would like to hear Hall preach at Richmond the following Sunday. With trepidation Hall did preach, and again before the prince on the following Tuesday. At this point, the prince asked him to become one of his twenty-four chaplains who served, as the custom was, two at a time for one month each year in the palace. We can imagine the joy with which Hall returned to Suffolk, made his peace with Lady Drury, said good-bye to little Elizabeth, packed up his family, and moved to Waltham.[3] Here, only twelve miles from the centre of London, he lived and worked for the next twenty years.

At Waltham, Hall's first and one of his most important literary contributions was his book of so-called Theophrastan *Characters* (1608), dedicated to his new patrons: 'the right honourable my singular good lords, Edward Lord Denny, Baron of Waltham, and James Lord Hay, his right noble and worthy son-in-law', the latter so much a favourite at court that King James made him Lord Doncaster and finally Earl of Carlisle.

Character-writing, like casuistry, is a peculiarly seventeenth-century literary phenomenon. Although efforts have been made to identify the genre in Chaucer, Shakespeare and other predecessors, the real beginning of what we know as 'the Theophrastan character' was Isaac Casaubon's edition of Theophrastus in Greek and Latin (Lyon, 1592) and his commentary in 1599. The first English book of 'characters' is Joseph Hall's *Characters of Vertues and Vices*, composed in the aura of his initial acquaintance with the court-life of Prince Henry and King James. Hall was followed by Thomas Overbury (1614), John Stephens (1615), Geffray Mynshul (1618), John Earle (1628), Francis Lenton (1629), Richard Braithwaite (1631), Donald Lupton (1638), Richard Flecknoe (1677) and a host of others. Except for the possible reappearance of the genre in the *Spectator* papers of Addison and Steele, character-writing came to an end.

Theophrastus is the father. Following E. C. Baldwin early in this century, however, some scholars have emphasized the influence of Ben Jonson and the English background.[4] In 1924, E. N. S. Thompson related the 'character' to *descriptio*, familiar to the English schoolboy from Thomas Wilson's *Arte of Rhetorike* (1553).[5] Wendall Clausen wondered why seventeen years should elapse between Casaubon's edition in France and the first tangible evidence of Theophrastus in England – Hall's.[6] Although Sir Richard Jebb's introduction to his classic edition of Theophrastus (1870) began the custom of making parallels between Theophrastus and Hall, Warren Anderson, in the introduction of his newly translated *Theophrastus: The Character Sketches* (Kent, Ohio, 1970), brings out Hall's untheophrastan didacticism and lack of humour in order to point again to Ben Jonson's dramatic types as the real beginning of Theophrastus in England.

If *Heauen vpon Earth* is a preview of the *Characters*, and I have suggested ways (Christian and Ramistic) in which I think it really is, then we need to recognize other influences upon Hall besides Seneca, Theophrastus, and the English 'humour'. Fifty years ago Richard Aldington made an interesting conjecture, 'for anyone to verify or refute': that 'we owe the sudden vogue of character-writing in England to King James'.[7] Perhaps the first book of 'characters' in England has more to do with the Scottish king, with his self-promoted reputation as Solomon, and consequently with the Book of Proverbs in the Bible, than it has to do with the *Characters* of Theophrastus. The hypothesis may explain Hall's major deviations from the Theophrastan pattern.

Hall refers to the ancient Greek in his dedication, and in all likelihood King James had talked to him about Casaubon's scholarship. According to Mark Pattison, 'Even in 1601, Casaubon was sufficiently well known to be sought out by foreigners of curiosity who visited Paris.' Spotswood, later archbishop of Glasgow, told Casaubon that his learning and piety were well known to James VI. From Edinburgh the monarch wrote an invitational letter 'to his dearest Casaubon, telling him that, besides the care of the church, it was his fixed resolve to encourage letters and learned men, as he considered them the strength, as well as the ornament, of kingdoms'.[8] It was not until 1610 that Casaubon, an Anglican by instinct, was able to come to England, where he spent most of his time in theological ripostes (in French) with His Majesty, and, at royal behest, writing Latin diatribes against the Roman Catholics when he should have been teaching Greek.

James I, uniquely, brought to the throne of England a learning that extended from prosody to theology, a reading knowledge of Latin, Greek and Hebrew, an unusual skill in disputation, and an ability to speak fluently, if with a Scottish accent, Latin, French and English.[9] When he first dreamed of succeeding Elizabeth to rule over a country of wealth and power, he deliberately patterned himself after another king, distant in time, also with tremendous wealth, unlimited power, and a reputation of wisdom: King Solomon.

In 1599, James wrote *Basilikon Doron*. Like the biblical Proverbs (1:8) ascribed to Solomon, it too is addressed to 'my son' (Prince Henry, born in 1593), and is filled with moral and political sentence suitable for a future king. On reading the Bible, James advises his young son as follows:

Reade the Prophets, and likewise the books of the *Proverbes* & *Ecclesiastes*, written by that great paterne of wisdome *Salomon*: whiche will not onlie serue you for instruction, how to walke in the obedience of the Lawe of God, but is also so full of golden sentences, & morall precepts, in all things that can concerne your conuersation in the worlde, as amonge all the prophane Philosophers and Poets, ye shall not find so rich a storehouse of precepts of naturall wisedome, agreing with the will & diuine wisdome of God.[10]

James divides the whole of Christian teaching into two antithetical parts: a command to do good and a prohibition – abstain from evil. 'Remember also,' he writes, 'that by the right knowledge, and feare of God (whiche is *the beginning of wisdome*, as *Salomon* saith) ye shall know all the thinges necessary for the discharge of your duety, both as a Christian & as a king ...' (p. 27). His own religion, he adds, is clear and simple, 'grounded vpon the plaine wordes of the Scripture' (p. 31). He affects a folk-wisdom in the use of proverbial speech: virtue or vice is often inherited 'and runne on a blood (as the Proverbs is)' (p. 109); and in this treatise on statecraft he will refrain from English matters, not to 'fishe in other folkes waters, as the prouerbe is' (p. 21).

On style, James is very explicit:

In both your speaking and gesture, vse a naturall and plaine forme, not fairded with artifice: for (as the French-men say) *Rien contrefaict fin*: but ex-chewe all affectate formes in both. In your language be plaine, honest, naturall, comelie, cleane, short, and sentencious: eschewing both the ex-tremities, as well as in not vsing any rusticall corrupt leide, as booke-language, and pen and inke-horne tearmes: and least of all mignarde & ef-foeminate termes. But let the greatest parte of your eloquence consist in a natural, cleare, and sensible forme of the deliuerie of your minde ... [Again,] Now as to your writing, whiche is nothing else, but a forme of en-registrate speeche, vse a plaine, shorte, but statelie stile ... [pp. 179–80, 183]

Joseph Hall was one of the official chaplains to this Prince when he first conceived the *Characters*.

In addition to adopting Solomon's style, James deliberately followed his great predecessor in a wish for an 'understanding heart' (1 Kings 3:4–15), in the making of wise decisions (1 Kings 3:16–28), in choos-ing and properly elevating his wife as a 'Queen of Sheba' (1 Kings 10:1–10), in keeping peace with neighbouring nations (1 Kings 5:12), and in enlisting the aid of clever foreigners (1 Kings 6:13). Well known is the story of James settling a quarrel during his progress southward in 1603: two courtiers were about to fight over who should have the honour of carrying the new king's sword, so James quietly gave it to a neutral third man. That the original two were satisfied evoked a universal memory of the biblical wise king, the quarrelsome pair, and a sword (1 Kings 3:16–28).

Obnoxious in many ways though James was – in his pedantic egotism, his fear of plots, his guile, his self-indulgence and his in-corrigible display of affection for handsome young men[11] – our main concern here is that in panegyrical speeches, dedications and sermons throughout his reign, King James and King Solomon were constantly compared. For example, William Barlow fulsomely dedicated his glowing account of the Hampton Court Conference (in which the King James version of the Bible was born) to James with many a parallel to Solomon, particularly in respect to their speech. Barlow was sure that 'words as they are uttered by him, being as Solomon speaketh, [are] like apples of gold, with pictures of silver' (Proverbs, 25:11, Geneva).[12] On 30 April 1605, a sermon was preached before the king at Nonesuch by the Reverend Robert Wakemen entitled 'Solomon's Exaltation'. John Carpenter dedicated to James his *Schelomonecham, or King Solomon his Solace* (1606) with dozens of parallels between the two kings, including the fact that both were 'brief in their sentences' and both were the authors of a 'booke of sapience'. Bishop George Carleton of Chichester, in *A Thankful Remembrance of Gods Mercy* (London, 1624), gives a brief review of recent English history in providential terms, noting that Elizabeth was 'succeeded [by] our peaceable *Solomon*, King James' (p. 176). To welcome Queen Anne's brother, King Christian IV of Denmark, Robert Cecil first Earl of Salisbury put on a show at Theobalds (before he traded the sumptuous house to the king on royal demand) in imitation of 'King Solomon's Temple'. As the court lady representing the Queen of Sheba rose to present the visiting monarch with a cornucopia of fruit, she vomited in his lap; and James himself, attempting to dance with her, fell down from having tried to keep pace bowl for bowl with Denmark.[13] The story, told by Sir John Harrington, is hilarious, spiteful and sad; but the important point is Cecil's choice, so soon after James's coronation, of the Solomonic stage-setting and characters for his 'masque'.

Joseph Hall admired in his sovereign two of Solomon's traits: wisdom and peace-keeping. On James's erudition he said in his sermon before the king in celebration of the tenth anniversary of his accession: 'Let me begin with that which the heathen man required to the happiness of any state, his learning and knowledge: wherein I may safely say, he exeedeth all his one hundred and five predecessors ... What king christened hath written so learned volumes' (V, 106)? And in a sermon entitled 'The True Peace-maker', preached before the king at Theobalds on 19 September 1624, Hall quotes 'wise Solomon's' sayings: 'The crowne of the wise is their riches, the folie of fooles is foolishness' (Proverbs 14:24, Geneva), and 'When the waies of a man please the Lord, he wil make also his enemies at peace with him' (Proverbs 16:7, Geneva). Hall ends his sermon with this: 'What good hath the earth which God doth not couch under the name of peace? Blessed be God and his anointed, we have long and comfortably tasted the sweetness of his blessing. The lilies and lions of our Solomon have been justly worded with *Beati pacifici*' (V, 230) – an allusion to James's royal coat of arms. It is not unlikely that Joseph Hall had King James in mind when he ended his 'character' of 'The Good Magistrate' with: 'He is the Guard of good laws, the Refuge of innocency, the Comet of the guilty, the Pay-master of good deserts, the Champion of justice, the Patron of peace, the Tutor of the Church, the Father of his Country, &, as it were, another God vpon earth' (p. 161).

The sedulously cultivated image of James as Solomon could fill a book, but we must hasten to its end, the sermon preached at his funeral on 7 May 1625, entitled 'Great Britain's Salomon', by Bishop John Williams of Lincoln. The three texts of 1 Kings 11:41, 42 and 43 provide the division into the life, the reign and the death of the two kings. In their lives they both praised eloquence as a kingly virtue, performed great *acta* to match their *verba*, and became non-pareils of wisdom. Surely the bishop's list of similarities is exhaustive: both kings were only sons; both were infant kings (James at thirteen months); both kings had white and ruddy complexions; both rose above the difficulties that attended the beginning of their reigns; both wrote eloquent prose and poetry, etc. Of England's dead king, Bishop Williams concluded: 'In his *Style* you may observe the *Ecclesiastes*, in his *Figures* the *Canticles*, in his *Sentences* the *Proverbs*, and in his whole *Discourse, Reliquium verborum Salomonis*, all the rest that was admirable in the Eloquence of Salomon.' James's Solomonic reputation for wisdom continued in a macabre note on his being embalmed for burial. As reported by William le Neve in a letter to Sir Thomas Holland on 25 April 1625: 'The semyture of his head soe stronge as that they could hardly breake it open with a chissell and sawe, and so full of braynes as they could not, uppon the opening, keepe them from spillinge, a great marke of his infinite judgement.'[14]

Professor Clausen denies Aldington's suggestion that Hall owed his *Characters* to King James on the ground that neither in his dedication nor preface does he mention the king. One should remember, however, that an author cannot suddenly dedicate a book to royalty lest he be accused of *lèse majesté*. In 1603, Hall had fulsomely welcomed James in 'The King's Prophecie', and despite his witty career at Cambridge had decided at Hawstead to become a churchman within the establishment. With his move to Waltham he shows ambitions of becoming an ecclesiastical courtier. As chaplain at Nonesuch and Richmond he dedicated the 1608 volume of *Epistles* to Prince Henry, and in the same year his *Characters* to his two new patrons, gentlemen very close to the throne. After 1608, Hall became a favourite preacher before James at Theobalds, Whitehall and even Newmarket, or wherever James decided to go hunting. In his autobiography, Hall speaks as though from personal experience of the king's custom (witnessed by others) of surrounding himself at meal-times with theologians, who stood behind his chair and parried his questions. Small wonder that the first character in Joseph Hall's *Characters of Vertues and Vices* is 'The Wise Man'.

Now, Hall's almost sycophantic admiration for James's learning and sententious style may well have impelled him to restudy the books in the Bible ascribed to the king's adopted model, King Solomon. In 1609 there appeared under the name of "Jos. Hall" *Solomon's Divine Arts, of 1. Ethics: 2. Politics: 3. Economics. That is The Government of 1. Behaviour: 2. Commonwealth: 3. Family. Drawn into Method Out of His Proverbs and Ecclesiastes.* Though this biblical work was published a year after the *Characters*, the two works were registered the same year: the *Characters* on 7 March 1608, and *Solomon's Divine Arts* on 8 December 1608. Given the lightness of the *Characters* and the density of Hall's concordance (evidence of the research and pains required for its composition), I have no doubt that while composing the *Characters* Hall was deeply involved in Solomon's ethical wisdom, especially as it emerges in the Book of Proverbs.[15]

Dedicating the book to the young Robert Earl of Essex, Hall refers to Solomon as 'the royalist philosopher and wisest king', a description James no doubt applied to himself. Hall's method is to make a concordance of Solomon's wise sayings, placing them under certain heads for the easier finding. The parallel of major divisions with James's *Basilikon Doron* could not have been accidental. James had divided his advice to his son into (1) religion, (2) administration and (3) general behaviour. Hall's first division, 'Ethics', addresses itself to religion as it must govern all behaviour; thus it embraces James's first and final divisions. Hall's middle section, 'Commonwealth', exactly coincides with the middle section of King James's treatise. And Hall's third section, 'Family' or *oikonomia*, overlaps both 'behaviour' and 'administration' as consisting of those 'best rules' enunciated by Solomon for governing the hierarchical relationships between husband and wife, parents and children, master and servant.

Hall subdivides his initial division, ethical behaviour as prescribed by the world's wisest king, into end and means. The end is felicity, which is found only in obeying God's commands. The means to that felicity are prudence (being 'wise' in God's commands), justice, temperance and fortitude. Throughout this lengthy treatment the abstract virtues quoted and paraphrased from the Geneva version of the Proverbs are balanced with their opposite vices. Thus the opposite of 'felicity' is 'wickedness', the refusal to take God into one's heart, as the opposite of the wise man is the fool, from Psalm 14:1, 'The fool said in his heart there is no God.'

As my analysis of *Heauen vpon Earth* showed, this disjunctive habit of mind is not only biblical but also Ramistic in its reliance upon the either/or dichotomy. For example, in the very first sentence of *Solomon's Divine Arts*, Hall takes his definition of ethics from Ecclesiastes 1:17 (Geneva version): 'And I gaue mine heart to knowe wisdome & knowledge, madnes & foolishnes.' Since felicity is the end of wisdom, Hall defines it (a) negatively and (b) positively. To define 'virtue' he tells us (a) what it is and (b) how it is ruled. For 'discretion' he discovers from Solomon what it is *versus* how it works, and that it works *either* in our actions *or* in our speech (Wynter, VIII, 231). Being over-wise on the one hand, and foolish on the other, are two extremes of 'wisdom' (VIII, 232). The 'fear of God' as gathered from Solomon is defined in terms of (a) what it is and (b) what are its results; and the results can be *either* present *or* future (VIII, 234). 'Honour' can exist *either* in 'best things' *or* in 'best times'; and 'obedience' is *either* attending on God's will *or* performing it (VIII, 235). Two areas of 'fidelity in performance' are 'to God' and 'to man' (VIII, 236). Truth is defined in terms of such contraries as lies, slander, dissimulation and flattery (VIII, 236). 'Deceit' can be *either* indirect *or* direct, and when the latter it can be *either* public *or* private (VIII, 239). The contrary of 'liberality' is two extremes: (a) covetousness, not giving enough, *versus* (b) prodigality, giving too much (VIII, 243). 'Modesty' can exist *either* in words *or* in actions; and its contrary is loquacity, ill speech and im-moderate mirth (VIII, 247). There can be 'continency' of lust and of anger, and these two are defined by their opposites (VIII, 250). Finally, 'fortitude' is treated (a) in general and (b) 'in the specials of it'; the 'specials' are divided again into confidence and patience; patience is acquired through learning how to bear (a) God's afflictions and (b) men's injuries. This mere outline of the first three books of *Solomon's Divine Arts* is sufficient to reflect Hall's biblical and Ramistic turn of mind in 1608, at or very near the time when he was writing his *Characters of Vertues and Vices.*

As readers of the Bible have known for a long time, Proverbs itself contain several rudimentary 'characters' of virtues and vices. The wise man who so consistently runs through Proverbs is opposed to the foolish or wicked man (Proverbs 6:12-15). There is a character of 'The Drunkard' in 29:29-35. In *Heauen vpon Earth* (sec. xxii), Hall had included three one-sentence 'characters' – the covetous man, the glutton and the needy scholar. These are not dissimilar to the brief 'characters' in Proverbs 26, where we find 'The Fool' (1-12), 'The Sluggard' (13-16), 'The Trouble-maker' (17-22) and 'The Hypocrite'

(23–8). The most important and sustained 'character' in Proverbs is 'A Virtuous Woman' in the final chapter as part of the consistent hypostatization of wisdom. Opposite her are 'The Harlot' (Proverbs 7:6–27) and 'A Foolish Woman' (Proverbs 9:13–18). Hence, at the very end of *Solomon's Divine Arts*, when Hall comes to define the good housewife from the Bible's 'wise king', it is impossible for him not to combine her description with that of her opposite, the harlot (VIII, 266, and Proverbs 31 plus Proverbs 7:6–10). Both Solomon and Joseph Hall give us wisdom in many an opposition of virtues and vices; the wise and foolish, the honest and dishonest, the just and the unjust, and so forth.

To pass now from content to style, in arguing that the prose style of Hall's *characters* is also classical, it is customary to reproduce the familiar definition of 'Senecan' or 'curt style' as given to us by Morris W. Croll, with a few examples of asymmetry and balance and then a few 'exceptions' to the rules. We are reminded, however, that Hall read Hebrew, and that according to Bishop Robert Lowth, an eighteenth-century Professor of Poetry at Oxford, poetic parts of the Old Testament are written in distichs, of three kinds: (1) synonymous, in which the two elements are identical in meaning; (2) antithetical, in which they are contrary; and (3) synthetic, a combination of both.[16] An example of sustained synonymy is Psalm 114: 'The sea saw it, and fled: Jordan was driven back./The mountains skipped like rams, and the little hills like lambs.' Two examples of such synonymy ascribed to Solomon and thus appearing in Hall's concordance are: Ecclesiastes 1:18 – 'For in the multitude of wisdome is muche grief: & he that encreaseth knowledge, encreaseth sorrowe'; and Proverbs 9:10 – 'The beginning of wisdome is the feare of the Lord, & the knowledge of holy things is vnderstanding' (Geneva) – quoted by King James to his son. The most antithetical chapter of Proverbs, on the other hand, is Chapter 10; each of the thirty-two verses consists of two parallel statements connected with the adversative conjunction 'but.' A not unexpected part of Hall's method is to emphasize the oppositional character of Solomon's ethics by the constant use of the word 'contrarily' (for example, pp. 227, 228, 239, 249, 250, 251, 254, etc.) to define virtues in terms of vices and vices in terms of virtues. Sometimes he even separates the elements of an antithetical distich in order to place one element (Proverbs 10:6 – 'All blessings are upon the head of the righteous') under 'Felicity' (p. 226); and the other element of the same distich ('but iniquities shall cover the mouth of the wicked') under 'Wickedness', which is introduced thus: 'Contrarily, there is perfect misery in wickedness' (p. 227). When we consider how ardently Joseph Hall and his comtemporaries took the Bible to be the literal word of God, including the genealogy in Matthew 1:2–7, which traces Christ back in a direct line to King David and King Solomon, then we can realize the depth of Hall's commitment in 1608 to organize Solomon's ethical wisdom, with a courtly glance sideways at God's anointed vice-gerent, James I of England.

It is not surprising, then, that Hall's *Characters of Vertues and Vices* contain more parallels with the Bible than with Theophrastus. 'The Faithful Man' of the *Characters* is 'Fidelity' in *Solomon's Divine Arts*. Its opposite is the hypocrite and the flatterer in Proverbs, which become two of Hall's 'Vices'. Hall continues (p. 238) from the Book of Proverbs with the dissembler as being 'vainglorious', 'impenitent', 'envious', 'prodigal' and 'slothful' – each one of these five opposites finding its place among Hall's 'Characters of Vices'. Also, 'Fortitude' in Solomon's wisdom parallels 'The Valiant Man' in *Characters*, and Hall's account of Solomonic 'temperance' (pp. 246–8) includes 'Humility' and 'Patience', virtues that correspond with 'The Humble Man' and 'The Patient Man' in the *Characters*.

The two most glaring differences between Hall's *Characters* and those of Theophrastus are, first, their constant reminder that wisdom is to be found in worshipping God, and, secondly, their antitheses of virtues and vices. Just as in *Heauen vpon Earth*, Hall as a Christian went 'beyond Seneca', so, he says 'To the Reader' of his *Characters*: 'It is no shame for us to learne wit of Heathens; neither is it materiall, in whose schoole we take out a good lesson: yea, it is more shame not to follow their good, than not to lead them better. As one therefore that in worthy examples hold imitation better than invention, I have trod in their paths, but with an higher & wider step . . .' (pp. 143–4).

Wisdom, with which he starts the 'virtues', rests firmly on reason upheld by religion. All the virtues that follow centre not on morality but on God. For example, 'If [the honest man] see what he must doe, let God see what shall follow' (p. 150). The whole of the character of 'The Faithful Man' is an account of his relationship to God: 'He is allied so high, that hee dare call God Father, his Saviour Brother: heaven his Patrimony, and thinkes it no presumption to trust to the attendance of Angels' (p. 151). When '[the humble man] approcheth to the Throne of God, he is so taken up with the divine greatnesse, that in his owne eyes he is either vile or nothing' (p. 153). 'The Valiant Man' is 'afraid of nothing but the displeasure of the Highest, and runs away from nothing but sin' (p. 154). 'Gods best witness' is 'The Patient Man' (p. 155), and 'The True Friend' is motivated by 'the best of vertues, Religion' (p. 156). 'The Truly-Noble' man 'is more carefull to give true honour to his Maker, then to receive civill honour from men' (p. 159), while 'The Good Magistrate' 'is the faithful Deputy of his

Maker, whose obedience is the rule whereby he ruleth' (p. 160). Surely David's 'broken and contrite heart' for sins committed defines Hall's 'The Penitent Man', the longest of the characters, for 'Hee is a thankfull Herauld of the mercies of his God' (p. 163). At last, 'The Happy Man', which Hall added to his second edition in 1614, is happy because 'He keeps ever the best company, the God of Spirits and the Spirits of that God' (p. 166). Thus, as wisdom begins the virtues, felicity ends them – both in God.

The denial of God gives rise to the vices, and not one of them can possibly be 'happy'; they are all 'Malcontents'. Not only is vice the opposite of virtue but individual vices are demonstrably set against individual virtues. As the 'fool' is the opposite of the 'wise' in Solomon's book, so in Hall's *Characters* the final virtue, happiness, is deliberately added in opposition to the final vice, envy: 'Whatsoever God doe for [the envious man] he cannot be happy with company; and if he were to chuse, whether he would rather have equals in a common felicitie or superiours in misery, hee would demurre upon the election' (p. 195). Several vices oppose the virtuous 'Faithful Man': 'The Distrustful Man', 'The Prophane Man' (who worships no God) and 'The Superstitious Man' (who worships many gods). Both 'The Hypocrite' and 'The Flatterer' are the opposite of 'The Honest Man', whereas 'The Presumptous Man' is the opposite of 'The Humble'. The antithesis of 'The Patient Man' is 'The Busie-bodie'. Finally, Hall's 'Truly-noble Man' is opposed by such vicious characters as the slothful, the covetous, the ambitious and the envious – all of whom, like the last one named, are 'enemies to Gods favours' (p. 197). The religious content, then, and the insistent use of antithetical pairs, both to be found in the biblical books of Solomon, differentiate Hall's *Characters* from those of his classical predecessor. Both traits were embraced by 'the English Solomon', James I, to whose theological and literary inner circle Joseph Hall, in his early thirties, had just been admitted.

To be sure, Hall had read Seneca and admired his style. He gained the sobriquet of *le vrai Seneque Chrestien* from Loiseau de Tourval's dedication of the 1610 translation into French of Hall's 1605 *Meditations and Vowes*. Thus another link between Joseph Hall and James I is that they were the first two English authors to be translated into French.[17] The sobriquet became popular in English through Thomas Fuller, who (quoting Henry Wotton) referred to Hall as 'our Christian Seneca'. The emphasis is placed on the adjective, for the ethical content of the *Characters* and most of their sententious style come not from Athens but from Jerusalem.[18] Their 'African' and 'Baroque' essence, rather than the classical, was caught by Overbury when he defined a 'Character' as 'a picture ... quaintlie drawne in various colours, all of them brightened by one shadowing'.[19] In his own 'Characters', however, except for the inclusion of some virtuous types, Overbury leaned more upon Casaubon's Latin than upon Hall's English, and, as Clausen says, 'Had it not been for the chance publication of Overbury's Characters in 1614, Character-writing might never have become a vogue in England, or certainly would have been deferred for many years' (p. 43).

Through Edward Lord Denny and his son-in-law Sir James Hay, Hall was introduced to many a noble personage; and he begins to show an ambition in ecclesiastical, social and financial affairs. From now on he addresses his books to people who are to help him in the future, particularly members of the Denny family, Prince Henry and finally the king. For example, the twenty-four separate 'books' of his *Contemplations* written at Waltham allowed him flowery dedications to people he would never have met had he remained in the village of Hawstead. These include Sir Edward Cecil, first Earl of Exeter, a soldier-courtier to Prince Henry; Sir Henry Danvers, page to Sydney, on whose tomb are lines by George Herbert; Sir Thomas Egerton Baron Ellesmere, Lord Keeper, to whom Sir John Davies had dedicated *Orchestra*; Sir Fulke Greville, friend of Sydney, created Knight of the Bath at Jame's coronation; Sir Henry Yelverton, the successor of Francis Bacon as solicitor-general; Sir Henry Mildmay, grandson of Emmanuel College's founder, flatterer and spy; Philip Earl of Montgomery, who knew so much about horses and hounds that King James gave him Edward Herbert of Cherbury's castle in Wales; and Francis Lord Russell, later Earl of Bedford, Lord-Lieutenant in 1623 of Devon and the City of Exeter – a probable abettor of Joseph Hall's first bishopric.

Joseph Hall had never heard the catch-phrase 'Protestant work-ethic'. All he knew in this regard came from the Bible (Romans 8:28) – 'All things work together for good to them that love God'), and from experience ('The Lord helps those who help themselves'). So closely allied now, in Waltham and London, to the nobility and so-called 'great', he all the more appreciated his Emmanuel College education and decried the separation he was able to observe sometimes between noble birth and behaviour. In a letter to 'Mr I. B.', published in 1610 in order that his complaint might be heard by more people, he laments the miseducation of so many sons of noblemen. Having failed to profit at our 'common nurseries of knowledge', they are 'transplanted to the collegiate inns of our common laws', where they study 'fashions and licentiousness'. 'And now, they so live, as if they had forgotten that there were books. Learning is for priests and pedants; for gentlemen, pleasure. O, that either wealth or wit should be cast away thus basely! that ever reason should grow so debauched, as to think any thing more worthy than knowledge' (Wynter, VI, 299–300)!

At Waltham, Joseph Hall, on the other hand, seemed never to rest for a day or leave a minute of each day unaccounted for.

> First [he reports to his new patron] I desire to awake at those hours, not when I will, but when I must ... My first thoughts are for him, who hath made the night for rest and the day for travel; and, as he gives, so blesses both ... While my body is dressing, not with effeminate curiosity, not yet with rude neglect, my mind addresses itself to her ensuing task; bethinking what is to be done, and in what order; and marshalling, as it may, my hours with my work.

He then describes how he first goes into his study but never reaches for a book without craving God's favour to receive profit from it. He sweetens the hours by variety: first some church father, then a classical text in Greek or Latin, and always the Bible. By this time the Denny family is up, and joined by Hall's own children, they all meet in the chapel of the great house, which stood on the ruins of the ancient abbey buildings. Today one can see the proliferation of the Denny family on the ornate tomb in the church of Waltham Holy Cross. Beneath the recumbent figures of Queen Elizabeth's courtier, the old Sir Edward Denny and his wife, are the ten Denny children – four daughters on the right and six sons on the left: the oldest being Joseph Hall's present patron, and the youngest son, born blind, led by his brothers. After these family devotions, Joseph Hall returns to his study.

> One while, mine eyes are busied; another while, my hand; and sometimes my mind takes the burden from them both ... One hour is spent in textual divinity; another, in controversy; histories relieve them both. Now, when the mind is weary of others' labours, it begins to undertake her own: sometimes, it meditates and winds up for future use; sometimes, it lays forth her conceits into present discourse; sometimes for itself, ofter for others. [VI, 280–81]

With a schedule like this it would seem that Hall had little time for his wife and family. Looking back, however, when he was past seventy, he gives us a lovely picture of his home life:

> I remember a great man coming to my house at Waltham, and, seeing all my children standing in the order of their age and stature, said, 'These are they that make rich men poor:' but he straight received this answer: 'Nay, my lord, these are they that make a poor man rich; for there is not one of these whom we would part with for all your wealth.' [VII, 82]

There were four boys – Robert, Joseph, Samuel, George; and one girl, Ann.[20]

At Waltham, Hall continued to preach three times a week, writing out each sermon beforehand. For his new and enlarged parish he prepared a *Brief Sum of the Principal Points of Religion* (1607), highly commended by his successor there, Thomas Fuller, as a 'little Catechisme [which] hath done great good in that populous parish; and I could wish that Ordinance more generally used all over England'.[21] From Waltham, in addition to the volumes of *Contemplations*, Hall published his own *Epistles*. Prince Henry asked him to give up his one-month-a-year attendance at his court in order to become his full-time chaplain, but Hall was too busy. Editions of the *Collected Works of Jos. Hall, D.D.* began to appear. Meanwhile he showed administrative skill in settling various lawsuits, particularly one in which he reclaimed for the church at Wolverhampton monies which had been illegally appropriated by Sir Walter Leveson. While at Waltham, Hall was sent three times on embassies abroad by James, 'the wise and peace-loving King'. Hall was on his way to becoming a bishop, a reward for the energy devoted to literature and religion while at Waltham.

As for King James, Solomon's two leading antithetical terms, combined in a witty paradox, ensure that he go down in history as 'the wisest fool in Christendom'.[22] A more charitable, self-chosen memorial is the great ceiling painted by Rubens for the Whitehall Banqueting House, finally delivered to Charles I in 1635. Whitehall itself was rebuilt by James for his great state occasions, and James had made contact with Rubens as early as 1619.[23] The first and central in the series of large paintings celebrates James's early and most signal stroke of peace, the union of England and Scotland by proclamation in 1604. Rubens depicts James as Solomon leaning forward in his throne, pointing with his sceptre (like a sword) at two ample women (England and Scotland) wrestling over a boy-child (Charles) while attempting to place on his head parts of two crowns. Minerva (Wisdom, Solomon's major trait) stands behind, binding the crowns together with an iron band at the command of the king, while two winged *putti* carry above her head the emblazoned escutcheon of the new era of 'PEACE'. Thus James claims his biblical 'type'. The three large central pictures and the six smaller ones on the sides develop a counterpoint of rectangular and oval shapes, the whole group based allegorically on such oppositions as Abundance *v.* Avarice, Government *v.* Rebellion, Wisdom *v.* Lust, Union *v.* Separation and so on. For Joseph Hall, Bishop of Exeter, we may be sure that Ruben's design for apotheosizing James I on the ceiling of Whitehall was itself a 'character', that is, a piece of depictive language expressing the victory of virtues over vices.

5. *The* Epistles *and Early Controversies*

As Joseph Hall at Waltham moved closer to the centre of England's political and ecclesiastical power, his writings in prose became less imaginative and more serviceable. This tendency emerges in the publication of three volumes of *Epistles*, begun soon after he arrived at Waltham and continued for the space of three years. The first two decades were registered on 20 November 1607; the second volume, consisting of Decades III and IV, on 17 October 1608; and the final volume, Decades V and VI, on 4 October 1610.

It is fitting that a Cambridge man became the first Englishman to publish his own epistles, for it was from his tower in Queens, Cambridge, that Erasmus in 1516 published the *Epistolae Erasmi*. He had edited Seneca the year before. Erasmus' letters are personal, spiced with complaints, dashes of humour, and affirmations of friendship.

As a 'letter'-writer Hall falls far behind this, in charm and interest, as well as behind two of his seventeenth-century countrymen: Nicolas Breton early in the period and James Howell in the middle. In his *Epistles* he does not evince the easy-going nature and the capacity for small talk that make some peoples' intimate correspondence such delightful reading. Sir Henry Wotton, for example, had the leisure, the wit and the skill in communication to make his letters a continual joy; Wotton's professional life as ambassador, furthermore, was largely spent in correspondence and conversation. Logan Pearsall Smith's summary admirably sets him against Hall:

> For Sir Henry Wotton was endowed with one gift, that of a letter-writer, which none of his more famous contemporaries possessed. Indeed, the very qualities of faults that stood in the way of his complete success, either as a statesman or author; the witty frankness that caused him to be a somewhat indiscreet diplomatist; a certain desultoriness of mind, combined with a great love of leisure and conversation, which hindered the completion of most of his literary tasks, all these made him an admirable correspondent.[1]

61

Strikingly absent from Hall's personal characteristics were love of leisure and desultoriness of mind.

John Donne, writing to his friend Sir Henry Goodyer in 1604 or thereabouts, reflects the literary tradition as well as a distinction between the familiar letter and the more serious and structured epistle; one being for love, the other serving knowledge. Donne writes:

> If you were here, you would not think me importune, if I bid you good morrow every day; and such a patience will excuse my often Letters. No other kinde of conveyance is better for knowledge, or love: What treasures of Morall knowledge are in *Senecaes* Letters to onely one *Lucilius*? And what of Naturall in *Plinies*? How much of the storie of the time, is in *Ciceroes* Letters? And how of all these times, in the Jesuites Eastern and Western Epistles ... The Evangiles and Acts, teach us what to beleeve, but the Epistles of the Apostles what to do. And those who have endevoured to dignifie *Seneca* above his worth, have no way fitter, then to imagine Letters between him and *S. Paul* ... The Italians, which are most discursive, and think the world owes them all wisedome, abound so much in this kind of expressing, that *Michel Montaig[n]e* saies he hath seen, (as I remember) 400 volumes of Italian Letters.[2]

Joseph Hall did not publish 'letters'; he published 'epistles'. The distinction is a real one, for the epistle, based on continental, classical and ecclesiastical models, is more formal, more rhetorical and more argumentative; and yet not to the degree of a polemical tract. Hall's epistles are serious exercises in persuasion on serious subjects, and again he is conscious of introducing a new genre into English literature. In dedicating them to Prince Henry, he writes: 'Your Grace shall herein perceive a new fashion of discourse, by epistles; new to our language, usual to others; and, as novelty is never without some plea of use, more free, more familiar. Thus, we do but talk with our friends by our pen, and express ourselves no whit less easily; somewhat more digestedly' (Wynter, VI, 126–7).

In calling the prince's attention to the 'variety and worth' of these epistles, Hall echoes the classical concept of *dulce et utile*. At the time he was still being influenced by Christian Stoicism, and thus they do reflect something of Seneca. Like Hall's letters to various people Seneca's letters to Lucilius could all have titles, such as 'On the Seclusion of Philosophers' (VIII). 'On Travel as a Cure for Discontent' (XXVIII), or 'On the Good which Abides' (XXVII). Both men distrust Fortune. Seneca argues for Stoicism with an Epicurean friend, as Hall attempts to win his Roman Catholic or Separatist friends to the Church of England. Like essays, the epistles of both men make the recipient secondary to the purpose, but Hall's epistles are never just like conversation. His definition of the epistle would deny that particular ingredient, which Seneca speaks of in his famous Epistle No. LXXV – '*Minus tibi accuratas a me epistulas mitti quereris* ... I prefer that my letters should be just what my conversation would be if you and I were sitting in one another's company or taking walks together, – spontaneous and easy; for letters have nothing strained or artificial about them.'[3] Though Hall's epistles are rarely spontaneous and easy, nevertheless a classical strain is evident.

The other strain is Christian. As in the mass, the reading of an epistle is always a 'lesson', a connotation that would ruin a friendly 'letter'. Just as Hall's *Characters* started with those of Theophrastus, but went beyond 'with a wider step,' so his epistles imitate those of Cicero and Seneca, the Italian and the French, but they are also instinct with the epistles of the church fathers of the first four centuries. These fathers were his daily companions in the study at Waltham, along with the treasures of classical literature. Almost ecstatically, Hall writes to Matthew Milward, his scholarly friend at St John's College, Cambridge:

> To find wit in poetry; in philosophy, profoundness; in mathematics, acuteness; in history, wonder of events; in oratory, sweet eloquence; in divinity, supernatural light and holy devotion; as so many rich metals in their proper mines; whom would it not ravish with delight! ... What an heaven lives a scholar in, that at once, in one close room, can daily converse with all glorious fathers and martyrs. [VI, 223]

In style, Joseph Hall has access to 'sententious Tertullian', 'grave Cyprian', 'resolute Jerome', 'flowing Chrysostom', 'divine Ambrose', 'devout Bernard' and that one father who is all of these – 'heavenly Augustine' (VI, 224).

These worthies furnished Hall with a precedent for including his female friends in a literary exercise. Writing to Sir John Harington on continence in marriage, he cites St Augustine 'in that serious epistle' to his Ecdicia (VI, 273). Again, he says in an epistle to Lady Honoria Hay, the sorely beset daughter of his patron Lord Denny:

> Thus have I endeavoured your Ladyship's satisfaction in what you heard, not without some scruple. If any man shall blame my choice in troubling you with a thorny and scholasticall discourse, let him know that I have learned this fashion of St Jerome, the oracle of antiquity; who was wont to entertain his Paula and Eustochium, Marcella. Principia, Hedibia, and other devout ladies, with learned canvasses of deep points in divinity. This is not so perplexed, that it need to offend; nor so unnecessary, that it may be unknown. [VI, 260]

These are Hall's models, and yet Douglas Bush, in comparing Hall's epistles unfavourably with Breton's 1602 'mad-cap letters', adds quite understandably, 'We cannot give heed to [Hall's] clerical, anti-Romish, and Senecan exhortations when livelier authors are frisking before us.'[4]

Unlike a 'letter', an 'epistle' does not frisk. Unless Joseph Hall conversed with his friends as if he were constantly delivering a prolusion, his epistles have nothing conversational about them. Apparently what he meant by 'no less easily, somewhat more digestedly' than conversation was the choice of a theme that is less serious than that of a sermon or controversial tract, and a treatment of that theme in a briefer compass. For example, Hall justifies the epistle to his Emmanuel College friend, Mr John Whiting, on clerical marriage by asserting that 'this argument seems shallow enough for an epistle' (VI. 162). As for treatment, writing to Sir Edmund Lucy in order to 'discourse on heaven', he affirms that the Bible proves that there are degrees of excellence in heaven and that the fathers witness to the proposition that there we shall have knowledge of each other; then he abruptly ends by saying this 'is a letter, not a volume' (VI, 205). The *dulce et utile* criterion is echoed in the dedication to Prince Henry of the third and last volume: here 'the pleasure of the variety shall strive with the importance of the matter' (VI, 244). Thus Hall's epistles are semi-personalized, well-written pieces of persuasion on topics that are or ought to be of general interest. The nearest thing to such a genre today might be the 'Letter to the Editor', let us say, of the London or New York *Times*. This literary kind is vital, important and, in capable hands, highly persuasive. Where else would you publish it? Hall's last editor, Wynter, placed the *Epistles* under 'Practical Works'.

That their purpose, whether directed to men or to women, is persuasion rather than mere communication is shown by the kinds of titles Hall placed at the head of every one. Sometimes the title is a noun followed by a preposition that gives us the key to the contents of the 'essay' to follow, like 'A Discourse on', which he uses thirteen times. Other noun-phrases are 'A description of', 'A report on', 'A complaint of', 'A preface to', 'The benefit of', 'Advice on', 'The estate of', 'Consolations of', 'A direction for', 'A particular account of' and 'Remedies against'. The verbs in his titles declare even more strongly the rhetorical bent: for example, 'Discoursing on' (eight times). 'Expostulating', 'Showing that', 'Dissuading', 'Encouraging', 'Preparing for', 'Discussing', etc. Many of the *Epistles* have titles similar to those Bacon gave his essays, beginning with 'Of the', such as 'Of the Contempt of the World' or 'Concerning', reminiscent of the Latin *de* or Greek *peri*. For years the English grammar-school curriculum had required the writing of arguments in epistolary form. A few years after the publication of Hall's *Epistles*, his nephew John Brinsley urged the exercise upon his pupils of 'how to make Epistles, imitating Tully, short, pithie, sweet Latine and familiar; and to indite Letters to our friends in English, accordingly'.[5]

Mr Jacobs found problems in dating the *Epistolae* of James Howell,[6] but there are very few puzzles in the dates of Hall's. Thanks to his conception of the 'epistle' as opposed to an 'intimate letter', there was little need of concocting circumstance to make a particular piece look 'real'. In effect, as Hall's Cambridge literary youth recedes, 'art' yields to 'nature'. In writing to his friends and acquaintances essays on general subjects, bits of controversial matter or religious counselling, Joseph Hall rarely had any need to mention current events that would either date the letter for us or reveal that a date had purposely been made for it. Most of the letters were evidently written very close in time to the publication date appearing on the title-pages and, more minutely, in the *Stationers' Register*. These dates, as well as the groups of addressees – such as those serving in Prince Henry's household, members of the large Denny-Hay family at Waltham – show that all of Hall's epistles were composed between 1607, when he took up his duties at Waltham and intermittently at the court of Prince Henry, and 1610, the publication date of the last volume. Only one letter (VI, 307) is actually dated, and that merely by the year, to John Mole, who for thirty years was kept prisoner by the Inquisition at Rome, a notorious case. The letter is headed '1607' and was perhaps carried to Venice by William Bedell for posting. Three years later, Hall published it apparently without change.

Among the current events he mentions is the assassination of Henri IV of France by Ravaillac, in a letter to Pierre du Moulin in Paris (VI, 263). This event took place on 14 May 1610, and the letter was registered for publication on 4 October 1610. In 1608, Hall published an epistle (VI, 160) congratulating Sir Edmund Bacon in retirement on being free from worrying about 'the Emperor's truce with the Turk', an allusion to the treaty signed in Austria in 1607. A letter to Mr Jonas Reigesberg (VI, 301) of the Dutch church is identified by Hall as having been 'written somewhile since' concerning opinions broached by 'Arminius, then living'. Arminius died in 1609 and the letter was published the following year.

An allusion is made to some current ecclesiastical history in Decade IV, epistle iv (registered 17 October 1608) 'To Mr J. P. – A Discourse of the increase of popery; of the oath of allegiance [1606]; and the just sufferings of those which have refused it.' The recipient is evidently a Norfolk recusant. Hall boasts that among those that 'we have sent into their heaven' are 'your second Garnett' who 'lived to proclaim himself a martyr' (VI, 225). His name is given on the next page as 'Drewry', which identifies him as Robert Drewrie, a priest who was hanged and quartered at Tyburn on 26 February 1607. With cruel relish, Hall mocks the joy with which Drewrie met his death: 'How many malefactors have we known that have laughed upon their executioner, and jested away their last wind! You might know. It is not long since our Norfolk Arian leaped at his stake.' The 'Norfolk Arian' is probably Francis Kett, graduate of Corpus Christi, Cambridge, and friend of Christopher Marlowe. On 14 January 1590, he was publicly burned at Norwich for his anti-trinitarian views, and a spectator wrote that 'he went leaping and dancing ... clapping his hands into the flames.'[7]

Even fewer than the current events in Hall's *Epistles* are allusions to his personal life which might give some indication to the exact date of writing. 'Since I saw you, I saw may father die,' Hall begins a serious epistle to Sir Andrew Asteley on the preparation for death (VI, 188). The elder Hall was buried at Ashby-de-la-Zouch on 17 May 1608;[8] consequently this letter was composed between that date and the date of its registration in October 1608. Thus very little evidence exists that Hall fabricated dates and occasions for his epistles, the reason being that given his definition and philosophy of the literary genre there was no need.

One exception to this rule may lie in a letter to William Bedell, registered for publication on 20 November 1607: 'Since your departure from us, Reynolds is departed from this world' (VI, 149). Thus Hall begins an elegy for deceased churchmen in the form of news. Now we know that Bedell left England for Venice in 1607 and that Reynolds died in 1607. His death seems to be the occasion for telling Bedell of the other clerical losses despite the fact that Bedell must have been already aware of them: Richard Greenham had died in 1594, Whitaker in 1595, Junius in Leiden and William Perkins in England in 1602. 'Dr Reynolds is the last,' writes Hall to his absent friend. Apparently the other deaths were added to the original letter for a wider public – a rare Howellian concoction.

As for autobiography, in addition to the one or two details already mentioned and the one long letter recounting his first trip to the continent, there are several allusions to his fondness for study. One of these is interesting in that it has to do with his health. Despite its precarious state whenever he went abroad, Hall did live to be eighty-two, for he knew how to take care of himself. As he writes to his old Ashby and Emmanuel friend, Hugh Cholmley:

> Fear not my immoderate studies. I have a body that controls me enough

in those courses: my friends need not. There is nothing whereof I could sooner surfeit, if I durst neglect my body to satisfy my mind: but, while I affect knowledge, my weakness checks me, and says, 'Better a little learning, than no health.' I yield, and patiently abide myself debarred from my chosen felicity. [VI, 171–2]

In general, the recipient of an 'epistle' is not as rhetorically functional as the recipient of a 'letter'. Rarely, as we try to frame our correspondence to *the* friend or *the* official, does Hall guide his address to a particular person despite the subscription. The majority of his printed epistles might have been written first as essays and then, either to reach a larger audience or to claim acquaintanceship with the nobility or court, addressed to a single person, posted, and then published.

A few of the letters are addressed to persons by initials only. One reason for this is that Hall wished to conceal identity depending upon the delicacy of the subject discussed. A case in point is Epistle III, vii, 'To Mr T. L. Concerning the Matter of Divorce in the Case of Apparent Adultery.' In other cases, the reason for initials is not clear. For example, as originally published, Epistle V, ix, was addressed 'To S. H. I.'. As often happens in this period, the initials are reversed, and intend 'Sir I. H.'. In the edition of 1614, the name of 'Sir John Harington' is substituted, but the identification is of no real significance.[9]

The 'person' is less important than the 'thing'. Hall's epistles are valuable as showing his major concerns, so largely the concerns of his age, and as demonstrating his skill in persuasion. Their subject matter is not gossip or banter, but primarily morality and religion, and these as they emerge in personal counselling, the challenges of a Christian life and Anglican apologetics. Trained as he had been in argumentation, Hall used the epistles, with royal sanction from his dedicatee Prince Henry, to uphold the liberal Puritanism, the Anglican order and peace abroad which James I made central in his policy.

Among Hall's early contentions, two that began in epistolary form proclaim his desire to protect the *via media* from the two extremes that threatened it: one argument directed against the Roman Catholics, and the other against the 'separating' Brownists. Though no Protestant Englishman living through Queen Elizabeth's reign and into that of James could be oblivious of 'Popery' as a danger from without and of 'sedition' from within, it was not until Joseph Hall travelled to the Low Countries with Sir Edmund Bacon that he began to argue in writing against one church from which his own had 'reformed' and another which was trying, unjustly he felt, to 'reform' him. 'How senseless are these two extremes', he cried; 'of the papists, that one man hath the keys; of the Brownists, that every man hath them!' (VI, 293).

Each of these arguments started small and grew large, such was the epistolary energy with which Hall began them; and both arguments prepared him for his most important polemics to come: the upholding of monarchy and the established church, in which he crossed swords with John Milton.

Typical of small beginnings is his plea for marriage of the clergy. In 1608 he published an epistle written to his Emmanuel friend, the Reverend John Whiting, rector of South Luffenham in Rutland, entitled 'An apologetical discourse of the marriage of ecclesiastical persons' (VI, 162). Whiting had evidently been challenged on the subject by a Catholic and had asked for Hall's aid in formulating an answer. Hall responds with a confession that he does not know whether to treat the 'Roman cavil' with silent scorn or, if he should answer, whether to be merry or serious. Nevertheless he does write an epistle of eight printed pages with over fifty footnotes in Latin and Greek. As usual with Anglican apologists, he depends upon antiquity, Scripture and reason; but mostly on the church fathers in that, as pre-Trent Catholics, their sanction of clerical marriage makes a shambles of the more recent Roman strictures.

This, Hall believed, ended the argument. But twelve years later the Reverend Edward Coffin, an English Jesuit whom James, in a gesture of coronation amnesty, had released from the Tower and banished, published a huge book directed against Joseph Hall's views on priestly marriage. That which Hall had written in 'three hours on three leaves,' he complains, is now refuted in twelve years and four hundred pages. Such pother makes him furious. Reviving some of his Cambridge rhetoric, he asks whether the kingdom of heaven and all religion should rest on marriage and maidenhead (VIII, 481). Nevertheless he replies point by point in a book entitled *The Honour of the Married Clergy, Maintained against the Malicious Challenges of C. E.* [Edward Coffin, S. J.], *Mass-Priest* (1628), and dedicated to Archbishop George Abbott. Not to be outdone, Hall's reply in a modern edition occupies 132 pages in two 'books' comprising forty-seven sections. There is no need to summarize the arguments on each side. The spirited style that Hall evinces on a subject like this against a detested Jesuit who owed his freedom to the royal magnanimity of England is evident in the following example:

But in speaking of the impossibility of some men's continency, it was not possible for my refuter to contain himself from a scurrilous invective against Luther, Pellican, Bucer. And it becomes him well. His fathers, like sepulchral dogs, tore up the graves of God's saints, and gnawed upon their dead bones; and now, this whelp of theirs *commingit cineres*, 'bedribbles their ashes'. The heroical spirit of Luther, for I cannot be flouted out of that word, hated the brothelry of their cloisters, and chose rather, which galls them to the heart, to be an honest husband than a fornicating friar. [VIII, 503]

As for the Brownists, in 1610 Hall had published an epistle 'Written long since to Mr J. W., dissuading him from separation, and shortly oppugning the grounds of that error' (Epistle VI, v). He quotes from an earlier epistle he had written to Mr Smith and Mr Robinson, 'ringleaders of the late separation in Amsterdam' (Epistle III, i), but there, he confesses, he had only touched upon the danger with a light hand. Now he will get down to real argument, in which his idea of epistolary 'brevity' is 5,400 words. He is responding to a letter from 'J.W.', for he quotes from it and answers it graciously and pointedly. 'J.W.' is not going to turn papist, but he is so filled with doubts about the Church of England that he is leaning towards sectarianism. Hall congratulates him for his doubts, which can lead to satisfaction as well as to error. The most serious doubt is that a body like the church which can allow even one sinner in it is guilty of sin. Guilt by association means that if one is guilty all are guilty. But, replies Hall, each of us must bear his own record; no human being, only Christ, can bear the record of all. So you may well doubt, says Hall, but don't doubt that Christ came to save us all from sin. Again, you doubt whether, even if sinners are present within the church, the Church of England is the true church. Why don't you doubt that there was no true church until Barrow and Greenwood, hanged at Tyburn in 1602 for sedition, came along to found it? We are as true a church as God ever made, going back in time to Christ and the Apostles, and has any separatist sect come up with anything so broad in its appeal to all consciences as our Thirty-nine Articles? Do Francis Johnson, or Henry Ainsworth, or Smith, or Robinson, or any of the three hundred 'Congregationalists' in Amsterdam use enough of their God-given reason to differentiate between peripheral and essential texts in the Bible? Does any sect possess our discipline? Finally, you doubt that we have the best form of worship. True, we are sacramental, and we love liturgy. But these are only the outside, the clothes of the church. Our body and substance is sound, for we worship through these the One God.

As in the former controversy, Hall thought his argument would end here. But almost as soon as it was published there appeared a pamphlet by Smith and Robinson of Amsterdam entitled *An Answer to a Censorious Epistle*. So, eighteen months after his first epistle to these two, Joseph Hall published his *Common Apology of the Church of England against the Unjust Challenges of the Over-Just Sect, commonly called Brownists, where the Grounds and Defences of the Separation are Largely Discussed* (1610). Quoting the whole of the Amsterdam pamphlet for refutation, Hall's book requires 113 pages of print. The footnotes mention almost every piece of

6. *The Art and Practice of Protestant Meditation*

In an earlier chapter we noted that while at Hawstead, before going to Waltham, Joseph Hall had written two books besides *Heauen vpon Earth*. These two books and his first trip to the continent we shall now discuss as leading up to a religious-literary preoccupation that lasted far beyond his sententious *Characters* and polemic *Epistles*, in fact to the end of his life. This was a form of meditation for Protestants that would match in effectiveness the Jesuitical contributions of the Counter-Reformation.

He had yet to discover his philosophy and his form of meditation in the early *Meditations and Vowes* (1605). Dedicating the first 'century' to Sir Robert Drury, he calls what is to follow 'homely Aphorismes'. They are indeed more ethical than devotional, more Senecan than biblical, more little Baconian essays on proper conduct than fervent pleas to God in secret for aid in arousing one's self from earthly lethargy to contemplation of heavenly things. Hall's initial experiments in the genre more often begin with a moral in proverbial language and end with self-admonition. Number 9 is typical: 'Expectation in a weake minde, makes an euill, greater; a good, lesse: but in a resolued minde, it digests an euill, before it come, and makes a future good, long before, present. I will expect the woorst, because it may come the best, because I know it will come' (1605, pp. 14–15). No actual address to God appears until the 'century' is half-way through, in Numbers 49 and 51: '. . . but thou, Lord, maist giue what thou wilt,' and 'Though there were no Heauen, O Lord, I would loue thee' (pp. 57–8). The book strikingly asserts at times the paradoxes of Christianity, but almost invariably for self-improvement rather than for the salvation of one's soul.

In the accompanying second 'century' of *Meditations and Vowes* dedicated to Lady Drury, there are one or two exceptions to this moralistic pattern, and perhaps in these we can perceive one kind of meditation which Hall was to define in his *Arte* and actually write, that is, the 'occasional meditation' as in Number 25:

> We pitie the folly of the Larke, which while it playeth with the feather, and stoopeth to the glasse, is caught in the Fowlers net; & yet cannot see our selues a-like made fooles by Sathan, who deluding vs by the vaine feathers, and glasses of the world, suddainly enwrappeth vs in his snares; wee see not the nets indeede, it is too much that we shall feele them, and that they are not so easily escaped after, as before auoyded: O Lord keep thou mine eyes from beholding vanity, and though mine eyes see it, let not my heart stoope to it; but loathe it a farre off. And if I stoope at any time, & bee taken, Set thou my soule at liberty ... euen as a birde out of the snare of the Fowler ... [1605, pp. 148–50]

That book was registered on 12 February 1605. About two months later, Hall was invited by Sir Edmund Bacon of Suffolk, Lady Drury's brother, to accompany him as chaplain on a mission to escort the English ambassador to the court of Archduke Albert in Brussels. Hall accepted the invitation, he tells us, 'for the great desire I had to inform myself ocularly of the state and practice of the Romish church, the knowledge whereof might be of no small use to me in my holy station'. He left his clericals behind.

The small party landed at Calais, and went by coach to Gravelines, Dunkirk, Winnoxberg, Ypres, Ghent, Courtray and Brussels. In the Lowlands, Hall saw farms, villages and Protestant churches recently ravaged by war, but Jesuit colleges springing up everywhere. He and Sir Edmund went from Brussels to Namur, up the Meuse river to Liège, and thence to the hot waters at Ardennes.[1] Resting there, Hall added a third 'century' to his *Meditations and Vowes*, this one dedicated to his travelling host. It contains Baconian echoes in compliment to Sir Edmund's illustrious kinsman like the following: 'I observe three seasons wherein a wise man differs not from a fool; in his infancy, in sleep, and in silence; for in the two former we are all fools; and in silence, all are wise' (No. 82, Wynter, VII, 513). Some of these 'meditations' sound like a 'character', for example:

> The prodigal man, while he spendeth, is magnified; when he is spent, is pitied; and that is all his recompense for his lavished patrimony. The covetous man is grudged while he lives, and his death is rejoiced at; for when he ends, his riches begin to be goods. He that wisely keeps the mean between both, liveth well and hears well; neither repined at by the needy, nor pitied by greater men. I would so manage these worldly commodities as accounting them mine to dispose, others to partake of. [No. 68, VII, 509]

At one point in his 1605 travels, Hall tangles with an old Jesuit named Costerus and, in his own delighted view, humiliates his adversary in argument. He scoffs at the statues of the Virgin at Halle and

Zichem, and refutes Lipsius' *Diva Virgo Hallensis* (1604), commissioned by the Jesuits to ascribe to the statues incredible miracles. He scorns (in his third 'century') the Roman Catholics for clinging to things rather than to ideas, to sensibly perceived realities rather than to intuited 'realities' that lie behind them:

> Those that travel in long pilgrimages to the holy land, what a number of weary paces they measure! What a number of hard lodgings and known dangers they pass! . . . and when they are come thither, what see they, but the bare sepulchre wherein their Saviour lay, and the earth that he trod upon, to the increase of a carnal devotion? What labour should I willingly undertake in my journey to the true land of promise, the celestial Jerusalem, where I shall see and enjoy my Saviour himself! What tribute of pain or death should I refuse to pay for my entrance, not into his sepulchre, but his palace of glory, and that not to look upon, but to possess it! [No. 34, VII, 500]

The kind of 'labour' he should 'willingly undertake' to achieve this goal was the art and practice of meditation. His first theoretical work in the genre was entitled *The Arte of Divine Meditation* (1606), written at Hawstead after his trip. In the dedication to Sir Richard Lea, he writes: 'Wherefore after those sudden Meditations which passed me without rule, I was easily induced by their successe . . . to send foorth this Rule of Meditation, and after my Heauen vpon earth, to discourse . . . of heauen aboue.'[2]

The work was initially conceived in a Protestant continental setting at a time of high anti-Jesuitical feeling in England, and registered in London three days after the first anniversary of the Gunpowder Plot.[3] That year Hall wrote a eulogistic poem on his friend William Bedell's *A Protestant Memorial or the Shepherd's Tale of the Pouder Plott*.[4] In the earliest sermon by Hall that was printed (1608), preached at St Paul's Cross, he denounced, after the name of their founder, 'those Loyolists' as enemies of English church and state.[5] Throughout his life, like most Englishmen in his time, he characterized Roman Catholics as 'Romish', 'Papisticall', 'idolatrous', 'superstitious'; and made scoffing remarks about 'hugging their crucifixes' and 'tossing their beads'.

Thus, after the trip to the Low Countries, Hall's view of meditation is instinct not with St Ignatius of Loyola but with a much older tradition: the Bible, the devotional spirit of Windesheim, the medieval naiveté of the Augustinian monks, and Neoplatonism rather than Thomism. Instead of the strict one–two–three pattern of the *Spiritual Exercises*, Hall's theory and practice insist upon diversity in subject matter, form and individual psychological occasion. Martz distinguishes this 'Protestant' tradition, as opposed to the post-Trent Roman Catholic, in his chapter entitled 'The Augustinian Quest' of

The Paradise Within: the one stemming ultimately from Plato and Augustine; and the other through St Thomas of Aquinas, to burgeon in the Jesuitical spearhead of the Counter-Reformation. Martz writes:

> Here the hint of the presence of something like innate ideas in the deep caves of the soul leads directly to a long account of what might be called the dramatic action of Augustinian meditation. It is an action significantly different from the method of meditation later set forth by Ignatius Loyola and his followers; for that later method shows the effects of medieval scholasticism, with its powerful emphasis upon the analytic understanding, and upon the Thomist principle that human knowledge is derived from sensory experience. Ignatian meditation is thus a precise, tightly articulated method, moving from the images that comprise the composition of place into the threefold sequence of the powers of the soul, memory, understanding, and will, and from there into the affections and resolutions of the aroused will. But in Augustinian meditation there is no such precise method; there is, rather, an intuitive groping back into the regions of the soul that lie beyond sensory memories. The three powers of the soul are all used, but with an effect of simultaneous action, for with Augustine the aroused will is using the understanding to explore the memory, with the aim of apprehending more clearly and loving more fervently the ultimate source of the will's arousal.[6]

Written in this tradition, Hall's *The Arte of Meditation* is never quite so methodical as it sounds, and even throughout the practice of that art, Hall himself rarely depends upon the 'steps' that he himself delineated. 'Meditation', as he defines it at the beginning of Chapter 2, 'is nothing else but a bending of the mind vpon some spiritual obiect, through diuers formes of discourse, vntill our thoughts come to an issue' (pp. 6–7). There are, he continues, two kinds: extemporal, occasioned by some outward circumstance; and deliberate, or 'wrought out of our owne heart'. This latter kind, again, is divided into matters of the intellect, and matters of the affections or will. Chapters 3 and 4 describe the first kind of meditation, illustrated by many a psalm in which David the poet is impelled to worship the Creator through gazing, for example, upon 'the glorious frame of the heavens'. The rest of the book discourses upon 'deliberate meditation', beginning with the psychological preparation of the meditator, and proceeding to the choices of a proper time, a fitting place and a fruitful subject. The 'method' to be followed, outlined from Chapter 13 to the end of the book, is divided into 'steps' for the first part or kind, that of the understanding; and further 'steps' for the second and more important part or kind, that of the affections and will. The first series of steps come from the familiar rhetoric of the day: choose your subject, consider its qualities, define its contrary, draw a few similitudes to clarify it, amplify it by testimonies of Scripture.[7] The steps to be taken in whipping up our wills to act upon that which our minds have thus presented he takes from a book by Mauburnus.[8] For example, first we must taste and relish the thought, then bewail our 'untowardnesse' to follow it. This should make us heartily wish for that which we want, and induce not only a confession of weakness but also an earnest petition for strength. The 'affective' series of steps ends with confidence and thanksgiving.

As for the roots of Hall's meditational theory, the very first sentence of the dedication of *The Arte of Divine Meditation,* conceived, as we have said, in the Protestant setting of the Low Countries, echoes the spirit of medieval Roesbroek and the Augustinian 'Pre-Reformation Reformers' of the monastery of Windesheim: 'Sir, euer since I began to bestow my selfe vpon the common good, studying wherein my labours might bee most seruiceable; I still found they could bee no way so well improued, as in that part which concerneth deuotion, and the practise of true piety.' Hence the sources of Hall's fairly easy-going and pious 'rule of meditation' are Augustine, Bernard and Bonaventure, whom he often invokes as placing their emphasis upon the heart rather than the brain.[9]

Thus the 'Reformation' rather than the 'Counter-Reformation' character of Hall's theory of meditation emerges in the Platonic rather than Aristotelian ambience of his thought, a distinction so clearly and importantly made for St Bonaventure by Étienne Gilson that the passage must be quoted in full.

St Bonaventure fully realized that he was here in the presence of two irreducible mental attitudes, from which flow two absolutely irreconcilable interpretations of the universe. Aristole's universe, born of a mind that seeks the sufficient reason for things in the things themselves, detaches and separates the world from God. Plato's universe – at least if we may take St Augustine's interpretation as true – inserts between God and things ideas as a middle term: it is the universe of images, the world wherein things are at once copies and symbols, with no autonomous nature belonging to themselves, essentially dependent, relative, leading thought to seek beyond things and even above itself for the reason of what they are. If, then, we penetrate to what is fundamental in the doctrines in order to lay bare the spirit which animates them, it is clear that the human mind has already long since chosen between the two perspectives, one facing towards Christianity, the other turning its back upon it. Essentially pagan, because it sees things from the point of view of the things themselves, it is no marvel if Aristotle's philosophy has succeeded in the interpretation of the things of nature: from its first moment it was turned towards the earth and organised for its conquest. Plato's philosophy, on the other hand, was in its very first intention a philosophy of what is beyond, placing the reasons of things outside the things themselves, even sometimes going too far in denying them all sub-sistence of their own; it was, then, a philosophy directed from its very origins towards the supernatural, a philosophy of the insufficiency of things and the knowledge we possess of them.[10]

Among Hall's sources are those who, in Gilson's words again, 'repre-sent the affective life of the medieval west at its most intense and most beautiful' (p. x). Hall consistently repudiates the 'schoolmen' as logicians who prefer a too elaborate 'scale' to the simpler and more practical directions of those in the main Augustinian tradition. To the three Christian Platonists already mentioned, he adds Jean Charlier de Gerson (1363–1429), Chancellor of the University of Paris.[11] Long thought to have been the author of *The Imitation of Christ*, Gerson is best known for his *De monte Contemplationis*, from which Hall strengthens his metaphors of 'mount', 'ladder', 'scale' and so on. Like the three ar-ticulate saints before him, Gerson insisted that he could not write down a system for meditation (which remained for St Ignatius to do). The reason for this refusal was his reiterated distinction between scien-tific theology and the affections of the ordinary man. His *industriae*, or preparations for meditation, consist of knowing one's own temperament, avoiding vain learning and cultivating pious affection. Hence Gerson has been hailed as an early 'Protestant', and as a 'prac-tical' Christian rather than merely a logician. 'It was a just answer, that John Gerson reports, given by a Frenchman,' Hall wrote, 'who, being asked by one of his neighbours if the Sermon were done; "No," saith he, "it is said, but it is not done, neither will be, I fear, in haste"' (Wynter, VI, 531). And within *The Arte of Divine Meditation*, Hall writes: 'Whereupon not unfitly did that worthy Chancellour of *Pairs*, make the first staire of his ladder of Contemplation, *Humble Repen-taunce*' (pp. 25–6). A few pages later, in a literal translation of Gerson's most famous title, Hall adds: 'It must bee a free and a light minde that can ascend this Mount of Contemplation' (p. 29). Though Hall deplored the part Gerson had taken at the Council of Constance in condemning the doctrines of Wyclif and Huss, he admires his plain-spoken appeal to the average mind, not the unusually subtle or militarily disciplined. He depends upon Gerson as an early 'Protestant', and uses him as an authority 'because our adversaries [the Jesuits] disclaim him for theirs' (p. 46).

The most direct source of Hall's theory of meditation, he confesses in the dedication of his *Arte*, is 'one obscure namelesse Monke which wrote some 112. yeeres agoe'. Martz rightly identifies Hall's marginal 'scale of meditation' in Chapter 16 as coming from Mauburnus (the Dutch Jean Mombaer), whose *Rosetum* was published anonymously in 1494, exactly 112 years before the publication of Hall's *Arte* in 1606.

But Mauburnus could not be the 'obscure namelesse Monke' because Mauburnus is consciously quoting from Wessel Gansfort's *Opera*, as Pierre Debongnie has shown.[12] Mauburnus introduces his author as 'doctor', and whether recognized by Hall or not, Gansfort was known to the faculties of theology, law and medicine in the universities of three nations as *Lux Mundi*.[13] In reproducing his scale, Hall merely says that it is by an 'author, ancient but namelesse' (p. 87), not that he is a monk and 'obscure'. Moreover, Hall asserts that this complex method is 'allowed by some authors, [but] reiected by vs' (p. 85). And though he does take over the second half of it, that having to do with the heart, in view of the fact that the *Rosetum* of Mauburnus (in Martz's words) is a book 'whose labyrinths of meditation easily lose the reader' and which, 'directly or indirectly, came to exert a strong influence upon the creation of the *Spiritual Exercises* of St Ignatius',[14] it is not likely that it or this quotation from it is more important than, as Hall confesses, 'the directions of all other writers' – including Augustine, Bernard, Bonaventure and Gerson. Such an acknowledgement could hardly be accorded to one half of a quoted *scala* whose treatment, even by a commendatory Joseph Hall, commands in his *Arte* only nine chapters out of thirty-seven and only thirty-six pages out of a total of 193.

Hall seems to be acknowledging a source of inspiration rather than of text. Let us look again at his dedicatory words: 'In this Arte of mine, I confesse to haue receiued more light from one obscure namelesse Monke which wrote some 112 yeeres agoe, then from the directions of all other writers: I would his humility had not made him niggardly of his name, that wee might haue knowen whome to haue thanked.' For this unknown person there are at least two better candidates than the ancient but nameless doctor whose *scala* Hall quotes.

It so happens that also 112 years before 1606, that is, in 1494, an anonymous and 'obscure' author 'wrote' the famous *Meditations on the Life of Christ*. He has been called 'the Pseudo-Bonaventura'. One 1494 appearance of the book is the translation by Nicholas Love, *Incipit Speculum vite Christi, The Myrroure of the blessyd Lyf of Ihesu Christ*, printed by Richard Pynson in London. Another is *Incipit Speculum vite Christi*, with woodcuts and Caxton's device on the title-page and 'Westmonsteri, Wynkyn the Worth, 1494'. This is the devotional work of the Middle Ages that rivals in popularity that of Thomas à Kempis. According to Marcel Viller and the editors of *Dictionaire de la spiritualité*, the original Latin piece exists in two versions, the longer one including the *Meditationes de passione* by St Bonaventura and the *De ministeris Marthae et Mariae*.[15] The versions and manuscripts of English provenance invariably have in their title the word 'glasse' or 'speculum'. This 'unknown Franciscan', as Martz fittingly calls him in a chapter on George Herbert,[16] brings together in the art of meditation Hall's favourite predecessors, as Mauburnus' isolated quotation of Wessel Gansfort's *Scala* does not.

An even stronger candidate for Hall's unidentified leader in the art of Christian meditation is the man we now know as Thomas à Kempis, the author of *De Imitatione Christi*. Some of its innumerable editions appeared under his own name, others under the name of de Gerson, and significantly for us, still others were 'namelesse'. In the year 1492, close enough to Hall's 'some 112. yeeres agoe' since he became aware of meditation in 1605, an edition of the *Imitatio* appeared, with no place of origin on the title-page, combining (not unusually) two separate works. It assigns the second piece, *Tractulo de meditatione cordis*, to Gerson (note Hall's emphasis upon the heart and his many allusions to the Chancellor of Paris), but gives no author for the first piece, *Tractatus de Ymitatione Christi*.[17]

Apart from the fact that Hall's Reformation instincts were reaffirmed during his trip to the Lowlands in 1605, there are several reasons why we should think this 'namelesse' *Imitation of Christ* is Hall's major source. Hall calls his writer a monk, and the author of the *Imitation* is obviously a member of a monastery living under a rule which he gladly embraces (I, 9). Chapters 17 to 20 of Book I describe the monastic life with enthusiasm and yet a warning: 'Never promise yourself security in this life, even though you seem to be a good monk or a devout hermit.'[18] The 'Disciple' speaks to Christ in III, 10: 'It is a great honour and glory to serve You, and to despise all else for Your sake; for grace will be given to those who have willingly entered Your most holy service . . .', having 'set aside all worldly interests' (pp. 104–5). The life of a monk fills him with Joy: '. . . I have accepted it, and will bear it until death,' he cries; 'the life of a good Religious is truly a cross, but it is also a guide to Paradise' (III, 56, p. 172). Joseph Hall seems to confess in his first chapter that he had found the best practice of meditation among the medieval monks, and that his purpose was to bring meditation out of the monastery into ordinary Christian life: 'And how euer of olde some hidden Cloysterers haue ingrossed it to themselues, and confined it within their Celles . . .,' every Christian, he asserts, should practise it, particularly those Christians who cannot devote their entire lives to religion (pp. 4–5).

The adjective 'obscure', meaning 'unknown to fame', that Hall applies to this monk is expanded in the phrase, 'I would his humility had not made him niggardly of his name.' Christian humility is reflected on almost every page of the *Imitation*. One of the rules of the Augustinian canons regular required the monk 'To learn the lesson of

Humility, according to the most perfect pattern set forth in the life of Christ, and in that of his nearest and most faithful followers; and especially in this, that the greatest among them should be the younger, and he that is chief as he that doth serve.'[19] Christ speaking to the 'Disciple' in *Imitatio*, iii, 24, on the evils of curiosity, says: 'Be ready; watch and pray. Above all be humble' (p. 124). And elsewhere the 'Disciple' says, 'Lord, I submit myself in all humility to Your unfathomable judgments; I acknowledge my utter nothingness' (III, 14, pp. 109–10). Hall's emphasis upon the heart over the mind and upon instinctive simplicity over borrowed unintelligibility is more likely to have sprung from *The Imitation of Christ* than from Mauburnus. 'Blessed is that simplicity,' writes the author of the *Imitatio*, 'which rejects obscure enquiry, and advances along the sure and open road of God's Commandments' (IV, 18, p. 214). *Amo nescire*, 'I love not to know', was the motto of the Augustinians.

The constant division into pairs of contrary states, moreover, like the heart versus mind that is so characteristic of the *Imitation*, would appeal to Hall's Ramistic bent. One of Hall's favourite oppositions is that between 'natural' and 'Christian', which reappears so strikingly in Cardinal Newman's definition of a gentleman. Hall insists that we are 'natural' in our brains; all are born logicians. But it takes something above and contrary to 'nature' to learn how to love God in our hearts. One of the many notable oppositions of the *Imitatio* occurs in III, 54, entitled 'On the Contrary Workings of Nature and Grace', a chapter which proceeds by dozens of disjunctives built on the adversative 'but', like 'Nature is quick to complain of want and hardship; but Grace bears poverty with courage' (p. 167). A man is a man by his understanding part, writes Hall as he passes from his rhetorical *topoi* to what he calls 'the very soule of Meditation'; 'but he is a Christian by his will and affections' (p. 150).

In an epistle (epistle viii of Decade III) to Mr Robert Hay, the son of Lord Doncaster, registered for publication on 17 October 1608, Hall gives his young friend 'a discourse of the continual exercise of a Christian; how he may keep his heart from hardness and his ways from error'. It is a shortened account of the whole meditative process. 'The evening is fittest for this work,' counsels Hall; 'when retired into ourselves, we must, cheerfully and constantly, both look up to God and into our hearts, as we have to do with both: to God in thanksgiving, first; then, in request' (Wynter VI, 209). At the end, Hall says: 'Much of this good counsel I confess to have learned from the table of an unknown author at Antwerp. It contented me, and therefore I have thus made it, by many alterations, my own for form, and yours for the use: our practice shall both commend it and make us happy' (VI, 210).[20]

In the front of the 1492 anonymous *Imitation of Christ*, a 'table' (*tabula capitulorum*, not *scala*) divides the work into two parts: the 'Incipit', which recounts the specialities of God's grace, and the 'Explicit' or confession and devout petition for mercy. The book describes the 'outer' and 'inner' life of a Christian. Joseph Hall admired the combination of the active and contemplative life, the systasis of Mary and Martha. In the *Arte*, he praises 'those auncient Monks' for alternating at various times of the day the work in the fields and the meditation in the study – not, he adds, like certain 'religious at this day' who 'hauing mewd and mured vp themselues from the world spend themselues wholly vpon their beads and Crucifixe, pretending no other work but meditation' (pp. 41–2).

Finally, in favour of Thomas à Kempis being the nameless, obscure, and humble monk from whom Hall learned so much about meditation, are two references in the *Arte* which Hall cites without name but with commendation. 'One sayes, (and I believe him),' Hall writes, 'that Gods Schoole is more of Affections, then Vnderstanding' (p. 9). Were this Bernard, or Bonaventure, or Augustine, or Gerson – all of whom could have said it – I think Hall would have named him. On the other hand, the thought is practically the thesis of *De Imitatione Christi*.

The second citation is this: 'Whither tendeth that ancient counsell of a great Master in this Arte, of three things requisite to this business, *Secrecy, Silence, Rest*: whereof the first excludeth company, the second noise, the third motion' (p. 53). Again, this is general and we do not know who the 'great Master' is. It could be Bernard or Gerson. Or it could be the anonymous monk (Kempis) echoing the Psalms in his cell, writing in I, 19, 'Of the Practices of a Good Religious'. Discipline is necessary, he says, but if for any reason you have to skip part of it, you can make it up the next day, as Hall himself says (*Arte*, p. 35). As for solitariness, Thomas writes, 'Whatever is purely personal is best done in private' (I, 19, p. 48); and 'The greatest Saints used to avoid the company of men whenever they were able, and chose rather to serve God in solitude' (I, 20, p. 49). Part of the day, we have seen, the monk is working with others in the field or the refectory; when he meditates, however, Thomas says, 'Seek out a place apart, and love the solitary life. Do not engage in conversation with men, but instead pour forth devout prayer to God, that you may preserve a humble mind' (III, 53, p. 164).

Why Joseph Hall as a student at Cambridge apparently had never come across either the *De Imitatione Christi* or Richard Whytford's translation of it as *The ffolowynge of Christ*, we do not know. Thomas à Kempis, as we now know the author, stated his conception, in De

Montmorency's words, 'in such a form that it could appeal to almost every type of mind, and make the simple peasant as well as the great philosopher realise that Christianity is philosophy at its highest exhibited in action.'.[21] It is difficult to resist the conviction that in 1605 in Holland, just before composing his *Arte of Divine Meditation*, Joseph Hall had come upon and had read with rapt attention the 1492 anonymous *De Imitatione Christi* bound up with Gerson's *De Meditatione Cordis*.

So much for Hall's theory of meditation and its sources. We consider now his mature practice in the kinds of meditation that followed from it. Throughout a long, busy and useful life, Hall wrote three kinds of meditation as first distinguished in the *Arte* of 1606: (1) the 'occasional meditations', induced by something external to one's self; (2) the 'deliberate meditations' which are 'rational'; and (3) the 'deliberate meditations' which are 'affective'. Examples of these three kinds are (1) the meditations 'On a Spider' or 'On a pair of spectacles'; (2) the studied *Contemplations* upon stories in the Bible; and (3) the often dithyrambic addresses to his own soul.

Thus Hall followed first in theory and then in actual composition a long Christian tradition of 'reading' about God that stems from the Bible, the early church fathers and medieval community-religious life. Two of the so-called 'books' are familiar: 'The Book of Creatures' and 'The Book of Scriptures', the two, for example, from which Sir Thomas Browne 'collected his divinity' (*Religio Medici*, I, xv). But there is a third 'book' through which God speaks, 'The Book of the Soul', or the heart, mind, conscience. Biblical precedent for such a 'book', independent of nature or the written word, lies in the Psalms and in such phrases as 'I will put my laws into their mind, and write them in their hearts' (Hebrews 8 : 10, echoing Jeremiah 31 : 33; cf. Hebrews 10 : 16). Hall's earliest theoretical statement of three 'books', not two, comes towards the end of Chapter 12 of his *Arte of Diuine Meditation*, entitled 'Of the Matter and Subject of our Meditations'. Here he specifies [1] the meditations on 'thy wonderful works'; [2] the meditations 'concerning Christ ... his incarnation, Miracles, Life, Passion'; and [3] meditations on 'those matters in Diuinity which can most of all worke compunction in the hart' (1606 edn, pp. 70–1). The three powers of the soul, as Martz points out in his classic account of the Augustinian tradition, all come into play: memory, as we study 'The Book of Creatures'; understanding, for 'The Book of Scriptures'; and will, in the final command over 'The Book of the Soul'. God spoke directly, without the medium of created nature or the Scriptures, to certain biblical figures; many a Christian in the past and even today believes that He still so speaks.

In theoretical arrangement, the 'Book of Scriptures' usually comes in the middle since through its 'glass' we can *sense* 'The Book of Creatures' and *know* that which in our own souls is most akin to God. And if any one book in the Bible were central to this, it would be the Psalms. Every use, in the King James version, of the term 'meditation' occurs there, and the process, in the biblical mind of the Protestant, is linked with poetry and fervent ejaculatory address rather than with mental discipline. The Psalmist's most famous religious address (Psalm 19 : 14) does not mention paradigm or even intellect: 'Let the words of my mouth, and the meditation of my heart, be acceptable in thy sight, O LORD, my strength, and my redeemer.' Joseph Hall had sung the psalms from his boyhood, and while writing on meditation tried his hand at 'metaphrasing' a few of them. 'Indeed, my Poetrie was long sithence out of date,' he writes in the 1607 publication of the result, '& yielded hir place to grauer studies; but whose vaine would it not reviue to looke into these heauenly songs? I were not woorthy to be a Diuine, if it should repent me to be a Poet with DAVID, after I shall haue aged in the pulpit.'[22] The Psalms contain all three kinds of meditation: some praise the Lord for His 'creatures' (Psalms 33, 104, 148); others cogitate His written commands (Psalm 119, § 5); and still others seek God by looking into the poet's soul (Psalms 6, 22, 38, 42). One of the Psalms that combines all three kinds is Psalm 19, the final stanza of which on 'the meditation of my heart' we have just quoted. The psalm is divided into three parts: the first six verses meditate on 'The Book of Creatures'; the next five verses on 'The Book of Scriptures'; and the last three verses open up 'The Book of the Soul', that is, the individual conscience. Psalm 19, in the King James version, follows:

1 The heavens declare the glory of God;
   and the firmament sheweth his handywork.
2 Day unto day uttereth speech,
   and night unto night sheweth knowledge.
3 There is no speech nor language,
   where their voice is not heard.
4 Their line is gone out through all the earth,
   and their words to the end of the world.
   In them hath he set a tabernacle for the sun,
5 Which is as a bridegroom coming out of his chamber,
   and rejoiceth as a strong man to run a race.
6 His going forth is from the end of the heaven,
   and his circuit unto the ends of it:
   and there is nothing hid from the heat thereof.

7 The law of the LORD is perfect,
   converting the soul:
   the testimony of the LORD is sure,
   making wise the simple.
8 The statutes of the LORD are right,
   rejoicing the heart:
   the commandment of the LORD is pure.
   enlightening the eyes.
9 The fear of the LORD is clean,
   enduring for ever:
   the judgments of the LORD are true
   and righteous altogether.
10 More to be desired are they than gold,
   yea, than much fine gold:
   sweeter also than honey and the honeycomb.
11 Moreover by them is thy servant warned:
   and in keeping of them there is great reward.

12 Who can understand his errors?
   cleanse thou me from secret faults.
13 Keep back thy servant also from presumptuous sins;
   let them not have dominion over me:
   then shall I be upright,
   and I shall be innocent from the great transgression.
14 Let the words of my mouth, and the meditation of my heart,
   be acceptable in thy sight,
   O LORD, my strength, and my redeemer.

This Hebraic pattern for the 'Three Books' has been Christianized, quite naturally, by ideas of the Trinity. 'The Book of Creatures' stems from God the Father; that of the Scriptures, on the types and the antitype of Christ, tells of God the Son; and the Book of the Soul, as the soul becomes sanctified, is the effect of God the Holy Spirit. The Book of Common Prayer (in the order for the visitation of the sick) commends 'the Christian soul' 'in the Name of God the Father Almighty who *created* three; in the Name of Jesus Christ who *redeemed* thee; and in the Name of the Holy Ghost who *sanctifieth* three.' (I underscore the words that bring out the three avenues.) When the three 'books' are put into the order of Creatures–Scriptures–Soul, the invariable dichotomizing of a tripartite structure takes several forms. We have said that the first two books are means; the third, end. Again, the first two books are past tense (God did create the world and Christ did die to free us from the bondage of the law), but the third book is present tense or even future since the soul attains its real sanctity when it leaves the body. The first two books are 'read' in time and in this world; the third is 'read' out of time and in the 'next world' as the soul gains glimpses of eternity. The first two are *outer*, the eye being used for the creatures and the ear for the Scriptures; these take us to the *inner* 'eye' and 'ear' of our own conscience. The movement in all three kinds of meditations as well as in many of the individual meditations, no matter of which category, is from protasis to apodosis. They pass from sensibles to intelligibles; from the exterior, into the interior, up into, finally, the superior.

Certain metaphors cling to such a 'reading' of God. The most obvious is the book metaphor: 'writing', 'alphabet' (as in the *Alphabetum Divini Amoris* ascribed to Gerson), 'God's A.B.C.', 'the hand-writing on the wall', 'emblems', 'hieroglyphs', 'characters', 'volume' and so forth. Then there is the metaphor of 'digestion'. As the body needs daily sustenance from real food, so the soul must 'feed' daily by 'taking in' the books of the Creatures, the Scriptures and the Soul. Significant here is the phrasing of the Collect in the Book of Common Prayer for the first Sunday in Advent, denominated 'Bible Sunday'. The people are enjoined to 'read, mark, and inwardly digest' the Holy Scriptures. In *The Devout Soul* (1643), Joseph Hall wrote: 'The food that is received into the soul by the ear is afterwards chewed in the mouth thereof by memory, concocted in the stomach by meditation, and dispersed into the parts by conference and practice' (Wynter, VI, 530–31), which is pretty complex alimentation. But the biblical manna, symbol of Grace, is heavenly food. The secular Francis Bacon uses the metaphor in a familiar passage on the reading of books.

A final metaphor is that of the 'glass' as both a mediating instrument and a reflector. It mediates between man and the sun, whose radiance is too bright for human eyes. It is partially a condition of our mortality, as in St Paul's words: 'Now we see through a glass darkly.' The favourite medieval term was *speculum*, used also in the sense of a mirror in which God appears as image and the things of nature as 'vestiges'. Donne wrote in his last sermon, 'Death's Duel', 'Our medium, our glass, is the Book of Creatures, and our light, by which we see him, is the light of Natural Reason.'[23] In an 'Occasional Meditation' on his own spectacles, Hall wrote: 'Many such glasses my soule hath and useth: I looke through the glasse of the creatures, at the power and wisedome of their maker: I looke through the glasse of the Scriptures at the great mystery of redemption and the glory of an heavenly inheritance: I look through God's favours, at his infinite mercy; through his judgments, at his incomprehensible justice' – a one-sentence 'mirror' reflecting the 'three books'.[24]

We shall now look in more detail at Hall's meditations that contemplate God in 'The Book of the Soul' and in 'The Book of Scriptures', reserving for a separate chapter, because of their intrinsic literary interest, his meditations on 'The Book of the Creatures'.

Problems of God's 'incomprehensible justice' must be settled in the individual's soul, in his conscience, the 'paradise [or else hell] within', where the Christian as a completely free agent alone confronts his God. In volume, time-span and intensity, Hall's meditations on 'The Book of the Soul' rank highest, for they represent the end-all of the meditative process.[25] Only two of these obey his own rules set down in *The Arte of Divine Meditation*: one on the saints which accompanies his theoretical text, and the other 'On Death' in which the steps are named as if to show the beginner that it can be done. In the rest, one can occasionally recognize certain 'steps' in the 'Ladder of the Affections', but hardly ever the same steps and rarely in the same order. With his theroetical emphasis upon the heart rather than the brain, it would appear that Hall, always psychologically aware of the practitioner, paid less and less attention to the rungs than to the ladder itself which would lead him and his readers from earth to heaven.

At the beginning of the seventeenth century and through the Civil War the art and practice of devotion became for Hall the central Christian duty. Throughout his life he called attention to his own 'often and serious meditation', to his constant practice of looking into his soul to know God, and his hope that by setting these meditations down he could show the way to others. He composed *The Devout Soul* amid the Civil War's drums and tramplings, a time above all times when it is proper 'to direct our address to the throne of God'. 'Blessed be my God,' he adds, 'who, in the midst of these woful tumults, hath vouchsafed to give me these calm and holy thoughts; which I justly suppose he meant not to suggest that they should be smothered in the breast wherein they were conceived, but with a purpose to have the benefit communicated to many . . . I direct the way: God bring us to the end' (VI, 503).

Because of the belief in 1643 that England's civil broils may be a visitation from God, psychologically this kind of meditation is the sinner's awareness of having erred and strayed from God's ways: 'It is fit the exercise of our devotion should begin in an humble confession of our unworthiness,' Hall writes; 'Now, for the effectual furtherance of this our self-dejection, it will be requisite to bend our eyes upon a three-fold object: to look inward, into ourselves; upward, to heaven; and downward, to hell' (VI, p. 516).

Next to the Protestant Christian's emphasis upon the conscience, is his belief in the sufficiency of the Holy Bible.[26] Though his meditations on 'The Book of Scriptures' are called *Contemplations upon the Principal Passages in the Holy Story*, in his dedication of their beginnings to Prince Henry, Hall refers to them as 'these meditations' and 'these holy speculations' (I, 2). Their purpose is to 'give light to the thoughts of any reader [;] let him with me give the praise to Him from whom that light shone forth to me' (I, 3). May 'that Spirit', he adds, 'which hath penned all these things for our learning . . . sanctify these my unworthy meditations to the good of his church' (I, 25). They differ from his exegetical work, *A Paraphrase upon the Hard Texts in the Whole Divine Scriptures*, in that they contain very little citation of authority or etymological and historical explanation. Their signature as meditation rather than exegesis or sermon is the reiterated phrase 'O my God' or 'O my Saviour' or 'O my soule'. Their tone is exemplified by the meditation on Jacob's 'sweet vision of angels climbing up and down that sacred ladder which God hath set between heaven and earth' (I, 325). They are filled with joy: 'What is this, other than the exaltation of Isaac's delight to walk forth into the pleasant fields of the Scriptures, and to meditate of nothing under heaven?' (ibid.). After a period of polemical writing, Hall returns to this healing work with the wish 'that all the professors of the dear name of Christ might be taken up with nothing but holy and peaceable thoughts of devotion' (I, 400).

Chronologically, the meditations on Scripture were begun after the *Occasional Meditations* on God's creatures (published later) and occupied a far longer period of Hall's creative life. He started writing them after he had become the rector in Lord Denny's benefice at Waltham. 'None can challenge so much right in these Meditations,' Hall writes in dedicating Book XIX to Denny, 'as your lordship, under whose happy shade they received their first conception'. Offering 'the 7th and last volume' to King Charles, Hall writes: 'Now at last, thanks be to my good God, I have finished the long task of my meditations upon the historical part of the Old Testament' (II.141). And dedicating his initial meditation on the New Testament again to the king, he asserts: 'More than twenty years are slipped away since I entered upon this task of sacred Contemplations' (II, 291).

The second volume of meditations on the New Testament is introduced thus: 'To the honour and glory of God my Saviour; and to the benefit and behoof of his blessed Spouse, the Church; I do in all humility devote myself and all my Meditations' (II, 409). Just as the *Occasional Meditations* begin with an emblem and end in a little homily and an affectionate devotion to God, so these meditations on the Bible usually begin with the story and end with application to our lives and a heart-felt adoration. The whole body of them, also, rises in emotion from the Old Testament to the New. The last meditation is the longest and most fervent of them all, hardly falling in attention and zeal throughout all of its 288 pages.

> My reader shall find the discourse in all these passages more large [warns their author]; and in the latter, as the occasion gives, more fervent: and if he shall miss some remarkable stories, let him be pleased to know, that I have purposely omitted those pieces which consist rather of speech than of act, and those that are in respect of the matter coincident to these I have selected. I have so done my task as fearing, not affecting, length; and as careful to avoid the cloying my reader with other men's thoughts. [II, 410]

Again, in *The Devout Soul* of 1643, Hall expands his theory of a meditation based on 'The Book of Scriptures' by citing the experience of David:

> Before we put our hand to this sacred volume, it will be requisite to elevate our hearts to that God whose it is, for both his leave and his blessing. *Open mine eyes*, saith the sweet singer of Israel, *that I may behold the wondrous things of thy law*, Ps. cxix. 18. Lo, David's eyes were open before to other objects; but when he comes to God's book, he can see nothing without a new act of apertion: letters he might see, but wonders he could not see, till God did unclose his eyes and enlighten them. It is not therefore for us presumptuously to break in upon God, and to think by our natural abilities to wrest open the precious caskets of the Almighty, and to fetch out all his hidden treasure thence at pleasure: but we must come tremblingly before him, and, in all humility, crave his gracious admission. [VI, 526]

These two categories of meditation, those based on 'The Book of the Soul' and on 'The Book of Scriptures', comprise Hall's major religious contribution to the practice of Protestant meditation. As we said, because of their special literary connections with seventeenth-century poetry and essay, we shall reserve his meditations on 'The Book of the Creatures' for a separate chapter. But it is not too early to generalize briefly on his method and to touch on his reputation as a writer of Protestant meditations.

In sharp contradistinction to the *Spiritual Exercises* of St Ignatius of Loyola, in Joseph Hall there is no single method, whether it consists of three steps, or seven or none, which can raise the soul of Everyman from earth to heaven. Nor does God work by miracle, but 'in such methods and by such means as may most conduce to his blessed ends'. The methods are those only of 'sweet conversation' or 'self-conferences' or 'heavenly soliloquies', or sometimes gentle and sometimes fierce arguments with one's own soul – all terms which Hall freely uses for what is technically called meditation. 'Devotion is the life of religion.' he wrote, 'the very soul of piety, the highest employment of grace, and no other than the prepossession of heaven by the saints of God here on earth' (VI, 504). Suspicious of two rigid a method though Hall is, he nevertheless insists that there is an 'art' of meditation which can be acquired by a mature person who is willing to practice. With no discipline at all, as he charmingly (and, in Croll's terminology, 'baroquely') puts it in another context, one's *cogitations* and *affections* (the two parts) can go astray:

> In this case it fals out with thee, O my soule, as with some fond child, who eagerly following a Bee in hope of her bag, sees a gay Butterflie crosse his way; and thereupon leaves his first chase, and runs after those painted wings; but in that pursute seeing a Bird flie close by him, he leaves the flie in hope of a better purchase; but in the meane time is disappointed of all, and catcheth nothing. It mainely behoves thee therefore to keep up thy Cogitations and Affections close to these heavenly objects; and to check them whensoever thou perceivest an inclination to their wandering.[27]

Hall believed that God's grace is furthered by art, but method is not everything. Many books have been written on chemistry, he remarks elsewhere, but few men have made gold (VIII, 7). Sometimes he begins a 'soul-meditation' with a biblical passage or with one of God's creatures, thus deliberately melding the three categories. In any one he may repeat from 'The Book of the Creatures' such outward occasions as the heavens, the spider, the bee and the worm. To these he may add such temporal occasions as the morning, or the evening, or Basil's lighting of the candles; and such inward occasions as affliction, remorse, doubt, gratitude and elation. These various psychological states with the ejaculatory prayers that accompany them remind one of the ups and downs of the Christian life as we read them in George Herbert's *The Temple*. Hall gains variety in his meditations as one literary genre flows into another. Thus a 'meditation' verges upon a 'vow', or a 'soliloquy', or a 'devotion', or a 'prayer'.

Joseph Hall, we have said, was a Calvinist who never left the Anglican church. As an Anglican he was devoted, of course, to the Bible, the tradition of the Apostolic Church, the Book of Common Prayer and reason. He was sufficiently free from Laudian restrictions not only to challenge his archbishop from his cathedral in Exeter, but also to bring to all his Christian writings, especially those that include his theory and practice of meditation, the assumption that all men are not built the same, that straitjackets impede the individual's free access to God. Protestant individualism and an Anglican capacity for adaptation, then, are the two most important notes in Hall's contribution to seventeenth-century meditation.

Along with these goes his insistence that any Christian can learn to meditate, not merely the professional or the recluse or the man who has the leisure. There is hardly a book of his that does not take time out to appeal to the 'unlearned', the beginner, whose heart can be taught to love God before his brain can understand Him. This is why Hall, in his *Arte of Divine Meditation*, rejected as far too subtle the step-by-step ratiocination which he found in Mauburnus. 'I doubt not,' he wrote, 'but an ordinary Reader will easily espie a double fault at the least, *Darkenesse* and *Coincidence*' (p. 87), that is, needless obscurity and an overlapping in logic that makes the thing more difficult than it really is.

Which brings us to Hall's clarity of style and his use of rhetoric. A person talking to himself or to God in the privacy of communion is really not conscious of style, yet Hall was constantly writing for others. He got his style for his theoretical and practical works partly from reading Seneca and mostly from reading the Psalms and the pithy sentences of the books in the Bible ascribed to Solomon. Not a little of it came from his education in Ramistic logic received from Dr Chaderton and other teachers at Emmanuel. The complexities of Aristotelian logic are made simple through a reduction to disjunctive dichotomies, so that the thought moves in a one-dimensional line independent of other levels of meaning.[28] This lies behind Hall's definition of meditation as *'a bending of the mind upon some spiritual object . . . until our thoughts come to an issue'*. Thus Hall's meditation is a conscious elimination of thoughts other than the single issue, an elimination based on firm Ramistic procedure. Hall, especially in meditation, is hardly ever the purely Senecan prose writer, a characteristic of his which, as we brought out in our discussion of his *Characters*, has been over-emphasized.

As for his reputation as a writer of meditations, though he helped to initiate several literary genres in England, he became most famous for this one.[29] In innumerable dedications, he calls attention to the need for writing and publishing meditations in view of the large number of sermons, exegetical works and controversy that kept pouring from the press. It was through his meditations that Hall became part of the inner circle of Prince Henry and King James's court. A volume of Hall's collected works published in 1617 (University of Michigan Library) has, pasted on the spine, a label in seventeenth-century hand that simply says 'Hall's Meditations' as though the volume contained nothing else. The meditations alone become the centre of John Owen's epigram on Hall, clumsily translated by John Vicars and published in 1619:

Doctor Ios. Hales Vowes and Meditations
Thou *Vowed'st Vowes*, fit to be *Vow'd*,
Worth *Reading Workes* dost write:
He's blest that *Reades* thy *Vowes*, if hee
To doe them take delight.[30]

The 1628 *Works of Joseph Hall Bishop of Exeter* has, under the
engraved portrait, lines by J. Sampson; after Hall has been publishing
books of various kinds for over thirty years, that which the eulogist
singles out is his meditations:

How farre beyond a Picture is his worth
Whom Pen, nor Pencill truly can set forth.
Behold his Reverend FACE; his better PART
Is left ungrav'd. This was beyond all Art.
His holy Thoughts in sacred MEDITATIONS.
His ravisht SOULE with heavenly CONTEMPLATIONS
Could not bee drawne. Here only are his Looks:
The Pictures of the rest are in his Books.

In his funeral sermon on Hall in 1656, the Reverend John
Whitefoot takes pains to praise Hall's major contribution to the Christian life of his time: 'He was one that conversed as much with God and
drew as nigh to Him in divine meditation, which is the ordinary way
of seeing God in the flesh, as any man of his time ... A great master he
was, and one of the first that taught this church the art of divine
meditation' (Wynter, I, lxxiii). The high place Hall's meditations held
among his many contributions to English prose was signalled by
Thomas Fuller as he nominated Joseph Hall one of England's
Worthies: the Bishop was 'not unhappy at *Controversies*, more happy at
Comments, very good in his *Characters*, better in his *Sermons*, best of all in
his *Meditations*'.[31]

Hall's works of meditation include *The Arte of Divine Meditation*, his
emblems on 'The Book of Creatures', his contemplations on parts of
the Scripture dedicated to Prince Henry and Charles I, and his continued publication of meditations on the individual's soul-hunger for
God. Faced with the political and religious necessity to resist the
Jesuits, in theory and practice he was completely independent of the
Spiritual Exercises of St Ignatius of Loyola. Joseph Hall became
seventeenth-century England's most eminent theorist and prose artist
in what he deftly called 'the slow proficiency of Grace'.[32]

7. *Hall's* Occasional Meditations *and Imaginative Literature*

Of Hall's three kinds of meditations, today the most appealing are those based on the 'Book of the Creatures'.[1] Of course Hall knew the story of Creation in Genesis, and for most of his literary-religious life had been influenced by the *Divine Weeks* of the French Protestant poet du Bartas and Sylvester's 1605 translation, as well as by King James's admiration for them both. Late in life, in *Select Thoughts* (No. 100), Hall cites many a biblical passage on God's creatures: Christ's calling our attention to the falling of a sparrow (Matthew 10 : 29), and Solomon's saying, 'A righteous man regardeth the life of his beast, but the tender mercies of the wicked are cruel' (Proverbs 12 : 10). There he also pays particular attention to David's poem in Psalm 104:

24 O LORD, how manifold are thy works!
   in wisdom hast thou made them all:
   the earth is full of thy riches.

25 So is this great and wide sea,
   wherein are things creeping innumerable,
   both small and great beasts.

26 There go the ships:
   there is that leviathan,
   whom thou hast made to play therein . . .

33 . . . I will sing praise to my God while I have my being.

34 My meditation of him shall be sweet . . .

Forty-two years before, Hall had written in *The Arte of Divine Meditation* (1606): 'God is wronged if his creatures bee vnregarded; our selues most of all if wee reade this great volume of the creatures, and take no lesson for our instruction' (p. 16).

That Hall is aware of hexameral and hebdomadal literature is clear from the selection of 'occasions' from which his *Occasional Meditations* arise. Every one of them (here we have room for only a few examples) can be placed in the order of the first creation, as follows:

(1) *The heavens* – Genesis 1 : 8 – 'And God called the firmament heaven': 'Vpon the sight of the Heavens moving', 'Vpon the small Starres in the Galaxie', 'Vpon view of the Heaven & the Earth'.

(2) *The earth and the waters* – Genesis I : 9–10 – 'and let the dry land appear . . . and the gathering together of the waters: 'Vpon the sight of a Raine in the Sun-shine', 'Vpon the sight of an heape of stones', 'Vpon Spring in a wild Forrest'.

(3) *The grass, flowers, shrubs and trees* – Genesis I : 11–12 – 'Let the earth bring forth grass, the herb yielding seed, and the fruit tree yielding fruit after his kind': 'Vpon sight of a Tree full blossomed', 'Vpon the sight of a Lilly', 'Vpon the sight of Grapes'.

(4) *The birds* – Genesis I : 20 – 'and fowl that may fly above the earth': 'Vpon occasion of a Redbreast comming into his Chamber', 'Vpon the singing of the Birds in a Spring-morning', 'Vpon the sight of a Larke flying up'.

(5) *The animals* – Genesis 1 : 24 – 'and the beast of the earth after his kind': 'Vpon the barking of a Dog', 'Vpon the sight of a Dormouse', 'Vpon the sight of an Hedge-hogge'.

(6) *The insects* – Genesis 1 : 25 – 'and everything that creepeth upon the earth': 'Vpon a Worme', 'Vpon Gnats in the Sun', 'Vpon the stinging of a Waspe'.

(7) *Man* – Genesis 1 : 26 – 'Let us make man in our own image . . . and let him have dominion': 'Vpon the sight of a Blackmore', 'Vpon the sight of Boyes playing', 'Vpon the sight of a Scavenger working in the channel'.

(8) *Man's crafts* – Genesis 4 : 22 – 'Tubal-Cain, an instructor in every artifice': 'Vpon the sight of a Diall', 'Vpon the sound of a crakt Bell', 'Vpon the hearing of Musicke by night'.

But it is their literary rather than religious content that makes these meditations based on 'The Book of the Creatures' interesting today. Resting on the *topos* of *Deus Artifex*, this kind of meditation attracted Joseph Hall as a creative artist in words; the genre is related to the seventeenth-century 'essay' and to 'metaphysical poetry'. As God created matter in an intelligently conceived and foreordained form, so, Hall wrote, 'that which we are wont to say of fine wittes, we may as truely affirme of the Christian hart: that it can make vse of anything' (*Arte*, p. 20). The whole world was seen by Plotinus and his followers as God's poem; and the Italians perceived God as a metaphysical poet who made the book of creatures, in witty metaphors, part of the poetic of correspondence.[2] 'The Book of the Creatures' is not that zoological one of Aristotle the biologist. Since an idea has been placed between the physical specimen and God, it is, rather, the world of Plato and

Hermes Trismegistus, the world of poetry, that allowed Sir Thomas Browne to wonder at the mystical mathematics of the city of heaven etched on the back of a turtle.

It is not known exactly when Hall composed his meditations of the creatures. From his own proem and from his son Robert Hall's dedication of the book to James Hay Viscount Doncaster, as well as from Hall's naming them 'Occasional', a term for one of the three varieties described in his 1606 *Arte*, it is safe to assume that the idea for them came early, and that they were probably composed at odd times during his first fifteen years or so on the Denny-Hay estate in Waltham. 'These Papers,' Robert tells us when Joseph Hall was the very busy bishop of Exeter, were found 'amongst others lying aside in my Father's study'.

There were printed editions of ninety-one of them in 1630, and again in 1631. A third edition in 1633 contained forty-nine additional meditations, and the printer evidently bound these on to the remaining copies of the 1631, with the notation on p. 233: 'Occasional Meditations not before set forth.' Appended to the title of No. XCI of 1631 is the phrase 'By way of conclusion'; and there are two 'tables', one at the end of the ninety-first and another at the end of the book. In 1633, the phrase 'By way of conclusion' is omitted, and there is only one table for all 140. That the extra meditations were bound in with the left-over copies of the 1631 edition is further shown by the fact that their orthography, punctuation and spacing are those of 1633, despite the date on the title-page. Except for these added meditations, there are no stylistic or substantive differences in the three editions. It was probably Robert Hall, their first editor, who translated all the *Occasional Meditations* into Latin and published them, in 1635, as *Josephi Halli Exoniensis Episcopi* [Gk *Autoschediasmata*] *vel Meditatiunculae Subitanae.*

After he was ousted by the Parliamentarians in the Civil War, Joseph Hall defined at greater length the meditation on 'The Book of the Creatures' in such a way as to allow us to see its relation to the literary traditions of the bestiary, the herbal, the fable, the proverb and the age-old human habit of thinking in similitudes:

> Every herb, flower, spire of grass, every twig and leaf, every worm and fly, every scale and feather, every billow and meteor, speaks the power and wisdom of their infinite Creator. Solomon sends the sluggard to the ant; Isaiah sends the Jews to the ox and the ass; our Saviour sends his disciples to the ravens, and to the lilies of the field. There is no creature of whom we may not learn something. We shall have spent our time ill in this great school of the world, if, in such store of lessons, we be non-proficients in devotion ... And indeed, wherefore serve all the volumes of natural history but

to be so many commentaries upon the several creatures wherein we may read God? and even those men who have not the skill or leisure to persue them, may yet, out of their own thoughts and observation, raise, from the sight of all the works of God, sufficient matter to glorify him. Who can be so stupid as not to take notice of the industry of the bee, the providence of the ant, the cunning of the spider, the reviving of the fly, the worm's endeavour of revenge, the subtlety of the fox, the sagacity of the hedgehog, the innocence and profitableness of the sheep, the laboriousness of the ox, the obsequiousness of the dog, the timorous shifts of the hare, the nimbleness of the deer, the generosity of the lion, the courage of the horse, the fierceness of the tiger, the cheerful music of birds, the harmlessness of the dove, the true love of the turtle, the cock's observation of time, the swallow's architecture; shortly – for it were easy here to be endless – of the several qualities and dispositions of every one of those our fellow creatures with whom we converse on the face of the earth? And who that takes notice of them cannot fetch from every act and motion of theirs some monition of duty and occasion for devout thoughts? [VI, 509–10]

The term 'creatures' includes more than the animals, the flowers and the rain; it embraces man. Also everything God has 'provided' for man by allowing him to create it – such as wine, a whetstone or a farm-wagon loaded with sheaves – becomes an occasion for meditating upon God. 'Holy mindes,' writes Robert Hall in the dedication, 'haue been euer wont to looke through these bodily objects, at spirituall, and heauenly; SO SVLPITIUS reports of S. MARTIN, that seeing a Sheepe newly shorne, he could say; Loe here's one that hath performed that command in the Gospell; hauing two Coats shee hath giuen away one.' Robert adds that Christ used the occasion of a feast to discourse on 'those Spirituall viands of grace and glory'. 'Thus,' he concludes, 'it pleased my Reuerend Father sometimes to recreate himselfe, whose manner hath beene, when any of these Meditations haue unsought offerd themselues vnto him, presently to set them downe.'

Those of us who may boggle at Hall's finding a ready sermon in every stone may be reminded of a sentence in C. S. Lewis's dedication to Charles Williams of *A Preface to Paradise Lost* (1942): 'Reviewers, who have not had time to re-read Milton, have failed for the most part to digest your criticism of him; but it is a reasonable hope that of those who heard you in Oxford many will understand henceforward that when the old poets made some virtue their theme they were not teaching but adoring, and that what we take for the didactic is often the enchanted.' We must come away impressed with the simplicity and clarity of Hall's prose style, and with the charm of these essays that arise from his own experience. Certainly they are livelier and more personal than Francis Bacon's. We have noted Hall's stand in favour of pacifism. He is also a staunch royalist in the politics of church and state; a well-tuned peal of church bells (LXXX) reminds him that domestic peace comes about only when each one keeps his due place of degree and order. At times Hall shows himself to be proud and independent: a crow, for example, can pull fleece off a sheep's docile back, but 'whosoever will be tearing my fleece let him look to himself' (XXVIII). He is an acute observer of nature in earth, sea and sky; but always devout. 'I desire not to comprehend, O Lord,' he writes; 'teach me to do nothing but wonder' (CXXI). He shows an interest in the growing science of his day; for example, in astronomy and magnetism. Still, he believed that since shellfishes have no sex, they are born of corruption, and this makes a fair pearl of greater price (CXI). Almost every page bears witness to his familiarity with the Bible, and this sometimes with humour as in his description of Elijah scanning the sky to see from what quarter of the heavens his uncouth caterers, the ravens, will bring him his breakfast (LXVIII). Hall shows himself to be a great student and lover of books; as he gazes around him in a 'great library' (probably the Bodleian), he could agree with Milton that you might as well kill a man as kill a good book (LXXI).[3]

Apart from the personality of the author, we get in these 'essays' of Joseph Hall an intimate view of the customs of the seventeenth century – in the city, on the farm and within the home. He pauses, as John Donne did, before a plague-stricken front door (LXXII). Corpses are placed in coffins made of fir to counteract the odour (LXXXVI). Ladies carry sweet-bags, into which they put the root of the fleur-de-luce (CXXVIII). A mob throws rotten eggs and insults at a whore being drawn in a cart (XCII). On separate occasions, Hall describes a beggar, a lunatic, a dwarf, a blind man, and a felon sentenced to be hanged. Mountebanks swallow dismembered toads and for a fee drink the juice (CXXXIX). A group of boys play a wild game of 'jacks' (XL). He watches a cock-fight (XXIV). And there is this description of a farmer's cart in prose that M. W. Croll would call 'Baroque': 'An empty cart runs lightly away, but if it be soundly laden, it goes sadly, sets hard, groanes under the weight, and makes deepe impressions; the wheeles creak, and the axeltree bends, and all the frame of it is put unto the utmost stress' (CXXXVI). These are meditations, but they are also literary essays that demand to be better known.

It has been thought that Protestants and 'Christian Platonists' are totally immersed in 'ideas' and that only the Roman Catholics in their sixteenth- and seventeenth-century religious writings taste, feel, touch and smell. But these meditations of Hall are not devoid of the senses, as even the few titles already quoted show. In the Renaissance hierarchy of senses, sight and hearing come at the top; smell, somewhere in the middle; touch and taste, at the bottom. Of the 140 *Occasional Meditations*, only fourteen are sensuously neutral; 103 use sight; seventeen, sound; three, smell; two involve the tactile sense; and only one (CXXXIX, 'Vpon a medicinal potion') refers to taste. And yet such exemplaristic use of the creatures and of man's common experience as emblems of the multiple attributes of God, as well as Hall's strong anti-Jesuitical stand, differentiates this part of Hall's matter from the Ignation *compositio loci*, which uses the senses to bring more sharply into focus a scene from the life of Christ, such as the manger, the crown of thorns or the *pietà*. To the Protestant poetic imagination, the 'Creatures', with all the sensuous imagery they may evoke, offer themselves in thousands of different ways.[4] And Calvinist though Hall was, nowhere else does his feeling for the synergistic principle more strongly emerge than from his *Occasional Meditations*: the double thrust of creature *and* creator, of man *and* God, of the world of things *and* of spirit. One is reminded of the singing lark and the 'lively din' of the cock in Milton's *L'Allegro*; and then the end of *Il Penseroso*:

> Where I may sit, and rightly spell
> Of every star that Heaven doth shew,
> And every herb that sips the dew;
> Till old experience do attain
> To something like prophetic strain.

Kitty Scoular is right: 'If any single English writer was responsible for popularizing the contemplation of the creatures as a religious exercise, it was probably Joseph Hall, Bishop of Exeter.'[5]

Hall's *Occasional Meditations* have not been reprinted since Wynter's edition in 1863, and then in a modernized text. Their literary flavour emerges not only in their style, but in their brevity, individuality and freshness. Of the 140 'essays' or 'prose poems' in this kind we have room here to transcribe only a very few, but these may give the reader relish for more:

XV
Vpon occasion of a Spider in his Window [Text, 1631]

THere is no vice in man, whereof there is not some analogie in the brute Creatures: As [35] amongst vs Men, there are Theeues by land, and Pirates by sea, that liue by spoyle and blood; so is there in euery kind amongst them variety of naturall Sharkers; the Hauke in the ayre, the Pike in the riuer, the Whale in the sea, the Lyon, and Tyger, and Wolfe in the desert, the Waspe in the hiue, the Spider in our window. Amongst the rest, see how cunningly this little Arabian hath spred out his tent, for a prey; how heedfully hee watches for a Passenger; so soone as euer he heares the noyse of a Fly a farre off, how hee hastens to [36] his doore, and if that silly heedlesse

Trauller doe but touch vpon the verge of that vnsuspected walk how suddenly doth hee seize vpon the miserable bootie; and after some strife, binding him fast with those subtile cords, drags the helplesse captiue after him into his caue. What is this but an Embleme of those Spirituall free-booters, that lie in waite for our soules: They are the Spiders, wee the Flies; they haue spred their nets of sinne, if wee bee once caught, they bind vs fast, and hale vs into Hell.

Oh LORD, deliuer [37] thou my soule from their crafty ambushes; their poyson is greater, their webs both more strong, and more insensibly wouen; Either teach mee to auoyd tentation, or make mee to breake through it by Repentance; Oh let mee not bee a prey to those fiends that lye in waite for my destruction.

XXX
Vpon the hearing of the street cries
in London [Text, 1631]

WHat a noyse doe these poore soules make in proclaiming their com-modities? Each tels what hee hath, and would haue all hearers take notice of it; and yet (GOD wot) it is but poore stuffe that they set out, with so much os-tentation; I doe not heare any of the rich Merchants talke of what bags hee hath in his chests, or what treasures of rich wares in his store-house; [76] every man rather desires to hide his wealth; and when he is vrged, is ready to dissemble his ability. No otherwise is it in the true Spirituall riches; hee that is full of Grace, and good workes, affects not to make shew of it to the world, but rests sweetly in the secret testimony of a good Conscience; and the silent applause of GODS spirit witnessing with his owne; whiles contrarily the venditation of our owne worth, or parts, or merits, argues a miserable in-digence in them all; O GOD, if the confessing of thine owne [77] guifts may glorifie thee, my modesty shall not bee guilty of a niggardly vnthankfulnesse; but for ought that concerns my selfe, I cannot bee too secret; Let mee so hide my selfe that I may not wrong thee; and wisely dis-tinguish betwixt thy praise, and my owne.

CXXI
Vpon the sight of a well-fleeced sheepe [Text, 1633]

WHat a warm winter coat hath God provided for this quiet innocent creature? as in- [302] deed, how wonderfull is his wisedome and goodnes in all his purveiances; those creatures which are apter for motion, and withall most fearfull by nature, hath hee clad somewhat thinner, and hath allotted them safe and warme boroughs within the earth; those that are fit for labour and use, hath hee furnished with a strong hide: & for man whom he hath thought good to bring forth naked, tender, helplesse; he hath indued his parents, and himselfe with that noble faculty of reason, whereby hee may provide all [303] manner of helps for himselfe; Yet againe so bountifull is God in his provisions, that he is not lavish; so distributing his gifts, that there is no more superfluity, then want; Those creatres that have beakes, have no teeth; and those that have shells without, have no bones within; All have enough, nothing hath all: Neither is it otherwise in that one kinde of man, whom hee meant for the Lord of all; Variety of gifts is here mixed with a frugall dispensation; None hath cause to boast, none to complain; Every man [304] is as free from an absolute defect, as from perfection; I desire not to comprehend, O Lord, teach mee to doe nothing but wonder.

XX

Vpon occasion of the lights brought in [Text, 1631]

WHat a change there is in the roome since the light came in, yea in our selues? All things seeme to haue a new forme, a new life; yea, wee are not the same we were: How goodly a creature is light, how pleasing, how agreeable to the spirits of man; no visible thing comes so neere to the resembling of the nature of the soule, yea of the God that made it; As contrarily, what an vncomfortable thing [49] is darknesse; in so much as wee punish the greatest malefactors with obscuritie of Dungeons; as thinking they could not be miserable enough, if they might haue the priuiledge of beholding the light; yea, hell it selfe can bee no more horribly described then by outward darknesse:

What is darknesse but absence of light? The pleasure, or the horror of light, or darknesse is according to the quality and degree of the cause, whence it ariseth; And if the light of a poore candle be so comfortable, which is nothing but a little inflamed ayre, gathered about a moystened snuffe, what is the light of the glorious Sunne, the great lampe of Heauen? But much more, what is the light of that infinitely resplendent Sun of righteousnesse, who gaue that light to the Sunne, that Sunne to the world; And, if this partiall, and imperfect darkenesse bee so dolefull, (which is the priuation of a naturall or artificiall light) how vnconceiuable, dolorous and miserable, shall that bee, which is caused through the vtter absence of the all-glorious GOD who is the Father of [51] lights? O Lord, how justly doe wee pitty those wretched Soules, that sit in darkenesse and the shadow of death, shut vp from the light of the sauing knowledge of thee, the onely true God; But, how am I swallowed vp with horror, to thinke of the fearefull condition of those damned soules, that are for euer shut out from the presence of GOD, and adiudged to exquisite and euerlasting darkenesse. The Egyptians were weary of themselues, in their three dayes darkenesse, yet we doe not find any paine that accompanyed their continuing night; What [52] shall wee say to those wofull soules; in whom the sensible presence of infinite torment shall meet with the torment of the perpetuall absence of GOD? O thou, who art the true light, shine euer through all the blinde corners of my Soule; and from these weake glimmerings of Grace, bring me to the perfect brightnesse of thy Glory.

At the end of Chapter 6 we spoke of the fame Hall achieved as a writer of meditations. It is fitting here that we briefly continue that history, particularly as it shows the impact these 'occasional meditations' may have had on some of the literary minds of the seventeenth century.

One of the Anglican clergymen in Hall's diocese of Exeter was the Reverend Robert Herrick. No record exists of the bishop's admonishing him on the use of sack; but it is interesting that in a poem addressed to Hall, the Hesperidian should have used a term close to that Hall himself often used for his meditations – 'a holy Rapture':

> To Jos: Lo: *Bishop of* Exeter.
> Whom sho'd I feare to write to, if I can
> Stand before you, my learn'd *Diocesan?*
> And never shew blood-guiltinesse, or feare
> To see my Lines *Excathedrated* here.
> Since none so good are, but you may condemne;
> Or here so bad, but you may pardon them.
> If then, (my Lord) to sanctifie my Muse
> One onely Poem out of all you'l chuse;
> And mark it for a Rapture nobly writ.
> 'Tis good Confirm'd; for you have Bishop't it.[6]

In 1665, Robert Boyle, 'the Christian Virtuoso', wrote a secular 'Discourse touching Occasional Meditations'. In the preface to his 'Dearest Sister Sophronia', he said:

> I know it is a new thing That I have ventured to put some Occasional Reflections into Dialogues. But the reader will be less startled at my deviating in this, and other things from *Bishop Hall's* way of writing *Occasional Meditations,* if I acknowledge, that not to Prepossess or Byas my Fancy, I purposely (till of late) forbad myself, the perusing of that Eloquent Praelates devout Reflections.[7]

Finally, that Richard Baxter depended almost wholly upon Hall for the last part of *The Saint's Everlasting Rest* (1650) shows how important Hall is in the Protestant and eventually English tradition of meditation, in prose and poetry, as opposed to the Roman Catholic and Latinate. Like Hall, Baxter quotes from an early continental 'Reformer': 'As *Gerson* ... saith, This Art or way of Meditation is not learned chiefly out of Books: but the spirit of God bestoweth it as he pleaseth: on some more plentifully, & on some more sparingly.'[8] The art of meditation, says Baxter like Hall before him, is 'The set and solemn acting of all the powers of the soul'; that is, not acting in separate stages as sensitive, intellectual and rational, but conjunctively. The acknowledgement in the margin is: 'Doctor Hall in his excellent Treatise of Meditation', and the whole of Baxter's section ix is practically a paraphrase of Chapter X of Hall's *Arte*. Baxter also is suspicious of too strict a methodology. 'What powers of the soul must be acted?' he asks. 'What affections excited? What considerations of their objects are necessary thereto? and in what order must we proceed? I joyn all these together, because though in themselves they are distinct things, yet in the practice they all concurre to the same action' (Chapter IX, p. 724).

Baxter's almost Herbertian metaphor for the proportion of thinking to feeling in a meditation is 'setting the instrument' and then 'the music'. Part of that 'music' as it affects the practitioner, to be sure, is the Protestant homiletic cast. He must argue with himself, plead, cajole by every means of rhetoric he can muster. A 'godly soliloquy' should have the parts and the ordering of a little sermon preached to one's self; a meditation is 'nothing but a pleading of the case with our own souls', says Baxter, and this allows and demands far greater variety of subject matter than the Ignatian scheme. With an unveiled thrust at *The Spiritual Exercises* of the Jesuits, Baxter writes: 'This is it that hath deceived Christians in this business; They have thought that Meditation is nothing but the bare thinking of Truths, and the rolling of them in the Understanding and Memory' (p. 692).

Baxter ends his disquisition on meditation by quoting Protestant poetry, not the kind of poetry written earlier by Southwell and later by Crashaw. He quotes two passages from Sylvester's translation of du Bartas,[9] and three poems by the Anglican priest George Herbert. The first Herbert quotation (on p. 814) is the final stanza of 'The Glance'.[10] This is followed (on p. 835) by the fourth stanza of 'Mans Medley':

> Not that we may not here
> Tast of the cheer:
> But as birds drink and then lift up the head:
> So must we sip and think
> Of better drink,
> We may attain to after we are dead – [11]

certainly a 'relishing' of heaven upon earth made memorable by a simple emblem from God's 'Book of the Creatures'. Finally, Baxter quotes in full for three pages (pp. 853–6) Herbert's poem 'Home', which begins, 'Come, Lord, my head doth burn, my heart is sick'; each stanza ends with the refrain, 'O shew thy selfe to me,/Or take me up to thee.'[12] We need not doubt that Baxter can visualize through Herbert's poetry the blood streaming down Christ's face (second stanza), nor look for ways in which Herbert must have been influenced by St Ignatius of Loyola.[13] The Protestant Baxter quotes Herbert's poem as an example of 'the poetry of meditation' at the climax of a treatise on meditation that is largely based on Joseph Hall.

As for the three 'books' in which the Protestant mind has sought God – as traditional as the poems of David and illustrated by Hall's distinguished meditations on the individual conscience, the 'Scriptures', and 'God's creatures' – it is inevitable that Professor Martz should include all three in his summary of 'Henry Vaughan and the Augustinian Quest': 'Such is the paradise within, compounded of the Bible, of Nature, and of the Self, which lies at the heart of Vaughan's *Silex Scintillans*, 1650 . . .'[14] Vaughan, Herbert, Traherne, Donne and Jonson and Herrick in their religious poems – all English, Protestant, ejaculatory, emblematic and meditative poets – may very well have been influenced, directly or indirectly, not by St Ignatius of Loyola, but by the art and practice of the Anglican Puritan Joseph Hall.

8. *Royal Embassies Abroad,*
Further Controversy

The serious yet out-going personality, broadness of view and skill in rhetoric led King James to choose Joseph Hall three times to represent England abroad: in 1616 with Lord Doncaster to France; then almost immediately to Scotland; and finally, in 1618, at the Synod of Dort.

Since the first trip produced no piece of writing, we can pass it by briefly. Its purpose King James conceived to be to congratulate Louis XIII of France on his marriage with the Infanta of Spain and to negotiate a marriage proposal for Prince Charles with Louis's sister Christine. Hardly anything was accomplished except show, for Lord Doncaster always demanded a tremendous retinue and the most expensive entertainment. All that Joseph Hall got out of it was another case of diarrhoea. He had to leave the embassy early, and even with the aid of Dr du Moulin, barely made it back to his home in Waltham. During his absence the king had presented him with the deanery of Worcester, a nice plurality.

Before the new dean had quite recovered, the king, again on an ill-conceived mission, insisted that he accompany him to Scotland. Other members of the party were Bishop Launcelot Andrewes, Dean William Laud of Gloucester, Dean Young of Winchester, and the luxurious Lord Doncaster again. Hall's presence assured a friendly response, for his liberal Calvinism was intended to pave the way for Laud's ecclesiastical formalism. But Hall was too popular; Scottish divines sought him out privately to aid them in securing some amelioration of 'the five points' which it was the purpose of the royal visitation to use as the basis of Scottish conformity with the Church of England. In particular, the Reverend William Struthers of Edinburgh raised doubts about them in a letter to Joseph Hall, and this made the king so suspicious of collusion that he commanded Hall to draft a defence of the five points to be read in the king's name at St Andrew's University, where much of the dissidence centred. Joseph Hall was thus simultaneously scolded for suspected insubordination and complimented by the trust the king put in his skill.

For reasons not clear, Hall returned to England before the others. Since the itinerary for a royal progress had to be made months in advance in order to allow time for the elaborate stop-overs, the party must have known that King James, on his way south from Hoarcross to Coventry, would spend the night of 1 September 1617 at 'the fine baronial Castle of the Earl of Huntingdon' in Ashby-de-la-Zouch.[1] It would have been a triumph for Joseph Hall, a native son, to return to his birthplace in the retinue of the king. Could it be that King James sent him back to Waltham as suitable punishment for a naughty boy? The letter to Mr Struthers was duly written from Waltham and dated 3 October 1617. The royal five points, as explained by Hall, were admitted by the Assembly at Perth on 18 August 1618, and confirmed by the English parliament in 1621.

Some things are to be done, Hall wrote to his Scottish friends, because they are commanded; and others, because they are to be done and therefore are commanded (Wynter, IX, 117–27). In this particular case, both authority and expedience meet in the single person of your king and mine. I confess, Hall adds, that never in my life have I so studied the whole history of ritual as I have in preparing this paper (you know my upbringing was 'Puritan'). These five points are only matters of ritual. They are on the outside. On the inside, which is of far greater importance, we are all in perfect agreement. You Scots allowed your universities to become careless, and His Majesty to your satisfaction and present pride tightened them up for you. Now he is attempting to do no more for your churches than he did for your seats of learning. The fundamentals are already there, scholarship in the one and devotion in the other. In both institutions you had strayed a bit far from the path of tradition. These five points of ritual are part of that great tradition, sanctioned by usage from the earliest days of the Christian church. Take, for example, the point of solemn festivities; you celebrate Christmas and Easter, so why not Pentecost or Ascension, which have equal historical weight? Points two and three have to do with the private celebration of Eucharist and baptism. Unlike the Romanists, you and I agree that the sacraments ordained by Christ are these two and not seven, and what is the difference between celebrating the sacrament in a church of four walls and in a sitting room of four walls? The spirit is the important thing, not the architecture. Article four has to do with kneeling to make one's communion. (We didn't kneel back there at Emmanuel College, remember?) Really there is no harm in suiting one's outward gesture to the thought within: to stand while praising God; to sit while listening to His Word, and to kneel, like a suppliant, for the bread and wine.[2] Finally, you stick at confirmation by bishops on the ground that it is a Roman novelty. Actually it is as old as the Bible – see 1 Timothy 4 : 14, etc. There is no new-fangled Popery in the apostolic succession. What is to be gained by breaking it?

The argument worked – at least for a time. Being as close to King James as he was, Hall could not help becoming aware of his sovereign's foolish dabbling in foreign affairs, his unpredictable tantrums and wanton behaviour in both public and private life, but he never showed any signs that he was anything but loyal. The Scottish journey inspired him to write three poems, the first one of which welcomes the king to his native land with unrestrained hyperbole, while the last poem pleads with him to return south to his other home.[3] Hall had not written poetry for some time. Perhaps he was not to be outdone by Sir Henry Drummond of Hawthornden, who welcomed his sovereign to Scotland in 'Forth Feasting'. (Its classical allusions, heroic couplets and ardent royalism made Ben Jonson wish he had written it in order to get back into the king's good graces – so we learn from the bibulous *Conversations*.) After the king's death, in a letter to an unidentified 'Sir' on the subject of celebrating Christmas, Hall counters the profane suggestion that in his youth James had once decried the celebration of feast-days. 'I could . . . give you,' Hall concludes, 'other proofs of King James's zeal for these days: but what, should I spend time in proving there is a sun in heaven, and light in that sun? The name of that great king suffereth for his excess this way' (Wynter, IX, 137).

So well, in fact, did Joseph Hall get along with royalty and the Calvinists, that the king appointed this loyal, obedient and learned *servus ecclesiae* to be one of his four representatives at the Synod of Dort held at Dortrecht, Holland, from November 1618 to May 1619. There had been a long and passionate demonstration of the position King James would have his delegates take in the famous debate. I refer to the Vorstius affair of 1611–12.

It was as if, today, a foreign potentate were to demand that Oxford or Yale fire a particular professor. King James from across the sea insisted that the rector and professors at the University of Leiden purge their faculty of Konrad Vorstius (1569–1622), who had been appointed to succeed the late Arminius in 1609. Franz Gomarus (1563–1641), whose theology was much more to the king's liking, had resigned in protest. In 1612, James published *His Majesties Declaration Concerning his proceeding with the States General of the United Provinces of the Low Countries in the Cause of D. C. Vorstius*. While out hunting last August, the king says, he received two terrible books, *Tractatus Theologicus de Deo* (1610) and *Exegesis Apologetica* (1611). Within the hour he wrote to the States General through his ambassador at The

Hague, Sir Ralph Winwood, scoring the seditious and heretical notions emanating from Leyden. 'Our principall meaning,' the king wrote, 'was of Arminius who though lately dead yet had left many of his disciples behind him' (p. 4) – the worst being Vorstius. '*Latet anguis in herba*,' goes the tirade against the snake in the grass. Think of the danger, 'so long as you permit the Schisms of Arminius to have such vogue as now they have in the principall townes of Holland, and if you suffer Vorstius to be received Divinity Professor in the University of Leyden (the Seminary of your Church) who in scorne of the holy word of God, hath after his fancie, devised a new Sect, patched together of severall pieces of all sorts of ancient and moderne Heresies' (pp. 28–9). Sir Ralph Winwood laid his liege's protest before the assembly of the States General, ending with King James's threat to 'stop our youth from registering in your University'. The king got a long and polite answer. Vorstius had been hired, the States General said, after careful inquiry and a public debate, held at The Hague on 29 April 1611, in which Vorstius fully satisfied the six Calvinist theologians who were set to argue against him. But James kept on fuming, and was delighted when Joseph Hall, in a sermon at Paul's Cross on the king's tenth anniversary, 24 March 1613, compared James's case against Vorstius with the statesmenship of Constantine. The Synod of Dort was the occasion for reopening the battle, particularly as two loyal subjects, residents in Holland, had been sniping at Vorstius from closer range: Matthew Slade, rector of a public school in Amsterdam, and George Eglison, a Scottish physician at The Hague.[4]

To represent him at the Synod of Dort, King James chose, besides Dean Joseph Hall of Worcester, the newly appointed bishop, George Carleton of Llandaff; John Davenant, the Lady Margaret Professor of Divinity at Cambridge; and Dr Samuel Ward, Master of Sidney Sussex College, Cambridge. According to Thomas Fuller, the king called these men to Newmarket well in advance in order to instruct them: practice your Latin, agree among yourselves and speak for moderation. But it is clear that the purpose of sending an English delegation to Dort was to condemn Arminianism and other 'hellish doctrines' emanating from the University of Leyden. In keeping with his persistent bad luck when travelling, Hall with the rest of the party unaccountably missed the Dutch man-of-war especially sent for them; and he had to leave the Synod early on account of another serious intestinal infection.

This was an international synod, and the English delegation was as learned a group as any there present. Samuel Ward was perhaps the best English scholar, and Hall, not far behind in scholarship, the best orator – both trained at Emmanuel. Hall had often voiced his pride in the intellectual stature of the Anglican clergy: 'This happy island abounds ... with store of incomparable divines,' he wrote. 'So as the messenger of Pyrrhus, long since, called your Italy "A country of kings," and Egypt was wont to be called, "The country of physicians;" so may this blessed island of ours justly merit the title of, "The region of divines"' (VIII, 484). The English delegates were held in great respect and were entertained at the expense of the States General of Holland. One of the proudest moments of the synod, Hall later recalled, was the speech given by Bishop Carleton after Hall had left which convinced his listeners that the absence of episcopacy in Holland was the cause of her divisions. The President responded with greater gravity than mere politeness would have demanded that they were not as fortunate in Holland as 'we in England' (IX, 155).[5] Carleton had been arguing that the way to get the Remonstrants to soften their demands was to ask the Calvinists to soften theirs, particularly on the points of predestination and election. Hall, on the other hand, thought that the two sides could come to an agreement by simply allowing the 'Word of God' to speak for itself.

Hall's view emerges in a key-note sermon preached before the Synod as early as the fifth day, 29 November 1618, from Ecclesiastes 7:16 – 'Be not righteous over much, neither make thyself over wise.' Unlike a sermon by Andrewes or Donne, so often tripartite in structure, Hall's is, expectedly, in two divisions.[6] Part One, on righteousness, he addressed to the civil authorities, the States General; it concerns the morality of governing. Part Two, addressed to the professors of theology, deals with wisdom in seeking religious truth. What is needed is the proper kind of *justitia* for the one part of his auditory, and the proper kind of *sapientia* for the other. But Hall wittily combines the major terms as he builds his propositions into an argument (in vain, it turned out) for peace between the Calvinists and the Remonstrants.

The first part gives us King Solomon's ideal for justice. There is positive or absolute justice, which no man possesses (Ecclesiastes 7 : 20); there is imperfect or self-fulfilled justice, and in this the 'just' man dies (7 : 15); and there is an in-between justice – *ne sis justis nimis*, 'be not righteous over much' (7 : 16). Hall illustrates this golden mean with an apparent allusion to his own *Characters of Vertues and Vices*: the too-liberal man is a spendthrift, the too-bold man is headstrong, and the too-frugal man is a miser (p. 471). In reminding the law-givers that we live in morally parlous times, Hall divides *justitia* into thought and action. Action again is divided into public and private. Private action under the rule of justice can be either abstaining or enduring, and so on. 'You, Governors of the State, censors and judges,' Hall demands, 'should be in your judgments, like the wise King Solomon, neither too severe or too lenient.'

Which brings him to Part Two. Here Hall leaves his neat disjunctions so that, it would seem, he can speak more passionately from the heart to his fellow theologians on the second part of his text: *neque sis sapiens nimis* – 'make not thyself over wise.' The scholastics, in being over wise on the exact ordering and number of the angels, displayed too little knowledge. We, on the other hand, are over wise in too much knowledge, rushing headlong into the most secret councils of God. 'I know that I am now touching the sore place of this age, which, however, I will do with a gentle hand,' Hall says (p. 479). St Paul himself exclaimed, 'O the depth' (Romans 11 : 33), yet we 'presume to reason concerning the most abstruse doctrine of Predestination' (p. 481), and are thus responsible for the two things that are most injurious to the church: an excess of talent in study and an excess of licence in preaching. Were St Paul to return he would not understand 'the crabbed theology of the Jesuits and Dominicans,' nor perhaps our vain disputes. St Paul cared only to preach Christ and Him crucified.

So let us leave our 'over wise' theological distinctions and return to the Bible. 'For if brothers dispute concerning the title to their inheritance, to what have they recourse but the testament of their father' (p. 483)? Hall's remedy, then, is for each theologian present to make as honest a paraphrase of the ninth chapter of Romans, on Predestination, as he can. 'It cannot but happen, that, with this heavenly light for your guide, the truth will freely expose itself to the eyes of the pious and unprejudiced' (p. 485).[7] 'We are brothers, Christians, not Remonstrants, Contra-Remonstrants, Calvinists, or Arminians.'

> Our King, [Hall concludes proudly], our most serene King James, in whose name the whole church of God appears to me to exult, the wisest King that the sun ever saw, except the heaven-taught Solomon, has, in his golden Letter, recommended these illustrious States, and has commanded us, to strive with all our force, and exclusively to inculcate, that you should all adhere to the belief which has hitherto been received, and to the confession which you hold in common with the other Churches! [p.485]

In a double sense, then, Hall preached from Solomon, from the author of Ecclesiastes and from the English sovereign who appointed him a delegate to the Council of Dort. As in the first part he seemed too cowed before the officialdom of the States General, so in his second part he appeared naively unaware that word-splitting would continue among professors of theology. But his sermon, which could not have taken more than forty-five minutes to deliver, won instant and lasting approval, for the official minutes call it *doctissima atque accuratissima exhortatio Latina* – 'by the Reverend and most distinguished Dr Joseph Hall, Dean of Worcester . . . For which he received public thanks.' It was published in Latin (1619) and in French (1621) at Geneva.

Had Hall been able to stay until the end, he might have been able to make his message stick. But after being in Dort for only two months, he was forced by his old disposition to leave the meetings in order to rest at the home of the English ambassador at The Hague, Sir Dudley Carleton. Hall's condition did not improve, and the Embassy physicians advised that he return to England. Arrangements were made to send Dr Thomas Goad, chaplain to Archbishop Abbott, in Hall's place; and James added to the English delegation Dr Walter Balcanquel to represent the Scottish church. Meanwhile Sir Dudley's secretary, the 'ever memorable' Mr John Hales, was in constant attendance at the proceedings and in his *Golden Remains* has given us an account which expresses the dilemma the English representatives found themselves in.

They were careful at Dort not to assent to the discipline of the continental churches, but were ready with some reluctance to subscribe to the Calvinistic canons adopted by the heavily weighted majority. Franz Gomarus and his 'five doctrines',[8] which by 1618 had become far more rigid than John Calvin had ever intended, swept over the liberal views of the Arminian 'Remonstrants'. Politics, beyond the reach of the English delegates, played an important part. The Remonstrants had been for peace with Spain and at home for a limited central government, directly opposed to Maurice of Orange, who stood for war with Spain waged by practically absolute power. At Dort, Maurice had on his side no less than eighteen of his secular commissioners.[9] So there was no *via media*. The Remonstrants were defeated. Barneveldt, their most vocal political leader, was executed; 'Arminian' ministers and professors were banished from Holland; and Hugo Grotius, the father of international law and a great encourager of the rational element in Anglicanism, was imprisoned.

Joseph Hall's trip home had been harrowing, and at times (so he wrote later to Dr Ward) he thought he would never complete it (X, 503). The queen, he added, was dead; and the king, ill himself, had gone off to Royston to seek solace in his own way. Again writing from Waltham to Dr Ward, Hall says: 'I could not till within these two days present myself to the king, of whom I was received exceedingly graciously. All the last Sunday's dinner he spent in discourse with me about our synodal affairs. Some busy information hath moved him against the president as undiscreetly hot and rigid in the dismission of the Remonstrants. I have fully satisfied him' (X, 504–5). King James, quite in character, had wanted the Remonstrants defeated at Dort, but he wanted the defeat to be peaceful. Hall was seriously ill. Three months after his return from Holland, he reports on 25 April 1619 to Sir Dudley at The Hague that he has 'been twice dead in general rumor', and that rivals like vultures are even bidding for his Deanery (X, 506).

In view of the sweeping Calvinist 'victory', some thought that the English Divines had been made to sign an oath in advance to help put the Remonstrants down. The charge was made so strong by John Goodwin in his *Redemption Redeemed* (1651) that Thomas Fuller, while preparing his *Church History,* thought it best to inquire into its truth from the last surviving member of the English delegation at Dort, Bishop Joseph Hall, by then evicted from his Bishop's Palace at Norwich. Writing back to Fuller from Heigham on 30 August 1651, Hall vigorously denies the allegation: 'Sir, since I have lived to see so foul an aspersion cast upon the memory of those worthy and eminent divines, I bless God that I yet live to vindicate them, by this my knowing, clear, and assured attestation; which I am ready to second with the solmnest oath, if I shall be thereto required' (X, 525).

Though the English delegates at Dort knew better than most Englishmen (including perhaps the king) that Arminianism and 'Socinian gangrene' were not identical, nevertheless they had to side with the Calvinist majority because of their ordination vows to uphold the Thirty-nine Articles of the Church of England. Writing on this question to Bishop Davenant, Hall said: 'I will live and die in the suffrage of that synod of Dort; and I do confidently avow that those other opinions (of Arminius) cannot stand with the doctrine of the church of England.' To which his fellow delegate replied: 'I know that no man can embrace Arminianism in the doctrines of *predestination* and *grace,* but he must desert the Articles agreed upon by the Church of England.'[10]

After it was all over, the Synod of Dort sent Joseph Hall a beautiful medal of solid gold (the other delegates received silver replicas), almost three inches in diameter and an eighth of an inch thick. Hall wore this medal as a pectoral ornament to the end of his days, never suspecting that it might have been a cynical advertisement on the part of the States General that they loved moderation. Hall included in his will: 'My Golden Medall, which was given to me by the States General of the Netherlands, for my assistance at the Synod of Dort, I give and bequeathe to the male issue of any one of my Sonnes (if any such be) according to the order of their birth; or in default thereof to

Joseph Weld the son of my daughter [Ann], as a memorial of that worthy employment.'[11]

Today the medal is in the Fitzwilliam Museum at Cambridge, having been permanently loaned in 1938 by the Master and Fellows of Emmanuel College. It was engraved by the Dutch artist, Jan van Bylaer.[12] On one side is an unusually clear representation of the synod in full session: in the centre at the head sit the five professors from Amsterdam University; below them, the twenty-one lay elders. On the left are the five English delegates, but the seats next to them are vacant, Louis XIII having forbidden the invited Huguenot delegates to attend. Below, in front, are the representatives of the Palatinate, Hesse, Switzerland, Geneva, among others, and around them the Dutch and Walloon spectators. On the circumference of the medal are the words "Religione Asserta". The picture on the other side is as dramatic as the first picture is historical. A steep rock, looking like that described by John Donne at the end of Satire III, extends towards the sky, where is enblazoned amid sunbeams the Hebrew tetragrammaton. Four ill winds blowing upon the rock attempt to dislodge two pilgrims who are climbing towards the temple that crowns its top. On the circumference appear the words *Erunt ut mons Sion* – 'They shall be even as Mount Sion' – 'CXIX * CIƆ * IƆ [1619]'.

Joseph Hall's contribution to imaginative literature came to an early end, but this is not to say that he lived too long. He became all churchman – a sought-after preacher, a writer of meditations and an arch polemicist. In 1612, at their dissolution, he preached for Prince Henry's bereaved palace family of some five hundred persons. In 1613 he was selected by King James to preach the sermon on the tenth anniversary of the reign. Nominated by his church to give the Convocation sermon in St Paul's on 20 February 1623, he preached *Columba Noae*, later translated into English by his eldest son. He was chosen, 8 March 1623, to be substitute-preacher (Archibishop Abbott becoming suddenly ill) at the funeral in Westminster Abbey for the Earl of Exeter. He preached often before the court, at St James's, Theobalds, and elsewhere. The theme of these and most of the forty-two published sermons is peace.

At this point in the narrative, one may ask why my table of contents does not include a chapter entitled 'Hall as Preacher'. And why, if he preached three times a week for the twenty years he served at Waltham Holy Cross (as he says he did), only forty-two of his sermons survive? Hall had made his mark in the pulpit as early as his Hawsted years, and there is much evidence that he was in great demand. My guess is that in view of the fact that he had found his peculiar vein as a devotional writer in 'meditations', he 'mined' his own sermons to furnish his major writings. A mere glance at the columns of his publications in the *Short Title Catalogue* or in that of the British Museum convinces one that no man could have published so much and still have written out by hand well over 3,000 sermons preached before congregations. Preachers like Launcelot Andrewes, John Donne, Jeremy Taylor and many others gained their fame in sermon literature. Joseph Hall, on the other hand, found his homiletic niche, as we have seen, in the written Protestant meditation. Those sermons which he did save for publication, all of them persuasive and often eloquent, are mostly of a ceremonial character. We have already looked at some of them where he is less preacher than orator. There was in his nature, perhaps arising from his humble birth, an ambition, devout Christian though he was, for worldly acclaim.

To reward him for public service, in 1624 James offered him the bishopric of Gloucester, which Hall surprisingly 'refused with much humble deprecation'. Perhaps because this was the diocese where he had successfully entered into litigation on behalf of his kinsman Samuel Burton against Sir Walter Leveson, he felt he still had too many enemies there. Perhaps, since William Laud had been dean there, Hall had sense enough to stay away. Or perhaps he had begun to distrust James's alternating moods; and having been scolded and flattered by the king for the same deed surmised that there were more thorns on this particular rose than those he was aware of.

A recent instance of His Majesty's inexplicable action in this regard lingered in his mind. One of the aftermaths of the Synod of Dort was the 'Quinquarticular Controversy'. For a moderate Calvinistic Anglican like Hall, such extreme tenets as total depravity and supralapsarianism were difficult to reconcile with his catholic concepts of benevolence and free will. In the wake of the defeat at Dort of the Remonstrants, the Reverend Richard Montagu (1577–1641), then rector at Stamford Rivers, Essex, in 1624 attributed to the Church of England five points taken by English Calvinists to be identical with the five raised at Dort by the Arminians. There arose immediately from the Puritan press and pulpit what Hall called 'busy and bootless brabbles' (Wynter, IX, 517). The moderate spokesman for his church, Hall wrote *Via Media: The Way of Peace, in the five Busy Articles, Commonly Known by the Name of Arminius*. Boldly dedicating his manuscript to King James as the head of the Church, Joseph Hall said: 'May it please Your Majesty: There needs no prophetical spirit to discern, by a small cloud, that there is a storm coming towards our church: such a one as shall not only drench our plumes, but shake our peace. Already do we see the sky thicken, and hear the winds whistle hollow afar off, and feel all the presages of a tempest' (IX, 489). To his chagrin, King James forbad him to publish it.

The *via media* in the quarrel, Hall had argued, is the past writings of the learned Bishop John Overall of Exeter, one of the translators of the Bible for King James. Hall takes up 'the five busy articles': (1) predestination, (2) Christ's ransom by His death, (3) election as synergistically dependent upon both God and man, (4) freedom of the will and (5) perseverance of the saints as not being automatic. For each one of these he quotes Bishop Overall to show that Montagu has really not said anything different, that his sense is not dangerous and newly brought in from Arminius but an historical and quite reasonable part of Anglican thought. Only Montagu's style is 'tart'. In a discursive conclusion, Hall asserts that both sides believe in God, in Christ and in common sense: 'Both will grant that the apothecary's shop hath drugs enough for the cure of all diseases, which yet can profit none but those that are willing to make use of them' (IX, 510).

That Hall was proud of this work, and particularly of the method he used to argue it, is shown by the amount of space he gives to its description in his autobiography. The anonymous editor of the 1660 edition of *The Shaking of the Olive Tree*, which contains *Via Media* (pp. 351–88), says: 'And if he shall suffer in the Opinion of hotter heads, as too lukewarm and temperate, yea, as a close Abettor of Arminianisme, because he hears it speak, and doth not spit Fire and Brimstone upon it, we enter this protestation: He was no Remonstrant, but against the Monster Smectymnuus' (1660, p. 2v).

Referring to His Majesty's injunction, Hall confesses: 'I was a little scorched with this flame, ... yet this could not stay my hand from thrusting itself into an hotter fire' (I, xliv). There were renewed taunts from continental Jesuits during the ill-fated negotiations for 'the Spanish match', that the Church of England was as new as Luther's Reformation and thus of the same ilk as Calvinists, Arminians, Familists, Brownists and other spawn of that 'schism'. Apologists for the Church of England had consistently argued that Rome had broken away from the Church, not that England had broken away from Rome. Under Henry VIII, England, 'reformed and Biblical', had only declared herself against certain intolerable Roman innovations. Had not Joseph Hall just got through saying, again: 'We have departed from the church of Rome but in those things wherein they have departed from Christ: what good thing they have is ours still; that scripture which they have, that creed which they profess, is ours; neither will we part with it for their abuse' (IX, 487)? As he wrote 'To a Worthy Knight' who was 'ready to revolt from the religion established': 'It is a killing word with those Romish imposters, "Where was your church before Luther?" than which, there was never any plea more idle, more frivolous, when it falls under a wise and judicious discussion' (VIII, 764).

Just such a discussion, he believed, was his pamphlet called *The Old Religion*, which caused 'the hotter fire' he mentions in his autobiography. In arguing the antiquity of the Anglican church by asserting the newness of the Roman, Hall needs only two of the familiar grounds, applying first Scripture and then reason to twelve 'new' Roman Catholic doctrines.[13] To gather this many so-called innovations that cannot be found in the Bible and which defy reason means, from our present vantage point, that Hall is being carried away by partisanship. Transubstantiation, invocation of saints, indulgences and purgatory, for example, were then real issues, perhaps; but the Roman Catholic Church no more 'worshipped images' then than it does now, nor can the Anglican church show that it had always used a colloquial language in its worship or that Rome's use of Latin is 'new'.

Nevertheless Joseph Hall doggedly went through the dozen 'innovations' and sent his treatise, in how many transcripts we do not know, to persons who would profit by it. To his surprise, opposition came from a peculiar quarter and on an issue that fell far outside the argument he was making. He had asserted quite casually, since it stands to reason, that Rome is a 'visible church': 'The true principles of Christianity which it maintains, maintain life in that church . . . As it is a visible church then, we have not detracted to hold communion with it; though the contemptuous repulse of so many admonitions have deserved our alienation: As Babylon, we can have nothing to do with it' (VIII, 717). This raised the ire of those Puritans who believed that to admit Rome to be a church at all was playing into the hands of the 'Papistical' clergy in the Anglican church. Hall, therefore, had to follow *The Old Religion* with two more pieces of writing, an *Apologetical Advertisement to the Reader* and *The Reconciler, An Epistle Pacificatory of the Seeming Differences of Opinion Concerning the True being and Visibility of the Roman Church*. He protested that he had never said Rome was 'the true church' but only 'truly visible' in its outer characteristics; in another of his common-sense aphorisms, he declared that a liar may not be a 'true man' but 'truly he is a man'. For his position he got letters of commendation from Bishop Thomas Morton of Lichfield and Coventry, Bishop John Davenant of Salisbury, Dr Prideau of Oxford, and Dr Primrose of the French Church in London. These letters, with the treatises that begat them, he then published together in 1627, shortly after he was made a bishop himself, and dedicated the volume, 'To my new and dearly affected charge, the Diocese of Exeter.' Thus, he tells us in his autobiography, 'I did by a seasonable moderation provide for the peace of the church, in silencing both my defendants and challengers in this unkind and ill-raised quarrel.'

But there was to be little peace for the church. And years later even John Milton, in assailing Bishop Hall, joined this non-issue of 'Rome-is-a-visible-church' to an accusation of venality: 'Doubtlesse, if need be, the Pope that owes you for mollifying the matter so well with him, and making him a true Church, will furnish you with all the fat oxen of *Italy*.'[14]

9. The Bishop of Exeter, John Milton, and the 'Modest Confutant'

James I died on 27 March 1625. As late as the *Humble Remonstrance to Parliament* (1640), which played its part in the quarrel between Hall and Milton, Joseph Hall said that King James was 'the learnedest king that ever sat upon this throne; or, as I verily think, since Solomon's time, upon any other' (Wynter, IX, 286). He was succeeded by his son Charles, whom Hall had known intimately as prince. From his new sovereign Hall accepted in November 1627 the bishopric of Exeter upon the death of Valentine Carey, incumbent.

How proud he must have been of his first diocesan responsibility! 'The county and city of Exeter,' as it is officially named, was the fifth most populous in England. Embracing the counties of Devon and Cornwall, it contained four archdeaconries: one of Cornwall itself, and the other three in Devon – Exeter, Barnstaple and Totnes; plus 'peculiarities of the Bishop'. Within were dozens of parishes, and we know the dates of the beginning of each register: Tavistock, 1614; Ottery St Mary, 1601; and so forth; but all the probate records of the diocese were destroyed by enemy action in 1942.[1] One parish now in Hall's charge was Tiverton, where, except for a 'speciality of Providence' a quarter of a century before, he might still be the schoolmaster. Not far off, in the parish of Dean Prior beyond Buckhurst Abbey, Robert Herrick by 1629 was celebrating his Lord, poetic mistresses and hock-carts, and wishing he were in London.

The city of Exeter was surrounded by a wall, and protected on the south by the River Exe and on the north by Rougemont Castle. 'When last I was at Exeter,' the king says in Shakespeare's *Richard III*, 'The mayor in courtesy show'd me the castle,/And call'd it Rougemont' (IV, ii, 106–8). A five-mile canal, cut when Shakespeare was an infant, brought great ships from the sea to the foot of Quay Lane at the south-west corner of town. The tavern named The Ship still stands; on it a plaque reads: 'Next to mine own shippe I do most love that old shippe in Exon a tavern in St Martins Lane – Sir Francis Drake, 1587.'

And the guildhall, one of the most beautiful and oldest in England, is still in use for state occasions. Within the walled town were no less than seventeen parish churches, with names like St Mary Arches, St Mary Major, All Hallows on the Walls, and St Mary Steps.

The cathedral itself is one of the world's glories. By virtue of its twin towers north and south and no tower where nave meets transept, it has the longest unbroken vaulted ceiling in England. The bishop's throne, made of Devon oak with no nails, stands sixty feet high, topped with the statue of St Peter. It is the custom that the bishop be consecrated not in this famous throne but in a bishop's chair placed behind the high altar. The cathedral's shield appears throughout, the two crossed keys of St Peter centred by an upright sword; and one of the parish churches adjacent to the close was appropriately named St Petrock.

In the north transept of the cathedral, the great clock marks the minutes, days, months, years and the phases of the moon which regulate the ecclesiastical calendar for Easter and other feast days. Its motto, familiar to Joseph Hall from Martial, is *Pereunt et imputantur* – 'The days pass and are reckoned to our account'. Now that Hall was a member of the House of Lords, in a letter addressed to the Commons a year after he became bishop, he seemed to recall the clock's motto: 'Gentlemen, for God's sake be wise in your well meant zeal. Why do you argue away precious time which can never be recovered?'[2] This was the year, 1628, in which the 'Third Parliament Petition of Right' became law, Buckingham was assassinated, the second expedition to Rochelle failed, and William Laud, rising rapidly, became Bishop of London.

Although Milton's later insistence that every Anglican bishop was venal, fat and rolling in wealth is unfounded, nevertheless history is hardly silent on how opportunities were open to an Anglican bishop in those days to make money, and Joseph Hall fared rather well in Exeter. He was particularly nagged on this score by one witty vicar with the unlikely name of Nansogge, who complained that out of the £88 a year the bishop was receiving for his parish, he himself was being paid only £12.[3] Twenty-five years before this, Hall himself had been telling Sir Robert Drury that a wage of £10 per year was insufficient. From one Philip Holditch, Hall purchased lands and tenements to the south of Totnes; and though he lived in the Bishop's Palace, he acquired 'house and grounds, with the appurtenances lying and being within the city of Exeter neare to the South gate of the said city'.[4] He persuaded the city fathers to cede land to the cathedral in order to expand its close. He complained of the stench emanating from the open ditch in St Martin's Lane and, we assume, got something done about it.[5] By 1631, Hall was famous enough to apply for and receive a coat of arms. The original grant, now in the Folger Library, is written and sketched by 'Clarenceux King of Arms in the name of Charles by the Grace of God King of England, Scotland, France, and Ireland. A shield to the Right Rev. Joseph Hall and to the descendants of his body.' On a sable shield are three talbots erased argent (three silver hunting hounds cut off at the shoulder), langued gules (crimson tongues extended). Above the shield are a helmet, a coronet and a lion rampant. Are the hounds in memory of James I?

Three of Hall's sons – Robert, George and Samuel – became 'learned, judicious, and painful divines'.[6] The oldest, Robert, was elected treasurer of Exeter Cathedral and, dying in 1667, lies buried in the north transept, his tomb adorned with the crest inherited from his father. There is a tradition that Robert dismantled the sixty-foot-high bishop's throne in order to preserve it from wanton destruction by Commonwealth soldiers. Sir Herbert Read, however, who actually dismantled the throne in 1941 when German bombs were falling, saw that it had never been taken apart before.[7] Apparently Cromwell's men did not need it for firewood. They did build a high brick wall across the centre of the nave where the organ and screen now stand, so that, simultaneously, Presbyterians could worship in one end and Independents in the other.

We have seen how energetically Joseph Hall had volunteered his talents in argument to bring peace, but the tides against him were strong. He took up his duties as Bishop of Exeter, he continues in his autobiography,

> ... not without much prejudice and suspicion on some hands; for some that sat at the stern of the church had me in great jealousy for too much favor of Puritanism. I soon had intelligence who were set over me for espials. My ways were curiously observed and scanned. However I took the resolution to follow those courses which might most conduce to the peace and happiness of my new and weighty charge. [Wynter, I, xlvi]

There were public and whispered complaints (probably spread by Nansogge) of his 'indulgence to persons disaffected' and of his custom of going about the churches of his diocese 'lecturing'. Three times, he confesses, he was on his knees before Charles I; and finally told Laud, by 1633 Archbishop of Canterbury, that if his 'misinformers' did not stop their slanderous tongues he would resign: 'I knew I went right ways, and would not endure to live under undeserved suspicion' (Wynter, I, xlvi). Despite his distrust of Laud and righteous condemnation of ecclesiastical spying, later he twice submitted his *Episcopacie by Divine Right* (1640) to his archbishop, who had commanded it in the first place, for revision. Hall subscribed to 'order and degree', submitting to it from above in order to demand it from below.

Rebuffed from one side for low churchmanship, he was accused from the other of being a 'Romanist', particularly by the crop-eared Henry Burton, whom Hall must have known years before in Prince Henry's household when Burton had been dismissed as an indiscreet Clerk of the Closet. In 1627, Burton was summoned by the Privy Council for the frontispiece of his *Baiting of the Pope's Bull* showing King Charles of England assailing the triple crown. From his pulpit in St Matthew's on Friday Street, London, he volubly scored in sermons and pamphlets the behaviour and views of the English prelates, including the Bishop of Exeter's calling Rome a 'visible church'. To Hall's embarrassment his own chaplain, Hugh Cholmley, boyhood friend from Ashby Grammar School and lodge-mate at Emmanuel, chose to defend his bishop in *The State of the Now-Roman Church, Discussed by way of vindication of the Right Reverend Father in God, the Lord Bishop of Exeter, from the weake cavills of Henry Burton. By H. C. London: Philemon Stephens. 1629.* In dedicating the 115-page pamphlet to Hall, Cholmley wrote, 'There are risen up, I know not what hot-spurres, and bold braggadochios in the Campe, who mutinouslie doe turne their weapons from Babel against you' (A 4 r). Burton had stated flatly that the Roman Catholics deny the saving Grace of Christ (p. 14), and Cholmley says, 'I deny your denial.' Burton, again, like many a 'prophesying' Puritan, makes the *blood in the sea* of Revelation 8:8 issue from the dead body of the Roman Church, and the *sea* itself, in which he descries Bishop Hall frantically swimming, becomes the Council of Trent. Cholmley responds, 'Theologia symbolica non est argumentiva.' But the new Bishop of Exeter could see that arguments and counter-argument were only troubling the waters. Signing a letter to Cholmley 'Your loving friend and ancient colleague', Hall wrote: 'I have perused your learned and full reply to Master Burton's answer; where you have, in a judicious eye, abundantly righted yourself, and cleared a just cause . . . But let me tell you, were it a book written by an angel from heaven on this subject, I should doubt whether to wish it public' (Wynter, VIII, 756).

Thus Bishop Hall, under King James a brilliant man of letters as well as a divine, was gradually forced to become all contender in a cause fated by history to lose. I refer to the tedious 'prelatical controversy' on the biblical, historical and functional difference between 'bishops' and 'presbyters'. As England was drawing up sides to engage in a tragic civil war, the Bishop of Exeter waged a battle of the pens first with the 'Smectymnuans' and then, somewhat lopsidedly, with John Milton. In the seventeenth-century manner of charge and counter-charge, the quarrel is contained in eleven publications between 1640 and 1642:[8]

1. Hall published *Episcopacie by Divine Right* (April 1640) at the behest and with the rivising hand of Archbishop Laud.
2. Hall continued his plea in *An Humble Remonstrance* (January 1641), supported by his friend Archbishop James Usher of Armagh, one of the most learned Anglican scholars.
3. Milton refuted the Anglican position in two pamphlets: *Of Reformation* [May (?) 1641], directed towards a general audience, and
4. *Of Prelatical Episcopacy* [May (?) 1641], directed against the 'antiquitarianism' particularly of Archbishop Usher.
5. Five Puritan divines, led by Milton's former teacher and combining their initials to make the eye-catching name 'Smectymnuus,' published an *Answer* to Hall's *Humble Remonstrance* [March (?) 1641].
6. Hall countered with a *Defence* of his *Humble Remonstrance* [April (?) 1641].
7. The Smectymnuans came back with *A Vindication* of their *Answer* [June (?) 1641].
8. Hall replied in *A Short Answer to the Tedious Vindication* [September (?) 1641].
9. Milton came to the aid of his five Puritan friends in *Animadversions upon the Remonstrant's Defence against Smectymnuus* [July (?) 1641]. Disgusted with the tactics of his many-headed opponent, Hall withdrew; but
10. An anonymous author in *A Modest Confutation* (February 1642) defended Hall against the *ad hominem* attack of *Animadversions*.
11. Milton, assuming this author to be Hall and/or one of his sons, published his *Apology for Smectymnuus* (May 1642) which combines for his opponent personal abuse and for posterity valuable self-revelation.[9]

Analyses of the argument have been made by such Miltonists (among others) as Barker, Chew, Emerson, Fixler, French, Hanford, Jochums, Masson, Parker and Taft.[10] A valiant defence of Milton's part has more recently been made in *Achievements of the Left Hand: Essays on the Prose of John Milton*.[11] Most important for Hall and Milton are the last three pamphlets: item 9, Milton's attack on Hall's person; item 10, the anonymous defence of Hall; and item 11, Milton's self-righteous rejoinder.

It has never been proved that the anonymous 'Confutation' (item 10) was written by Bishop Hall. Since much of the rhetoric towards the end of this story depends upon the drama of two unknown pamphleteers leaping at each other in the dark, each speaking for more important and publicly known persons, I shall call the author we now know as John Milton the 'Animadverter' and the 'Apologist', and the unidentified author who came between these two *personae* the 'Confutant'.[12]

Whoever he was, the Confutant did not know that he was arguing against John Milton. 'I have no further notice of [the Animadverter].' he writes, 'than he hath been pleased ... to give of himself; and therefore, as our industrious Criticks for want of clearer evidence concerning the life and manners of revived Authours, must fetch his character from scattered passages in his own writings' (A 3 r). Again, the Confutant cries. 'Beleeve me, whoever you are ...' (p. 4). That the Apologist took some of the arrows shot thus at random into his own breast has convinced a few critics that the pamphlet is scurrilous, underhanded, venomous and nasty enough to provoke the Apologist to answer in kind (Taft, I, 864).

The worst things the Confutant says about the defamer of his friend Bishop Hall come in the short 'To the Reader': '... there is thrust forth upon the Stage ... a scurrilous Mime, a personated, and (as himself thinks) a grim, lowring, bitter fool.' Having been 'vomited out' from the university,[13] this person is now living in a 'suburbe sinke about London, which, since his comming up, hath groaned under two ills, Him, and the Plague'. If you want to find him after dinner, the Confutant adds, search among the play-houses and bordelli. This is certainly close to libel, but the key to it is the play-house image, which is not the Confutant's but comes from the *Animadversions*. The Animadverter had announced in his Preface that he is purposely adopting a role; and the Confutant (p. 34) picks up further reference to that theatrical role in the Animadverter's use of 'Modena masks' and 'vizards', among other examples (I, 711). In accusing the Animadverter of writing 'a scurrilous and slanderous' attack on Bishop Hall, the Confutant tries in what follows not to open himself up to the same charge.

Of the twelve sections of his *Confutation*, the anonymous author requires the first nine to argue that the Animadverter's language ('scurrility') is unbecoming to religious controversy and that the incessant name-calling amounts to 'libel'. On the very first page the Confuter quotes a long list of such vituperations as 'spiritual fornication', 'cogging of dice into Heaven', 'gleeking and Bacchanalia', and concludes: 'Such language you should hear from the mouths of canting beggars, at an heathen altar; much lesse was it looked for in a treatise of controversial Theologie, as yours might have been thought, had you not thus prevented it' (p. 2). He confesses that 'there may be hid in my nature as much venemous Atheisme and profanation as hath broken out at his lips', but he is in fair control of it.

Even when he quotes his adversary's language, he omits its saltier aspects. For example, here for comparison are three of the Animadverter's original phrases with the Confutant's quotations of them (A 3 v): (a) Animadverter – '. . . a gallopping Nun, proffering her selfe, but wee heare of none that bids money for her' (I, 680); Confutant – '. . . like an English galloping Nun': (b) Animadverter – '. . . vain-glorious . . . like the desire of *Tamar*, who to raise seed to her Husband sate in the common road drest like a Courtesan, and he that came to her committed incest with her' (I, 688); Confutant – 'A Pharisaicall and vain-glorious project': (c) Animadverter – '. . . than a wife affecting whorish attire kindles a disturbance in the eye of her discerning husband' (I, 687); Confutant – '. . . than a wife affecting whorish attire.' The whore-of-Babylon conceit for Rome was a commonplace; but although he is as anti-Roman as any Anglican or Presbyterian, the Confutant sedulously expurgates the Animadverter's more sexual treatments of the metaphor. 'Christian,' he asks in possible mock-innocence, 'dost thou like these passages, or doth thy heart rise against such unseemly beastlinesse?' Is this what the Animadverter means by 'free-writing'? – that is, uncensored publication? 'I am free, as you,' cries the Confutant, 'or any true subiect may or need be: I have a fortune therefore good, because I am content with it: and therefore content with it, because it neither goes before nor comes behind my merit' (p. 6).

As the Confutant for the most part avoids scurrilous language, so in defending Hall against libel he steers fairly clear of the thing he condemns. Like the shocking vocabulary he quotes, most of what seems to be personal opprobrium consists of phrases taken from the *Animadversions* and turned back upon their author. For example, the Apologist is appalled (I, 883–93) at the Confutant's implying that he, the Apologist, had spent his youth in 'loytering, bezzelling, and harlotting' (*Modest Confutation*, p. 3 r); but it was the Animadverter who had first said that all prelates 'spend their youth in loitering, bezzling, and harlotting' (I, 677). Again, the Confutant's charge, 'You can be as bold with a Prelate, as familiar with your Laundressse' (p. 9), struck the Apologist as such calumny as to call for protestations of his own chastity; whereas the Confutant is merely alluding to the Animadverter's assertion that a bishop's 'surplesse' and the Priest of Isis' 'lawne sleeves' 'may all for holinesse lie together in the suds' (I, 729). To be sure, the Confuter paraphrases this as washing 'a Christian minister's surplice and an Egyptian Priests frock in the same suds'; but where did Hall's attacker get this bit of lavational knowledge? From his laundress? Nobody had accused the Animadverter of fornicating with his washer-woman.

Throughout, the Confutant makes it clear that what some later critics have taken to be personal vilification comes originally from the author of the *Animadversions*. He accuses the Animadverter of atheism and of sedition against king and Parliament on the grounds of the language used; you handle such matters 'in such a wretched, loathsome manner' as to jeer at 'religion, and God, and all' (p. 6). Quotations of that language carry his point. For example, 'If [Bishop Hall] write controversies, then he is a Swash-buckler against the Pope; ... If he preaches, then he sermonizes and dawbes with untempered mortar;[14] If he contemplates or meditates, then he playes with Lambeth kittens; If at Court, he is crowding for preferment, or accusing the people to the King; If at home, he is a belly-God, &c. O the love, and charity, and reverence of these times, to so holy, so deserving a Bishop' (p. 20). The *Modest Confutation* brims over with language like this, but it is the Animadverter's language. 'Neither in this point,' the Confutant says in another context, 'would I ever have condemned ye, had I not heard it from your owne mouths' (p. 21). Again, 'Forsooth you would give the world to know these two things: First, that you are no Bishop; Secondly, that you can pray ex tempore. Surely, a man of strong parts, and a mortified ambition' (p. 22). This is sarcasm, not libel.

The Confutant is justly shocked by the lack of Christian charity that lies behind the Animadverter's attack on Hall's person, especially (p. 5) in view of the Animadverter's self-expressed determination to write 'without all private and personal spleene' (I, 663); the Confutant concludes, nevertheless, that it 'is the greatest matter in your book'.

> We must go higher yet [he adds], and if we *will*, may believe the Remonstrant [i.e. Bishop Hall] to be *a notorious enemy to truth*, pag. 2. *a false Prophet*, pag. 3. *a belly-god, proud and covetous*, pag. 5. *squeezed to a wretched, cold, and hollow-hearted confession of some Praelaticall ryots*, pag. 15. *whose understanding nothing will cure but Kitchen-physick*, pag. 17. *a Laodicean*, pag. 24. *a dissembling Joab*, pag. 28[15] ... Good God! thou that hast promised to direct the steps of the humble, and to be with those that are of a meek heart, instruct me how to chuse some other path to walk towards my Eternity; for this my soul hates. [p. 17]

I think I have exhausted the Confutant's so'called venomous and scurrilous attack.[16] As for the Animadverter, most scholars agree that he over-stepped the bounds of propriety and fair play. Professor Kirk's statement speaks for many: 'We can scarcely condone the language he [Milton] initiated against a good man [Bishop Hall]' (I, 655).

Having spent three quarters of the *Confutation* on his adversary's scurrilous and libellous language, the anonymous author comes to the argument – a proportion he takes to be approximately that of tantrum to reason in the *Animadversions*. 'The scraps and offall that remain of your Libell, concern Liturgie and Episcopacie: both of which you have handled, as you esteem of them, unworthily and basely,' he says (p. 21). By 'scraps' he means the method of quoting disconnected passages from Hall out of context and answering them; and by 'offal' he means the disgust, obvious to every reader, that Hall's detractor evinces at the mere mention of the Book of Common Prayer and Anglican ecclesiastical polity. The Confutant takes the usual Anglican stance that under Henry VIII England returned to the 'Apostolic Church' after ridding herself of Roman encrustations. As for history and nationalism, part of the closing theme of *Animadversions*, the Confutant asserts that the Church of England can take more pride than those who cling to recent importations from Luther and Calvin. The Confutant parries 'the rude fist of your logic' (p. 34): for example, one bishop is bestial or tyrannical, therefore all are so (p. 35). The noble and patriotic dithyramb in *Animadversions* on the coming of the Reformation to England, Scotland, and Wales (I, 704ff.), he impudently dismisses as 'a long, tedious, theatricall, big-mouthed, astounding Prayer, put up in the name of the three Kingdomes' (p. 22) – spoken by a Book of Common Prayer man, but feelings ran high. The Confutant becomes soberly prophetic: 'You say that set forms of Prayers are quenching to the Spirit; whether it be so or no, I am sure your Extemporall will set such a fire on your Spirits, that they will need quenching, or the whole Kingdome will burn with them. Weigh these circumstances, and you will see that there is an expediency of set forms in a nationall Church' (p.30).

On the whole, the confutant's defence of liturgy and episcopacy is practical, moderate and eloquent – reflecting the temper of Hooker, whom (unlike Hall) he often appeals to. He defends his church as he defends his friend. Concerning the Court of High Commission at Lambeth, which, though founded in 1583 under Elizabeth, had by exceeding its mandate become anathema to the Puritans, the Animadverter had said: 'They had neither bin hal'd into your Gehenna at *Lambeth*, nor strappado'd with an oath *Ex Officio* by your bow men of the Arches' (I, 674–5). The Confutant responds: 'If that Court hath been illegall, either in the constitution of it, or in its proceedings, it is more than I know; but if so, the Remonstrant [Hall] is as guiltlesse of such illegalities, as I am ignorant' (p. 8). In his defence of Joseph Hall against the onslaught of the Animadverter's rhetoric, the Confutant includes some rare and valuable character-sketches of the bishop at the age of sixty-seven, a bit weary and harassed, but noble and still vigorous. He defends his friend in terms of Hall's widespread reputation for piety, learning and religious toleration, against the scandal, inept argumentation and intolerance of the Animadverter. When he comes upon a 'good' thought in the *Animadversions*, he compliments the unknown author for it and for the style in which it is expressed (p. 37).

The Animadverter's feelings when he read this *Modest Confutation* emerge from his response in the *Apology*. The Confutant's satire arising from a naturally biased reading of the *Animadversions* was so accurate as to touch the Animadverter's nerves. The *Modest Confutation* ripped Milton's cover, flushed Milton out, caused him to assume almost ridiculous postures of self-defence that would never have been necessary had he trusted his own anonymity. Did his five older friends, who had started the quarrel with wiser arguments and more Christian bearing, think the untried Milton had actually been caught in the Confutant's image, and did they then put pressure on Milton to speak out not for them but for his own *Animadversions*? And did Milton accept the challenge, now that he felt he was known, to protect his more solid work, *The Reason of Church-Government*, which he had signed with his name? We shall never know. But one cannot read the *Apology* without noting that there is more egotistical sublimity than the argument requires. Also, that neither the *Animadversions* nor the *Apology* quite comes off may be due to Milton's idealism-cum-uncertainty regarding the basic principles of the party he spoke for concerning religion and its social contexts, compared with the mastery he evinced two years later on the subject of censorship. Even in revealing their own personalities amid the flourishes of rhetoric, however, these two controversialists show that they are also speaking to high public issues with probity and grave responsibility.

Milton did not possess any more notice of the author of *A Modest Confutation* (as the Confutant said of the Animadverter) 'than he hath been pleased . . . to give of himself'. Since Milton was confused about his age, let us begin there. As evidence of authorship, Milton cites Bishop Hall's three anti-Smectymnuan pamphlets (*Apology*, I, 876). Elsewhere, however, he wonders whether the author of the *Remonstrance* (Bishop Hall) and of the *Modest Confutation* 'be not both one person, or as I am told, Father and Son' (I, 897). Throughout the *Apology* he seems to waver between the ageing bishop and a young collegiate whom he addresses as 'thou lozell Bachelour of Art' (I, 920).

The Confutant could not be Bishop Hall. He was in the Tower from

30 December 1641 to 5 May 1642, and had other things on his mind. These included Parliament, finances (he faced a £5,000 bail on release), winding up his affairs in Exeter, and readying himself for his new duties in Norwich. Also, he spent a good part of the five months in prison writing his autobiography. I doubt, moreover, whether Bishop Hall could be responsible for the sarcastic tone the Confutant at times takes against his opponent. Only once in a long career as polemicist had Hall used *ad hominem* argument, this to a 'detested Jesuit', Edward Coffin.[17] In the present Smectymnuan controversy he had specifically deplored it. 'I talk of "false and frivolous exceptions," ' Hall wrote, 'they [the five Smectymnuans] say, I call them false and frivolous men. I talk of "vain cavils"; they charge me to say they are vain cavillers.'[18] Hall withdrew from the contest conducted on this level. Finally, the *Modest Confutation* is so filled with praise of Hall that Hall himself, an unusually modest man despite his achievements, could not have written it; nor would he ever have authorized it.

Milton assumed there was a young collaborator from three passages in *A Modest Confutation*. When he justified his own 'grim laughter' as part of his mask in the *Animadversions* by saying that 'grave Authoures' recommend it as a pedagogical device (I, 663–4), the Confutant responds: 'I care not to know what your reading hath been; mine own is confest small' (p. 2). At this point he quotes one 'grave author', Sir Francis Bacon, against turning religious controversy into comedy or satire. A single author ('small reading') is pitted against Milton's failure to mention any. Again, the Confutant confesses that he is not very well read in the history of church councils: '. . . I conjectured your ignorance in that kind of learning to be . . . as much and great as mine' (p. 34). This could be a slur on the Puritan's usual rejection of patristics, an adept side-stepping in order to get into current affairs, and a 'modest' disclaimer of his own knowledge. Finally, to Milton's suggestion (I, 718) that all financial support by church and nobility of students at Oxford and Cambridge be stopped, the Confutant asnwers: 'It is one of those young Scholars that asks your Eldership . . .' (p. 36). This could mean that the Confutant is grateful for having once been such a scholar. 'Your Eldership' sounds like a humorous jibe at the comparative age of his unknown Smectymnuan opponent, say Thomas Young – with a pun on his name if he knew it.[19] These are the Confutant's only possible references to his own age.

If the author or collaborator was a young man, as Milton temporarily suspected, could he have been one of Hall's sons? Professor Taft summarizes the possibilities in a brief note: 'Masson (II, 393–8) says the Confutant was Robert Hall, two years ahead of Milton at Cambridge. Parker (pp. 266–9) questions Masson's identification.

Jochums, p. 3, argues for another son, Edward Hall' (I, 863, n. 4). Actually there is no evidence for either one, nor even an argument.[20] As for the three sons who became, as the bishop said of them in his will, 'learned, judicious, and painful divines', rarely have sons, particularly Robert, so followed the wishes of their father in choice of profession, scholarly inclination and general behaviour. It is most unlikely that any son of Bishop Hall would be so 'injudicious' as to write and publish *A Modest Confutation*.

As a matter of fact, the Confutant shows himself to be no 'college matriculant' at all, but mature in the range of his reading. He alludes to and quotes Persius, Martial, Juvenal, Aristotle's *Ethics* as well as the *Politics*, Macrobius, Pliny, Horace's *Ars Poetica*, Suetonius, Lactantius, Plautus. That he is literary minded and *au courant* with the times he lived in is shown by the large number of moderns he quotes from, ranging from Chaucer (incidentally he handles philology well) to his own contemporaries. Several times he quotes Hooker, Bacon and Sandys. He had read Donne's *Pseudo-Martyr*, Sidney's *Defence of Poesy*, Ben Jonson's *Catiline*, du Moulin, Meric Casaubon, Sir David Lindsey, Hugo Grotius, Junius (du Jon), Machiavelli and a host of others.

He writes a crisp, witty style, sprinkled with proverbial lore and some very beautiful images. He talks of 'bowmen quick in the delivery of their arrows [but] wide of the mark' (p. 8). To him, organs, anthems, copes and all the accoutrements of Anglican worship are only aids to devotion, not any part of the Christian creed: 'That soul that can soar aloft upon the strength of his own wings, or hath its flagging Pinions completely ymped with feathers from the *Dove*, the Spirit of God, shall little need such advantages as are these things ...; onely take you heed you do not, *Icarus*-like, over-dare, and give all the Christian world else leave to acknowledge and remedy as they may, their almost irremediable weaknesses' (p. 32). He seems to have learned something about English prose from Joseph Hall, whose *Occasional Meditations* (twice alluded to) in praise of God for his creatures possibly inspired a passage like this: 'He can raise Manna into our mouths, as well as dew upon the earth. Shall we be angry, because we have our Corn at the second hand? He could have sent us into the world with our cloathes on; is it not as well that he set the worm to the wheel to spin it for us?' (p. 39, misnumbered 38).

A few further hints of the life and character of the Confutant emerge from scattered passages in his brief. We can assume that he is a Royalist and an Anglican very probably in orders. He tells us that he has been abroad: 'I have seen beyond sea what the Jesuites of our own nation have carped at Master *Fox* for his History' (p. 7). He is intimate with Bishop Hall and with his writings. Above all, like the bishop whom he defends, he is large-minded and cannot make the Christian gate any narrower than Christ himself made it for those who do not in all points believe and worship as he does (p. 18). Such is the anonymous author who was responsible for Milton's combining in the *Apology* bitter, petty, sarcastic wrangling with noble passages of self-revelation. Who was he?

To repeat from an earlier chapter: where external proof of authorship is lacking, the literary scholar must argue by probability. He makes a hypothesis to stand or fall not by a chain of reasoning (which breaks at its weakest link), but rather by explaining more historical facts in the circumstances and more literary traits in the document than any other. The hypothesis is strengthened as it resolves other problems that have been hanging upon the solution of this particular one.

I shall argue, then, that the 'Modest Confutant' who got under Milton's skin in 1642 was the Reverend Robert Dunkin of Cornwall – a man whose connection with Milton was first pointed out, inaccurately, by J. Milton French, and tied more closely to my thesis, though with little supporting argument, by William Riley Parker.

In John Walker's *Sufferings of the Clergy* (London, 1714), appears under Bishop Hall's own diocese, consisting of Devon and Cornwall, this entry: 'DUNKIN, ROBERT, A. M. *St Stephens* in Branwell. He was one of the most learned of all *Cornish* clergy, lived to be Restored, and Preached the first *Assize-Sermon* at *Launceton* after his Majesty's Return. He published some things against Milton' (Part II, p. 229).

How trustworthy is Walker's information? John Walker (1674–1747) was himself born in Exeter, his father becoming mayor of the city; he was rector of Upton Pyne church in Devonshire, and lies buried in Exeter Cathedral. According to the *Dictionary of National Biography*: 'Walker collected particulars by help of query sheets, circulated in various dioceses; those for Exeter (very minute) and Canterbury are printed by [Edmund] Calamy (Church and Dissenters Compar'd, 1719, pp. 4, 10).' It is apparent that Walker made more compendious and more astute inquiries in his own diocese (which had been that of Bishop Hall, born exactly one hundred years before Walker) than for any other diocese.

Masson does not mention Robert Dunkin.

A. G. Matthews, in *Walker Revised* (Oxford, 1948), adds certain information, including Dunkin's university, Oxford, and a second parish, 'vicar of St Michael Caerhays, 1667' (a mistake for 1637). Matthews had evidently checked Foster's Oxford *Alumni*, but chose to omit the name of Dunkin's college. Foster's complete entry [*Alumni Oxonienses* (1891), I, 433] is as follows: 'Dunkin, Robert, of Cornwall, pleb. Wadham Coll., matric. 19 May, 1615, aged 16; B.A. 4 Feb., 1618–19, M.A. 25 June, 1621, Vicar of Caerhayes, Cornwall, 1637. See Foster's Index Ecclesiasticus.' The latter book reveals nothing, but Foster's following entry, another 'Robert Dunkin' who became a judge, shows that later in the century there were Dunkins living in Liscard, Cornwall.

J. Milton French, in *Life Records of Milton* (1949–53), discusses Robert Dunkin in relation to Phillips's reference to 'some little scribing quack in London', dating the reference to events of 1660 to 1674 (IV, 293–4; V, 56, 455). As Parker points out, however, in the two-volume *Biography* (1968, II, 1145), Phillips is plainly talking of events in 1673, too late for Dunkin, who was born in 1599. If Dunkin had anything to do with Milton (Walker), Parker is inclined to set his attack earlier, in the 1640s. Parker, therefore, comes closer to my hypothesis than anyone else: 'Dunkin may have been the anonymous author of the 1642 *Modest Confutation* or the 1644 *Answer to ... The Doctrine and Discipline of Divorce*' (1968, II, 1081).

I believe Robert Dunkin was the author of *A Modest Confutation* for the following reasons:

1. As for the age of the Confutant, I have shown that the imputations of youth are not well grounded. The Confutant was young enough to look upon Bishop Hall with filial reverence and yet old enough to enter a controversy of considerable significance. If Dunkin matriculated at Wadham College, Oxford, in 1615 at the age of sixteen (Foster), he was forty-three years old in 1642. Milton was thirty-three. By 1654 Milton himself had given up on 'Father and son' and so dismissed the 'lozell bachelour of Arte'.[21]
2. The *Modest Confutation* is not as 'scurrilous' and 'libellous' as it has been made out to be. The genuine shock at Milton's language befits a clergyman. He is obviously a Church of England clergyman.
3. His is a mature piece of writing, fulfilling Walker's estimate of Dunkin as 'one of the most learned of all Cornish clergy'.
4. The Confutant knows, admires and loves Bishop Hall. Dunkin had been serving probably for fifteen years in Bishop Hall's own diocese.
5. The absence of Calvinistic and Ramistic principles, on the one hand, and the presence, on the other, of strong royalist sympathies, including a ringing plea for Charles I may point towards the author's having been trained at Oxford rather than at Cambridge. Dunkin was an Oxford man and is remembered as giving 'the first Assize sermon in Launceton after His Majesty's Restoration'.

Of course, Milton scholars around the world and those indefatigable antiquarians in Oxfordshire and Cornwall must give us more facts about Robert Dunkin. Did he ever go to Exeter to consult with his bishop? Did he visit Hall in the Tower? Did he at one time travel on the continent? Does his record at Wadham College promise a learned career? Is Dunkin's Assize sermon extant?[22] Did he write anything else? Did Archbisop Laud from the Tower, after consultation with his fellow prisoner Joseph Hall, command the *Modest Confutation*, this being the reason for its careful anonymity?

The Confutant never revealed himself, for his job had been done. The world is thankful that his strike with the word 'bordello' brought forth the famous account of Milton's early reading of the poets who taught him to be himself 'a true Poeme' (I, 890ff.).

When we can agree that indeed Robert Dunkin was the author, what else could be gained besides the fact that the very process of attempting identification should make us read the *Modest Confutation* as carefully as we have read the *Animadversions* and the *Apology*? It would explain why Milton was confused as to the identity of the author: the manner is not as gentle as that of Hall, and yet too clever to be that of a mere youth. It would explain why Milton became so angry: before he had attained much confidence in his 'left hand', he had had his own words, not merely his arguments, thrown back at him by a man ten years his senior, wittier and more deft than he. It would identify the person who has given us a rare and valuable character-sketch of Hall at a climactic period in Hall's life. It would identify the earliest allusions we possess to Hall's valuable *Occasional Meditations* (1630–33). Finally, it would solve the puzzle in John Walker's notice of Robert Dunkin: 'He published some things against Milton.'

I have argued the late Professor Parker's suggestion that the Confutant was the Reverend Robert Dunkin. Until documentary proof either for or against Dunkin's candidacy comes to light, or until a different hypothesis explains more of the historical and literary facts than this one does, the case rests. Although we cannot *prove* that Dunkin was the 'Modest Confutant', at least we have strengthened the proposition that Joseph Hall was not. It remains for us to make three observations on the parts Joseph Hall and John Milton played in this drama, concerning prose style, logic and the temper of argument.

Few will disagree with the following description of Milton's sentence-structure by the eminent Miltonist Don M. Wolfe:

[Milton's] prose is like a hard pine log full of knots and unexpected twirls, rarely straight and smooth and easy to follow. Milton almost never strikes off a simple declarative sentence ... If Milton's diction has a tough, muscular quality communicating consistently the burning images of his many-faceted mind, his sentences, with exceptions of memorable beauty, are so bulky, cumbersome, and complex as to require often many readings for full comprehension.[23]

On the other hand, Milton complained of Joseph Hall as 'one who makes sentences by the Statute, as if all above three inches long were confiscat' (I, 873). Joseph Hall temporarily lost the ecclesiastical and political argument, but artistically he was marching with the history of English prose style, anticipating that of Dryden, whereas Milton was not.

As for logic, Milton's argument is vitiated by his dependence on syllogisms whose major premises are patently false. Not *all* Anglican priests were ignorant, libertine and 'Papistical'. The record of Anglican learning speaks so eloquently for itself that we hardly need Hall's admittedly partisan view. In his *Humble Remonstrance* he says that if some of our bishops are foul, it is our shame; even among twelve there was one Judas. 'Yet,' he continues, 'upon a just sway it will be found that not one clergy in the whole Christian world yields so many eminent scholars, learned preachers, grave, holy, and accomplished divines as this Church of England doth at this day' (Wynter, IX, 294). Milton's response to this, in full, is: 'Ha, ha, ha' (I, 726). Also, Anglican priests were not agents of the Pope. They shared with the Roman church an episcopal form of polity and the use of liturgy; but Hall preferred government by bishops as historically English, whereas Presbyterianism was newly brought in from overseas; and all his life be believed in the use of both formal and extemporaneous prayer. Milton's method of answering at length quoted fragments from Hall's pamphlets hardly lends itself to sustained reasoning. His argument frequently shows inconsistency,[24] and consistency, one would like to think, is as necessary in a single argument as in a man's whole life, if he himself is to be a 'true poem'. Hall was an Anglican of moderate Calvinistic beliefs for the last sixty years of his life, whereas the 'Puritan' Milton, in a later reversal, pronounced your 'new Presbyter' to be your 'Old Priest writ large', and finally became as Arminian in theology as many an Anglican intellectual.

Overshadowing Milton's often obscure prose and shaky logic, finally, is the bad temper he showed in the controversy with the person he took to be Hall. Peevishness is a sign of being out of control. It cannot be justified on grounds of 'my-opponent-hit-me-first' or of clever rhetorical shafts of 'grim laughter'. Even the most ardent Miltonists comment on it; typical is this observation by Frederick L. Taft: 'What is revealed . . . is not always pleasant; sharp sarcasm, bitter wrangling, unreasoning and even indecent vituperation, pettiness – all these aspects of Milton are made clear.'[25] Despite the noble passages of autobiography, perhaps Milton would have to plead guilty to Matthew Arnold's strictures made in a different context: 'This fatal self-righteousness, grounded on a false conceit of knowledge, makes comprehension impossible; because it takes for granted the possession of truth, and the power of deciding how others violate it; and this is a position of superiority, and suits conquest rather than comprehension.'[26]

Beneath the surface, personal reasons may have led Milton to become so angry with Hall as to forget his logic and his manners. Though he married Mary Powell in June 1642, he was far from attaining a firm marriage and the beginnings of a family. Joseph Hall, by contrast, was well established in reputation and profession, and in house as well as home. Hall had been born in humble surroundings and was now a bishop; Milton, born of a rich father, had been acclaimed in Italy as a poet but now in England was private tutor to a group of boys including his two nephews. He was earning his own living without the protection of church or crown; but though he had once thought himself destined for a position in the Anglican church, he was perhaps put off by his early Puritan teacher, Thomas Young.[27] Hall had sucessfully resisted the Presbyterianism of his boyhood tutor, Anthony Gilby, to become famous as a moderate Anglican and a bishop at that. Both Haller and Parker cite Milton's lack of standing in 1641–2.[28] Little known in England before his divorce tracts, Milton needed to slay a Goliath; he brandished rhetorical swords but drew no blood. In this argument he became angry, sarcastic and spiteful.

By contrast, Hall's temper is revealed in the following autobiographical passage: 'Methinks controversy is not right in my way to heaven, however the importunity of an adversary may force me to fetch it in. If truth, oppressed by an erroneous teacher, cry like a ravished virgin for my aid, I betray it if I relieve it not; when I have done, I return gladly to these paths of peace' (Wynter, I, 400) – that is, writing his meditations on the scriptures. In 1653, after Hammond and others had recklessly promoted the Laudian views of episcopacy, 'the Puritan saint of Kidderminster', Richard Baxter, must have had Joseph Hall in mind when he described

[the first of] two sorts of Episcopal men, who differed from each other, more than the moderate sort differed from the Presbyterian. The one was the old common moderate sort, who were commonly in Doctrine Calvinists, and took Episcopacy to be necessary *ad bene esse Ministerii & Ecclesiae* . . . . The other sort followe *Dr H. Hammond* and (for ought we know) were very new, and very few: Their Judgment was that all the Texts of Scripture which speak of Presbyters do mean Bishops.[29]

Ten years later, after the Restoration, Thomas Ken in *Ichabod: or Five Groans of the Church* deplored the disappearance of moderation in ecclesiastical matters: 'Devout Taylor,' he wrote, 'thou didst urge pathetically; . . . solid Sanderson, thou didst state clearly; holy Usher and Hall, you did offer moderately, heartily, and learnedly. But who, O ye Worthies, believed your report? Who would hear you? Who was convinced by you?'[30]

Though speculating on what might have happened is a pleasant and inconclusive game, the question arises why, when in the previous century Hooker had staked out firm grounds in expediency rather than in God's decree for the English way of governing her church and clothing her priests, the whole business had to be raised again, this time in hot words, bad logic and human blood? Much of the Smectymnuan controversy seems to echo the arguments of seventy years before between Archbishop Whitgift and the Puritan Thomas Cartwright. If King James had not been so affronted by his Scottish clergy's insistence that the church is forever above the state, he would not have been so adamant, from his ill-conducted Hampton Court Conference (1604) forward, on 'the divine right of kings'. James, England's Solomon, propounded the theory in his speeches and books from King Solomon himself: 'Where the word of a king *is, there is* power: and who may say unto him, What doest thou?' (Ecclesiastes 8:4). Charles, on the other hand, left the theorizing to others, including Bossuet and Salmasius, but acted on it throughout his reign, with tragic consequence.[31] Had royal father and son in their different ways not been so insistent on that score, Laud would not have needed to invent, and England might not have become divided. What Stuart monarch ever did understand English ways? These are the 'what-ifs' of history.

The facts are that the Civil War happened, and both Hall and Milton played parts in it.[32] Though Hall may have been blind, with many others, to the growing forces of democracy in church and state, he deplored revolution as political heresy; he threw his creative energy into arguing the 'ancient rights' of king and Apostolic Church. Unlike Milton, in this war of words he used his *right* hand; and though his efforts against Smectymnuus are no more literature than Milton's anti-prelatical tracts, as history turned out both men were half right and half wrong. Monarchy was restored and the Church of England re-established, but Parliament was ever to be above the divine right of kings, and 'prelatry', with its privileges, courts and pluralities, had to come to an end.

In view of Hall's life-long admiration for King James I, it would appear that he was buttressing the church by allegiance to the court. Dedicating the 1615 edition of his collected works to King James, he had written: 'As Kings are to the World, so are good Kings to the Church: None can be so blind, or envious, as not to graunt, that the whole Church of God upon earth, rests her-selfe principally (next to her stay above) upon your Majesties royal supportation.' If there was a weakness in Hall's character, as well as in his argument on episcopacy, it was in his reliance upon the principle of *de jure divino*, a reliance that he must have felt he owed personally to the personal rule of James I. No other capable moderate – like Bedell, Ward or Usher – had come under such close sway, and Laud knew this. Hall was pressed twice by Laud to speak, and then twice pressed by events to defend his speech. In all other things he depended upon the historic strength of Anglicanism (forfeited, it seems, under Laud) to bend, to accommodate, to give, to persuade. Hall sought peace with the French, German, Dutch and Scottish Protestants, despite his disagreement with many of their doctrinal beliefs. On the other hand, he did not hide his dislike of the quasi-Arminianism of Montagu and of the high-church uniformitarianism of his archbishop, and yet he defended Montagu against the fears of the Puritan segment of the Church of England, and dutifully collaborated with Laud in producing *Episcopacie by Divine Right*. And in contrast to his praise of James, he is strangely silent on Charles I.

In Bishop Ken's words, Hall did argue 'moderately, heartily, and learnedly' even in the Smectymnuan affair. After doing his best, he silently left the five authors to themselves, and did not defend his contributions to English literature against the savage jibes of the sixth author who joined them anonymously. Hall never mentions Milton's name, though he joined the chorus of shock at the *Divorce Tracts*. Had he lived to read *Paradise Lost*, he would have welcomed it, with the rest of the world, as being far above – in beauty, majesty and doctrine – the poems of his 'renowmned Spenser' and 'divine du Bartas'.

Recognizing the Smectymnuan hand in the personal attack on his sixty-seven-year-old friend, the 'Modest Confuter' (Robert Dunkin?) has given us an eloquent portrait of Hall at the point in his life when Hall had been released from prison and was translated by Charles I from the bishopric of Exeter to that of Norwich. The portrait is so rare and valuable that it must be quoted in full as an appropriate end to this chapter.

> Let me for ever be shut out of that heaven, that is the reward of such black calumny, such malitious and divellish slanders! And, O you my dear brethren, who are disaffected towards the Prelate, look upon and give evidence to the man! How is he an enemy to the truth, unlesse the Gospel of Christ be a lye? How is he a false Prophet, unlesse your selves who professe the same faith be imposters? View well that heap of age and reverence, and

say whether that clear and healthfull constitution, those fresh cheeks and quick eyes, that round tongue, agile hand, nimble invention, stay'd delivery, quiet calm and happy bosome, be the effects of threescore yeers surfeits and gluttony. What time could he steal to bestow upon Mammon, the God of this world, who hath given us so large an account of his idlest minutes? whose whole life hath been nothing but a laborious search after humane and divine truths, which having pickt out, (as that little miracle of nature doth honey) from weeds and flowers, he did not improper to himself, but liberally dealt them to the good of the publike; his toyl being impleasanted to himself, in that he loved the work he went about; and accepted of the world, because they knew he dished out nothing to them, but what he tasted of himself; penned nothing but what first he practised. How could he be lazie and idle, whose volumes are so many, whose preaching so frequent, whose studies so early and late; so that it is onely questionable whether his lips did drink in more grace than they distilled? I commend not, but vindicate. Must he be therefore luke warm, because his zeal burns not as hot as hell? must his conscience be therefore cauterized and feared, because he brands not every Christian out of the Church of England with the marks of reprobation? writes not the dreadful doom of God in the forehead of all Popishly given, in France, Spain, Italy, Germany? Sends not all Russian, Abassine, Grecian, Armenian, Ethiopick Churches, which all the day have flown different wayes, and laboriously cull'd (with the Bee) such sweets as they could light upon, in the evening swarming to hell; or presently sets not fire on their hives? Alas! how long hath this been the doctrine of the Church of England? and I cannot yet belleve it. Shall I ever think, with that foolish Anchorite, that the Sun shines no where but into my Cell? Or can I not enough enjoy and blesse God for the warmth of his great light, unlesse I consequently affirm that at no time, in no measure it shines beyond our Tropick? Let who will confine the mercies of God in Christ to so narrow limits; I dare not. [D 2 r-v]

10. *Norwich, Sequestration and Last Days*

On 31 July 1641, a committee in Parliament drew up articles of impeachment against twelve of its member-bishops, including Joseph Hall of Exeter. As if in defiance of Parliament's impeachment proceedings, Charles I, on 15 November 1641, translated Hall, on the death of Montagu, to the bishopric of Norwich. Declared guilty of high treason, the twelve bishops were taken to the Tower to join Archbishop Laud on 30 December 1641, subjected on the way to the indignities of the mob. After five months in prison, they were released on 5 May 1642, on bail of £5,000 each.

After making a triumphal visit to Exeter, gathering up his books and papers and saying farewell to as many of his former diocesan charges as he could, Hall travelled to Norwich, where he was welcomed by the High Steward of the cathedral, Thomas Earl of Arundel, as well as by the humblest parishioner. He settled himself, his family and his belongings in the Bishop's Palace eight months after his election, with emoluments amounting to £400 per year.

Norwich was then the second largest city in England, and its cathedral spire (except for Salisbury) the tallest. The thirty-three parish churches within the city walls are filled with relics of Reformation history. St Andrew's, for example, which entombs Bishop Underwood, the local burner of 'heretics' under Queen Mary, has inscribed in stone over the south door these lines:

> This church was builded of timber stone & bricks
> In the yeare of our Lord XV hundred and six
> And lately translated from extreme idolatry
> A thousand five hundred and seven and fourtie
> And in the first year of our noble King Edward
> The Gospel in Parliament was mightily set forward
> Thanks be to God Anno Dom 1517 Decemb.

And again:

> As the good King Josiah being tender of age
> Purged his Realm of all Idolatry
> Even so our noble Queene and Counsell sage
> Set up the Gospell and banisht Popery
> At twenty fower years began she her Reign
> And about forti foure did it Maintain
> Glory be Given to God.

But though the gates were closed to 'Popery', they were left wide open to the 'Sectaries'. By virtue of geography – close to Protestant Holland and far from the civil and ecclesiastical centre of London – East Anglia gathered an amazing variety of minority religions, speaking all the languages of the Reformation. The Brownists, whom Hall had argued with many years before, were plentiful. Besides them were Adamites, Anabaptists, Antinomians, Antisabbatarians. Antitrinitarians, Apollonarists, Apostolics, Arminians, Arians and Atomists (from Mrs Atomy), Barrowists, Behemists, Cerdonians, Divorcers, Enthusiasts, Expectants and Familists; Johnsonists, Marcionites, Millenaries, Pellagians and Perfectionists; Ranters, Sebellians, Sabbatarians, Schwenkefeldians, Seekers, Servetians, Socinians, Soul-Sleepers, Tertullians, Traskists, Valentinians and Vanists – and how many more it is impossible to say.[1] No wonder Elizabeth chose East Anglia as the starting point of her campaign to control them, but to little avail. King James was too indolent or too local in his own theories of ecclesiology to do much about the situation; but as the Church of England under Laud became more insistent upon national uniformity, efforts at control became stricter and consequent rebellion stronger. Laud sent Richard Corbett of Christ Church, Oxford, to Norwich to see what he could do, but Corbett's addiction to verse and drinking bouts with his chaplain Dr Lushington must have raised 'antiprelatical' horror. When Corbett died in 1635, Laud, on a visitation to the troubled diocese, determined that it needed a stronger bishop. His appointee, Matthew Wren, was so strict in applying uniformitarianism that he almost raised a rebellion among a large segment of the population, whose zeal was being fanned by the effective pen of William Prynne. So, in 1638, Laud translated Wren to Ely and sent the scholarly Richard Montagu to Norwich.

From the Nonconformists' point of view, Bishop Montagu was even worse, for in addition to being strict in ceremonies he was suspected of harbouring a theology that smacked of Arminianism. Within two years of his 'rule', a mob made up of Presbyterians, disaffected Independents and no doubt some protesting low-church Anglicans, threatened Norwich ˙Cathedral, as we learn from the following title-page:

> *True News from Norwich: Being a certain Relation how that the Cathedral Blades of Norwich . . . did put themselves into a posture of defense, because that the Apprentices of Norwich (as they imagined) would have pulled down their Organs. In which Relation the foolishness of these Cathedral men are to be understood, and deserve to be laughed at for this silly enterprise there being no such cause to move them thereunto. 1641.*

Ready to fight 'the rebellious Puritans, as they term'd them', the pamphlet says, about five hundred 'cathedral blades' (note the class distinction) formed a protective ring around the cathedral. 'Oh how they loathe to part with their Diana's, their Altars, Images, Crucifixes, Coapes, Surplices, and Romish vestments,' the pamphlet continues. In this very year, 1641, a public-minded bookseller in London brought out an irenic masterpiece entitled *Religio Medici*, by a prominent member of St Peter Mancroft Church in Norwich, but it was at first read by the wrong people. The Commons introduced a Bill condemning Richard Montagu, but the bishop died before any action could be taken.

The three high-Anglican bishops who directly preceded him, averaging less than three years in office, having utterly failed, the 'moderate' Joseph Hall became Bishop of Norwich. His great skill in diplomacy by person and by pen made him the man for the place. Aware of the difficulties that lay ahead, nevertheless an optimist by faith, Hall must have looked forward to serving his new and challenging diocese. Since a great part of it consists of waterways, and a canal once led from the Bishop's Palace to the water-gate on the River Wensum, he could even visit many of the parishes in the bishop's barge. This would include the two largest parishes outside Norwich, St Margaret's in Lynn and St Nicholas's in Yarmouth.

But such was not to be. In April 1643, commissioners arrived at the Palace to put into effect the Act of Sequestration. Since Hall had been released from the Tower in May 1642, he was an effective Bishop of Norwich for less than one year. After being evicted, it was difficult for him to sustain his faith in the 'specialities of Providence'. This we can see in *Hard Measure*, a continuation of the autobiography he had begun in the Tower. Though he gives in detail the insolences and difficulties he and his family were subjected to, nothing in the sad account compares in feeling to his description of the actual desecration of Norwich

Cathedral, which, having barely escaped under Bishop Montagu, was now his proud charge:

> It is no other than tragical to relate the carriage of that furious sacrilege whereof our eyes and ears were the sad witnesses, under the authority and presence of Linsey, Toftes the sheriff, and Greenwood. Lord, what work was here! what clattering of glasses, what beating down of walls! what tearing up of monuments! what pulling down of seats! what wrestling out of irons and brass from the windows and graves! what defacing of arms! what demolishing of curious stonework, that had not any representation in the world but only of the cost of the founder and skill of the mason! what tooting and piping upon the destroyed organ-pipes! what a hideous triumph on the market-day before all the country, when, in a kind of sacrilegious and profane procession, all the organ-pipes, vestments, both copes and surplices, together with the leaden cross which had been newly sawn down from over the Greenyard pulpit, and the service-books and singing-books that could be had, were carried to the fire in the public market-place; a lewd wretch walking before the train in his cope trailing in the dirt, with a service-book in his hand, imitating in an impious scorn the tune, usurping the words of the litany used formerly in the church. Near the public cross all these monuments of idolatry must be sacrificed to the fire; not without much os-tentation of a zealous joy, in discharging ordnance, to the cost of some who professed how much they had longed to see that day. Neither was it any news, upon this guild-day, to have the cathedral open on all sides, to be filled with musketeers, waiting for the major's return; drinking and tobacconing as freely as if it had turned alehouse. [I, lxvii – viii]

The Parliamentary forces tore everything out of the interior of the cathedral, including all but one of the beautifully painted chantries, leaving today only empty Norman arches. Meanwhile, in Hall's birthplace, Ashby-de-la-Zouch in Leicestershire, Parliamentary engineers with gunpowder reduced Hall's childhood vision of Lord Hastings's splendid Ashby Castle to ruins. After reading *Hard Measure*, one cannot agree with William Haller's estimate, written, to be sure, of a younger Joseph Hall: 'Steeped in Seneca's smooth and engaging moralizings, he shows how easily a prosperous man could compound Calvinism and Stoicism into the theory that all was for the best in the best of all possible worlds.'[2]

Ejected from the Bishop's Palace and garden adjacent to the cathedral, Joseph Hall, aided financially by a few neighbours, rented a house in Heigham, about one mile south-west of the centre of town. Today one goes there on Old Palace Road towards the ancient and well-known public house called The Dolphin. One tradition says that this was actually the bishop's home, and hence the name of the street on which it stands. But another, I think stronger, tradition places his house, a much smaller one, as having once stood on the opposite side of

Old Palace Road nearer the church of St Bartholomew's, where every Sunday he ministered. From this more modest 'Bishop's Palace', he had to watch his Anglican ministers one by one deprived of their livings, and Presbyterians or Independents assigned to their pulpits.

On 26 August 1646 there appeared in London a pamphlet entitled *Vox Populi, or The Peoples Cry against the Clergy, Containing the Rise, Progress, and Ruine of Norwich Remonstrance*. Written when only ten of Norwich's parish churches still held Anglican services, the tract accuses eight of their ministers of conspiring with the Mayor to suppress freedom of worship. In particular, a 'Romish' Mr Thornback, for exhorting his congregation to stamp out any other form of worship, 'deserves to be cut in pieces and his house to be made a Jaques'. The charges were almost immediately answered in *Vox Norwici: or, The Cry of Norwich, vindicating their Ministers . . . from the foule and false aspersions and slanders, which are unchristianly throwne upon them in a lying and scurrilous Libell, lately come forth, intituled, Vox Populi . . .* (London, 1646). The faithful communicants assert that their ministers do not fail to preach against sin, 'except only to Recusants and Separatists that never frequent our Congregations'. In the margin is printed the reason for their absence: 'they are in Mrs Ashwell's chamber'. That the Anglican ministers are not carnall or want only richer preferments is argued by a 'character' of each one; it is interesting that almost all of them had resisted the arbitrary encroachments of Bishop Wren.

> Master Carter [for example, of St Peter Mancroft] ever groned under Prelatical ceremonies . . . declaimed against them bitterly, both publikely and privately, and because his conscience would not suffer him to yield to their trash, he was unmercifully persecuted by Bishop Wrenn, and his Chancellour, suspended, deprived and molested: So he was forced to leave Norfolke, and seeke hiding places, he suffered with joy the spoyling of his goods, and counted exile a Paradice, only to be free from the base trash of Prelates. [1646, p. 15].

This is written by Anglicans. The Reverend Mr Carter is here spoken of as again preaching in St Peter Mancroft, and the person responsible for his restitution was probably Bishop Joseph Hall. The pamphlet is signed by fifteen members of the congregation, Dr Thomas Browne's signature being third from the top.

Although Hall had occupied the Bishop's Palace in Norwich for less than a year, nevertheless, living in retirement at Heigham for the thirteen years remaining to him, he still considered himself in all his acts as 'JN' (*Josephus Norvicensis*) or 'J. H. D.D. B.N.' (Joseph Hall, D.D., Bishop of Norwich). The plaque in the cathedral today that names its past bishops includes Hall as bishop from 1642 to his death in 1656. The next bishop, Edward Reynolds, was consecrated in 1661.

During his retirement he continued preaching and writing and even performing one of his best-loved episcopal functions, 'the imposition of hands'. Among those he ordained at Heigham, in defiance of Westminster, was Gipson Lucas, 'an Esquire of good estate, a great Commissioner, and Justice of the Peace in the County of Suffolk'.[3] Another was Simon Patrick, later Bishop of Ely, who in his post-Restoration autobiography gives us a hint as to why he sought out this old moderate Calvinist within the Church of England: 'Hearing a rigid sermon about reprobation of the greatest part of mankind, I remember well that when I was a little boy, I resolved if that were true, I would never marry; because most, if not all my children, might be damned.'[4] He describes the scene that took place in Bishop Hall's study in Heigham on 5 April 1654: 'There we were received with great kindness by that rev. old Bishop, who examined us and gave us many good exhortations.'

Most of the energy left to him after his eviction, however, Hall expended in his life-long consecration to writing. In addition to a few posthumous works, including *Hard Measure*, gathered by a friend in 1660 under the nice title of *The Shaking of the Olive Tree*, and a few letters considered important enough at the time to be made public either by himself or by others, he published the following works during his retirement:

1. *The lawfulness and unlawfulnes of an Oath or Covenant, set down in short propositions agreeable to the law of God and men, and may serve to rectifie the conscience of any reasonable man* ... (Dedicated to Charles I), Oxford, 1643.
2. *The Breathing of the Devout Soul* ..., London, 1643.
3. *The Peace-Maker; Laying forth the Right Way of Peace in Matters of Religion*, London, 1645.
4. *The Remedy of Discontentment; or, a Treatise of Contentation in whatsoever condition; fit for these sad and troubled times*, London, 1645. (A fourth edition was published in 1684.)
5. *The Balme of Gilead: or conforts for the distressed both moral and divine*, London, 1646. (Further editions appeared in 1655 and 1660).
6. *Christ Mystical: or, the blessed union of Christ and his Members* ... by *J.H.D.D.B.N.* [1647].
7. *Satan's Fiery Darts Quenched, or, Temptations Repelled.* By J.H.D.D.B.N., London, 1647.
8. *Select Thoughts, one century* ..., London, 1648.
9. *Pax Terris suasore et nuntio Jos. Hallo, ecclesiase Norvicensis servo*, London, 1648.
10. [Gk *Cherothesia*] *or, the Apostolique institution of imposition of hands, for confirmation, revised. By a lover of peace* [1649].

11. *Resolutions and Decisions of divers practical Cases of Conscience, in continuall use amongst men, very necessary for their information and direction. In foure decades. By J.H.D.D.B.N.*, London, 1649.
12. *Susurrium cum Deo . . .*, London, 1651.
13. *The great Mysterie of Godlines, laid forth by way of affectuous and feeling meditation . . .*, London, 1652. (Another edition in 1659.)
14. *Holy Raptures: or, Pathetical Meditations of the Love of Christ . . .*, London, 1653.

I have already shown why in his writing Hall had long since abandoned his brilliant beginnings in imaginative literature. A glance at this list shows also that he has ceased to be polemicist. His writing in retirement, some of the works 400 or 500 pages in length, shows two main trends. The first and more important is that of meditation, which was discussed in earlier chapters as his life-long preoccupation; six of the works mentioned above may be classified as 'soul-meditations'. The second trend is 'practical theology' or 'cases of conscience' (both terms being preferable to 'casuistry'). It became Hall's final contribution to a significant and peculiarly seventeenth-century genre.[5]

As one dips into seventeenth-century casuistry, consisting of thousands of cases dealt with in minute, often quibbling detail, it is easy to make fun of the whole enterprise, as some dismiss the theology of the Middle Ages by asking how many angels can dance on the point of a pin. At times casuistry appears to be a method of justifying sin, like the case Pascal in his sixth *Provincial Letter* found amusing: when can a religious escape excommunication for leaving off his habit? Answer: when he commits a burglary or enters a brothel, for detection under these circumstances would bring obloquy upon his order.[6] Again, one's conscience has to do with obeying or not obeying a law of God or a law of man (as in Hall's first title quoted just now). In any particular case we can be (a) right, or (b) wrong; and either (a) certain, or (b) doubting. Such neat correlatives and antitheses inspired me to compose the following:

On the Parallel between Seventeenth-Century Casuistry and the Heroic Couplet
> O might my Conscience flow like thine, O Priest,
> And grant Salvation, or some Sleep at least:
> Not Sure and Wrong; nor Doubting yet with Light;
> Never unable to decide; but always Sure and Right.

But man's conscience is a serious matter. Starting with the Jesuits (Bellarmine, Escobar) as a guide to confessional, then taken up by the Puritans (Perkins, Ames), and finally by the Anglicans (Hall, Taylor), a theology of cases of conscience embraced every one who at some time during his life had to take or else reject an oath. As Bishop of Exeter, Hall had never administered Laud's 'Etc.–Oath' of 1640, apparently making an exception to a law with a good conscience for himself and the clerics in his diocese. After sequestration, then, he began his serious thinking of casuistry (in the best sense of the word) with the first bibliographical item mentioned above, on oath-taking; and carried it forward in Item No. 11. For each of the religious groups – Catholics, Puritans and Anglicans (in that order) – casuistry came into being in times of persecution when most people (like us, not made of the stuff of martyrdom) had to survive under the powers that were.[7] First, the Jesuits were harried out of various countries but survived; next, the Puritans successfully and 'God-fearingly' resisted Laudian conformity; and finally, Hall's book on casuistry and the greatest Anglican contribution to the genre, Jeremy Taylor's *Ductor Dubitantium* (1660), were both written during the hardships suffered by Anglicans under the Protectorate and Commonwealth. As religious toleration gradually obtained, casuistry as a 'science' came to an end. A political and sometimes a religious counterpart, however, has come into being in our time for millions of conscientious people subjected to compulsory military service, enemy occupation and dictatorship.

In his book on casuistry Hall did not attempt to match the Jesuits or the Puritans in their exhaustive probings. He includes only forty of 'the most common and practical cases' divided into four 'decades': (1) of profit and traffic, (2) of life and liberty, (3) of piety and religion, and (4) of matrimony. It is obvious why, after living through the times he did, and after having to make the decisions as bishop that he did, he should direct his mind to the various laws that governed his actions and the justified or unjustified exceptions to those laws. Less obvious is why he chose these particular four categories and why he placed them in that order. Again, in a kind of neo-classical *concors* of balanced correlatives and antitheses he attempts to resolve the *discordia* each man is faced with. His stance is not that of the psychological theologian but of the practical religious counsellor. The first two categories have to do with 'Man', and the last two with 'God'. Under 'Man', the first is subsumed under the second, for if man's right to life and liberty is guarded by law, to what extent and under what circumstances can he extend that liberty to live by extortionate prices and usury? In a parallel but chiastic way, under God the fourth segment is subsumed under the third, for if we are enjoined to obey God's laws, do any extenuating circumstances permit us to dissolve a marriage 'made in heaven'? Jesus Christ said, 'Whosoever shall put away his wife, saving for the cause of fornication, causeth her to commit adultery' (Matthew 5 : 32). What if husband and wife are mentally and spiritually incompatible as Milton had argued back in 1644? Thus in the section on 'Matrimonial Cases' Hall seems to glance at his former opponent in a sentence which, despite Milton's twitting him on Senecan brevity, is more than 'three inches long':

> I have heard too much of, and once saw a licentious pamphlet thrown abroad in these lawless times, in the defense and encouragement of divorces ... to be arbitrarily given by the disliking husband to his displeasing and unquiet wife: upon this ground, principally, that marriage was instituted for the help and comfort of man; where, therefore, the match proves such as that the wife doth but pull down a side, and by her innate peevishness, and either sullen or pettish and froward disposition, brings rather discomfort to her husband; the end of marriage being hereby frustrate, why should it not, saith he, be in the husband's power, after some unprevailing means of reclamation attempted, to procure his own peace by casting off this clog; and to provide for his own peace and contentment in a fitter match? [VII, 371]

Hall admits this pamphlet is 'well penned' – he could recognize good writing and close argument – but he cannot understand how a Christian could have written it. He himself was married only once, and that for thirty-nine years. His wife died at Heigham in 1652.

Still preaching and writing, when he was not engaged in his own daily meditations, Hall weakened in his eighty-second year, and died on 8 September 1656.[8] In the words of the anonymous editor of *The Shaking of the Olive Tree*, he died '... after his prevailing infirmities had wasted all the strength of nature, and the Arts of his learned and excellent physician Dr Brown of Norwich (to whom under God, we and the whole Church are engaged for many Years preserving his life as a blessing to us)'.[9] Dr Browne has left this estimate of him: 'My Honord freind Bishop Joseph Hall ... was buryed at Heigham, where hee hath his monument, who in the Rebellious times, when the Revenues of the church were alienated, retired unto that suburbian parish, and there ended his dayes: being above four-score yeares of age. A person of singular humility, patience, and pietie: his owne works are the best monument, and character of himself ...'[10]

Bishop Hall had wished for the simplest kind of tomb, but his executors – Peregrine Pond, Margaret Hatley and Edward Camplin[11] – perhaps yielding to the demands of the faithful few, erected for him in St Bartholomew's Church in Heigham a horrendous emblem of *ars moriendi*: a full-scale human skeleton, gilded, on black marble, holding in his bony hands two legal documents. The antiquary Anthony Norris thus described it in the 1730s:

> Against the South Side of the Chancel is a Mural Monument on which is painted a Skeleton, holding in his Right Hand a parchment Deed, having a

Seal of the Arms of Hall hanging by a label to the Bottom of it, on the parchment is wrote Debemus Morti Nos Nostraque. In his Left Hand he holds a Cancelled Deed with the Seal torn of, in which is wrote Persolvit et Quietus Est [.] On the background behind the Skeleton [:] Obiit 8 Sep: Anno Aerae Xtianae 1656. Aet: Suae 82.[12]

Beneath the skeleton were the words 'JOSEPHUS HALLUS olim humilis Ecclesiae Servus', and towards the top of the monument were the arms of Joseph Hall, the three talbots on a sable shield; above that a bishop's mitre. The whole rested on a slab of black marble on which were carved the three mitres of the arms of the see of Norwich.

Bizarre though the design for this tomb may be to us, it makes some sense to readers of one of Bishop Hall's own *Occasional Meditations* written almost fifty years before. In No. XCIII, 'Vpon a cancelled Bond', using the two deeds as emblems, he speaks of his own death and of the parchments as a 'monument':

> VVhiles this obligation was in force, I was in servitude to my parchment; my bond was double, to a payment, to a penalty; now, that is discharged, what is it better then a waste scrole; regarded for nothing but the witnesse of its owne voydance, and nullity. No otherwise is it with the severe Law of my Creator; Out of Christ it stands in full force, and bindes me over either to perfect obedience, which I cannot possibly performe, or to exquisite torment, and eternall Death, which I am never able to indure; But now, that my Saviour hath fastened it cancelled to his crosse (in respect of the rigour & malediction of it) I looke upon it as the monument of my past danger and bondage: I know by it, how much was owed by mee, how much is payed for mee; The direction of it, is everlasting, the obligation (by it) unto death is frustrate: I am free from curse, who never can be free from obedience. O Saviour, take thou glory and give me peace. [Text: 1633]

On 30 September 1656, the Reverend John Whitefoot preached the commemorative sermon in St Peter Mancroft on the text 'And the time drew nigh that Israel must die' (Genesis 47:29). Though the actual funeral lacked certain 'ceremonies of deserved honour (which his own humility and the envy of the times denied him)', the preacher said, 'yet doth he not want ... *a good name*' (1657 edn, p. 78). 'He was noted for a singular Wit from his Youth: a most acute Rhetorician, and an Elegant Poet; He understood many Tongues, and in the Rhetorick of his owne, he was second to none that lived in his time.'[13] Recalling the recent hard measures, the preacher concluded, 'All men honoured the Doctor, though some loved not the Bishop.'

Among the soul-meditations he wrote after retiring, in 1651 appeared *Susurrium cum Deo, Soliloquies: or Holy Self-Conferences of the Devout Soul, upon sundry choice Occasions, with Humble Addresses to the Throne of Grace.* The book contains a new portrait, engraved the year before, of the old bishop in his robes, the heavy Dort gold medal hanging on his breast, his white spade-shaped beard pushed forward by the Elizabethan ruff, and a *round* cap on his head (the *square* cap was Laudian). Behind his right shoulder is a bookshelf lined with folios, and over his left shoulder his own coat of arms impaled with those of the see of Norwich. At the bottom are engraved these lines:

> This picture represents the Forme, where dwells
> A Minde, which nothing but that Mind excells.
> There's Wisedome, Learning, Witt: there Grace & Love
> Rule over all the rest: enough to prove,
> Against the froward Conscience of this Time,
> The Reverend name of BISHOP is no Crime.

In 1942 the section of Norwich where St Bartholomew's Church once held Bishop Hall's tomb was heavily bombed and the church ruined. Its shaky walls were razed in 1953 as a precautionary measure, leaving only the broken tower as a monument. At the same time, all the graves in the churchyard were moved elsewhere. Today a large block of cement beside the skeleton church-tower is inscribed: 'To the Glory of God and in memory of Bishop Hall.'

Notes

1. Beginnings

1 I am happy to express in this first note my gratitude to Dr O. B. Harbison and the Trustees of the Folger Library in Washington, D.C., for granting me a generous Fellowship in the spring and summer of 1970 for a project that was loosely entitled 'To begin a book on Bishop Joseph Hall'.

2 W. and J. Hextall, *The History and Description of Ashby-de-la-Zouch* (1852); N. Carlisle, *Endowed Grammar Schools* (1818), I, 742ff.; Levi Fox, *A Country Grammar School: A History of Ashby-de-la-Zouch Grammar School through Four Centuries, 1567 to 1967* (Oxford, 1967). Another famous graduate of the school was William Lilly, 'the Christian Astrologer'.

3 All quotations of the writings of Hall where the flavour of contemporary spelling and punctuation seems unimportant will be from the ten-volume modernized edition of Philip Wynter (Oxford, 1863), reprinted by AMS in 1969, the references by volume and page parenthetically incorporated.

4 cf. E. S. Schuckburgh, *History of Emmanuel College* (Cambridge, 1904); M. M. Knappen, *Tudor Puritanism* (Chicago, 1939), ch. XXVI.

5 Objecting to this provision, Charles I on 5 May 1627 suspended Emmanuel's statutes, but the grandson of its founder had them reinstated by furnishing several new benefices to the college (*Calendar of State Papers, Domestic, 1627–8*, p. 165).

6 Gordon Rupp, *William Bedell, 1571–1642* (Cambridge, 1971), p. 112.

7 Michael Grant, *Cambridge Illustrated* (London, 1966), p. 112.

8 The following anecdote has been attached to several divines, but George Lewis, *A Life of Joseph Hall, D.D.* (London, 1886), p. 32, tells it of Lawrence Chaderton. At one place, having preached for two hours, he said he would stop, fearing to tire his listeners; but the congregation cried out, 'For God's sake, Sir, go on, we beg you, go on!' Accordingly he went on for another hour.

9 cf. Wilbur S. Howell, *Logic and Rhetoric in England, 1500–1700* (Princeton, N.J., 1956), and Perry Miller, *The New England Mind* (Cambridge, Mass., 1954).

10 See the amusing account of James's visit, during which Emmanuel College, fearing the kind of royal drunkenness displayed at Oxford, refused to deck itself out, in D. H. Willson, *King James VI and I* (London, 1956), ch. XVI.

11 *Poems*, ed. J. A. W. Bennett and H. R. Trevor-Roper (Oxford, 1955), 'A Certaine Poeme . . .', p. 13.
12 *Lives*, ed. S. B. Carter (London, 1951), 'Sir Henry Wotton', p. 107.
13 *Acquisition Catalogue* (1915), p. 6: 'Statutes granted to Emmanuel College', etc. ff. 1–50.
14 *The Collected Poems of Joseph Hall*, ed. A. Davenport (Liverpool, 1949), p. 4.
15 Thomas Fuller, *The History of the Worthies of England* (London, 1662), 'Leicester-shire', p. 129.
16 Eugene E. White, 'Master Holdsworth and "A Knowledge Very Useful and Necessary" ', *Quarterly Journal of Speech*, LIII (1967), pp. 1–16.
17 *Ludus Literarius* (London, 1612).

2. *The Satirist in English Verse and Latin Prose*

1 My thanks go to my colleague and friend Ejner Jensen for giving an early version of this chapter his usual critical reading.
2 John Nichols, *Literary Anecdotes of the Eighteenth Century* (London, 1812–16), V, p. 654: Pope gave West a copy of *Virgidemiae*, telling him that 'he esteemed them the best poetry and truest satires in the English language, and that he had an intention of modernizing them, as he had done some of Dr Donne's'. cf. *The Works of Bishop Joseph Hall*, ed. Peter Hall (Oxford, 1837), XII, p. 137: 'Bp Warburton told Mr Warton that in a copy of Hall's satires, in the library of Mr Pope, the whole of the First Satire in the Sixth Book was either corrected in the margin, or interlined; and that Pope had written at the top, *Optima Satira*.' cf. Sir John Hawkins, *The Life of Samuel Johnson, LL.D.*, ed. C. H. Davis (New York, 1961), p. 74: 'So little was he [Pope] used to that kind of reading [in old authors], that, as himself confessed, he had never heard of the Virgidemiarum of Bishop Hall, a collection of the wittiest and most pointed satires in our language, till it was shewn to him, and that so late in his life, that he could only express his approbation of it by a wish that he had seen it sooner.'
3 Full reprint of Warton's *History* (1778 and 1781) in one volume (New York, n.d.), pp. 954–5.
4 *Palladis Tamia*, ed. D. C. Allen (New York, 1938), p. 283v.
5 A. Davenport (ed.), *The Collected Poems of Joseph Hall*, (Liverpool, 1949). All my quotations of Hall's satires will be from this text, the references incorporated by number of 'Book', number of 'Satyre', and number of page. I am indebted to the late Professor Davenport's erudite notes, and my present point of departure is the following modest disclaimer in his introduction: 'The purpose of this edition is not to discuss the literary qualities of *Virgidemiae*' (p. xxv). I have attempted just this.
6 'Satura and Satire', *Classical Philology*, VIII (1913), p. 192.
7 Hall's *Poems*, ed. Davenport, Appendix, p. 282.
8 cf. Arnold Stein, 'Donne's Obscurity and the Elizabethan Tradition', *English Literary History*, XIII (1946), pp. 98–118.
9 cf. Harold O. White, *Plagiarism and Imitation During the English Renaissance* (Cambridge, Mass., 1935), pp. 120–21.

10 *English Literature in the Sixteenth Century* (Oxford, 1954), p. 471.
11 *Poetices* (1581), III, p. 98 (Davenport's edn, p. 160).
12 For some of the adverse effects of enclosure when Hall was writing, see R. H. Tawney, *The Agrarian Problem in the Sixteenth Century* (London and New York, 1912), pp. 234ff.
13 The quoted phrase comes from John Peter, *Complaint and Satire in Early English Literature* (Oxford, 1956), p. 127.
14 On this point, cf. Jacques Perret, *Horace*, trans. Bertha Humez (New York, 1964), p. 43, where he scores those who mistakenly on historical grounds 'identify' Furius with a real person, whereas Furius is an artistically created character. I argue the same principle in my article 'On the Persons in Dryden's *Essay of Dramatic Poesy*', *MLN*, LXIII (1948), pp. 88–95, reprinted in *Essential Articles for the Study of John Dryden*, ed. H. T. Swedenberg, Jr (1966), pp. 83–90.
15 Davenport has complete bibliographical references to all these attempted 'identifications'.
16 The order from the *Stationers' Register* (Arber, III, 677–8) is reproduced by Davenport, p. 293.
17 Edwin H. Miller, *The Professional Writer in Elizabethan England* (Cambridge, Mass., 1959), p. 196. See also the accounts of this 1599 censorship order in Charles Edmonds, 'Destruction of Books at Stationers' Hall in the Year 1599', *N & Q*, 3rd series, XII, 436, 30 Nov. 1867; G. B. Harrison, *The Elizabethan Journals* (3 vols. in 1, London, 1938), III, 333; and John Peter, pp. 148–152 (see note 13 above).
18 E. A. Petherick, '*Mundus Alter et Idem*', *Gentlemen's Magazine*, CCLXXI (1896), pp. 66–87.
19 *The Discovery of a New World* (*Mundus Alter et Idem*), ed. Huntington Brown (Cambridge, Mass., 1937), pp. 142–3. Further quotations from Healy will incorporate references to this edition.
20 'Renaissance Influences in Hall's *Mundus Alter et Idem*', *Philological Quarterly*, VI (1927), pp. 321–34.
21 The satire against the Roman church comes, pointedly, in 'Fooliana'. cf. Claude Lacassagne, 'Le Satire Religieuse dans *Mundus Alter et Idem* de Joseph Hall (1605)', *Récherches Anglaises et Nord-Americaines* ('Ranam'), II (1972). Cf. the article on *Mundus* by Ian Laurenson in *La Trobe Library Journal* (Melbourne), V (1977), pp. 45–52.

3. *The Cambridge Parnassus Plays, John Marston and Hawstead, Suffolk*

1 The genesis of this chapter was my lecture at the Clark Memorial Library, Los Angeles, in 1972, which appeared in *Illustrious Evidence: Approaches to English Literature of the Early Seventeenth Century*, ed. Earl Miner (Los Angeles, Cal., 1975), pp. 3–32. The material is re-used by permission.
2 W. D. Macray (ed.), *The Pilgrimage to Parnassus with the Two Parts of the*

Return from Parnassus: Three Comedies performed in St. John's College Cambridge A.D. MDXCVII–MDCI (Oxford, 1886).

3 J. B. Leishman (ed.), *The Three Parnassus Plays, 1598–1601* (London, 1949), Introduction, pp. 26–34; cf. Marjorie L. Reyburn, 'New Facts and Theories about the Parnassus Plays'. *Publications of the Modern Language Association*, LXXIV (1959), pp. 325–35.

4 Leishman, p. 135. All quotations from the plays will be from this edition and the references hereafter incorporated.

5 John Weaver actually celebrated his native Cheshire river in *The Life and Death of Sir John Oldcastle, knight* [1601] (Roxburgh Club, 1873), p. 221. Oldcastle speaks:

> Through many bywaies, many countries fle[d,]
> In midst of Cheshire now I am on a river,
> By more crookt winding which her curr [ent led,]
> Then I had gone by wayes; her name the W [eev] er;
> On whose prowde banke such entertaine I had,
> As longer, if I might, I would haue staid.

6 Leishman, Introduction, p. 54.

7 All my quotations from Hall's *Virgidemiae* are from A. Davenport's edition, *The Collected Poems of Joseph Hall* (Liverpool, 1949). The references will come within my text. Here I omit textual italics in order to underscore verbal similarities.

8 Introduction, p. xviii, n. 1.

9 A. B. Grosart (ed.), *The Complete Poems of Joseph Hall* (Manchester, 1875), Introduction, pp. xxii–vi; A. H. Bullen (ed.), *The Works of John Marston*, 3 vols. (Boston, Mass., 1887), I, pp. ixx, xx.

10 Hall's *Poems*, Introduction, p. xxviii.

11 Anthony Caputi, *John Marston, Satirist* (Ithaca, N.Y., 1961), p. 35. cf. Arnold Stein, 'The Second English Satirist', *Modern Language Review* XXXVIII (1943), pp. 273–5.

12 See full documentation in Davenport, p. 263; and Caputi, pp. 34–5.

13 All my quotations of Marston are from A. Davenport's edition of *The Poems of John Marston* (Liverpool, 1961), the references again incorporated in my text. It is fortunate that a single editor of Davenport's ability should have edited both these satirists and thus have been able to 'spot' parallels more knowledgeably than anyone else.

14 Assuming that all three plays had been written by 1598, though the performance of the last play is recorded as later. For the exact chronology, see Leishman, Introduction, p. 26.

15 cf. *O.E.D.*: 'ivory-palm' refers to the nut of a palm (called also 'vegetable-palm') used for making an expensive glossy paper. Hall visualizes the slopes of Mount Sion covered with sheets of such paper, on which is printed 'religious' poetry so bad as to be tantamount to blasphemy.

16 See Philip J. Finkelpearl, *John Marston of the Middle Temple* (Cambridge, Mass., 1969), p. 90.

17 The problem of Hall's 'lost Pastorals' was invented by J. P. Collier (*Bridgewater Catalogue* (London, 1887), pp. 139); expanded by Thomas Corser (*Collectanea Anglo-Poetica*, VII (1887), p. 134); also by A. H. Bullen (*Works of John Marston*, III (1887), 286, n. 1). Davenport says that '[Hall's *Pastorals*] have not survived' (Hall's *Poems*, Introduction, p. xvii).

18 *Historical Manuscripts Commission, Twelfth Report, Appendix, Part I: The Manuscripts of Earl Cowper, K. G. Preserved at Melbourne Hall, Derbyshire*, vol. I (London, 1881), p. 19.

19 *The Returne from Parnassus*, second part, was assigned in the *Stationers' Register* on 16 October 1605, to Owen Gwynn, Fellow of St John's College and cousin to Richard Vaughan, Bishop of London from 1604 to 1607. See Miss Reyburn's article cited in note 3 above.

20 'Apology against a Pamphlet', [The Yale] *Complete Prose Works*, ed. Frederick L. Taft, I (1953), 868–953. This quotation comes from pp. 881–2. Details of the Hall–Milton 'quarrel' will come in Chapter 9.

21 ibid., pp. 887–8.

22 Hawstead Rectory was demolished in 1852; a picture of what it once looked like appears in the Roxburgh edition of Hall's *The King's Prophecy*.

23 In a sense the role of a great satirist requires that he outgrow it. For this reason Hall is superior as a satirical poet to Marston (or to any other candidate for the authorship of the Parnassan plays), although even Marston became ordained. cf. Hallett Smith, *Elizabethan Poetry* (Cambridge, Mass., 1952), p. 242; and Ejner Jensen, 'Hall and Marston: the Role of the Satirist', *Satire Newsletter*, IV, No. 2 (1967), pp. 72–83.

4. *Waltham, King James as Solomon* and Characters of Vertues and Vices

1 Rudolf Kirk (ed.), *Heauen vpon Earth and Characters of Vertues and Vices* (New Brunswick, N.J., 1948). Hereafter my quotations of these two texts will be from this edition, the page references incorporated.

2 I am strengthened in this opinion by H. Fisch's article, 'The Limits of Hall's Senecanism', *Proceedings of the Leeds Philosophical Society*, vol. VI (1950).

3 See Epistle I, ix, 'To Sir Robert Drury and His Lady, Concerning my removal from them' (Wynter, VI, 155). Hall probably went to London in June 1607, for he signs his prefatory letter to the publication of his metaphrased *Psalms* 3 July [1607] from Nonesuch, where Prince Henry had his court (cf. Davenport, Hall's *Poems*, 1949, pp. 128 and 272). The year 1607 also marked the departure of his Emmanuel College friend and neighbour, William Bedell, from Bury St Edmunds to Venice. Hall evidently served at Waltham for a full year before officially resigning from Hawstead. George Lewis, *A Life of Joseph Hall* (London, 1886), p. 108, cites from the Hawstead parish register: 'July 4, 1608 – Ezekiel Edgar, Clericus ... Roberti Drury Mil.: Vacan. per resignationem ult. incumb.' The last incumbent, of course, was Joseph Hall. I have not seen the register. For the £100 emolument at Waltham, see Jones, *Life of Joseph Hall* (1826), p. 44; and Davenport, p. xxi, n. 2.

4 E. C. Baldwin, 'The Relation of the English "Character" to its Greek Prototype', *Publications of The Modern Language Association*, XVIII (1903), pp. 412–24. Almost all we know about the 'character' lies in two books, both published by Harvard University Press in 1947: *The Theophrastan Character in England to 1642* by Benjamine Boyce, and *A Bibliography of the Theophrastan Character in England* by Chester Noyes Greenough. A recent and excellent estimate of Hall's *Characters* is Gerhard Müller-Schwefe (Tübingen), 'Joseph Hall's *Characters of Vertues and Vices*: Notes Toward a Revaluation', *Texas Studies in Language and Literature*, XIV (1972). pp. 235–51.

5 *Literary Bypaths of the Renaissance* (New Haven, Conn., 1924), p. 6. Sister Mary Tumasz connected the seventeenth-century 'Character' to the medieval and Renaissance emblem-literature (unpub. M.A. thesis, Catholic University, Washington, D.C., 1953).

6 Wendell Clausen, 'The Beginnings of English Character-Writing in the Early Seventeenth Century', *Philological Quarterly*, XXV (1946), pp. 32–45.

7 Richard Aldington, *A Book of Characters* (London & New York, 1924), p. 9.

8 Mark Pattison, *Isaac Casaubon, 1559–1614* (Oxford, 1892), p. 264. In 1608, the year after Hall joined the royal household as Prince Henry's part-time chaplain, Archbishop Bancroft gave King James a copy of *De Libertate Ecclesiastica*. His Majesty 'had been so delighted with it, that for many days he could talk of nothing but Casaubon' (ibid., p. 272).

9 One of many witnesses of James's learning, Bishop John Hackett in his *Life of Archbishop John Williams of York* (1693) describes the king's seeking knowledge with the same gusto he evinced while hunting: 'The reading of some books before him was very frequent, while he was at his repast; he collected knowledge by variety of questions which he carved out to the capacity of different persons. Methought his hunting humour was not off, while the learned stood about him at his board; he was ever in chase after some disputable doubt, which he would wind and turn about with the most stabbing objections that ever I heard; and was as pleasant and fellow-like in all these discourses, as with his huntsman in the field' (quoted by Pattison, *Casaubon*, p. 270).

10 James VI, *Basilikon Doron*, ed. James Craigie, The Scottish Text Society, 3rd Series, No. 16 (1944), p. 35.

11 One of the most devastating descriptions of James's character is that by William Harris, *An Historical and Critical Account of the Life and Writings of James I. King of Great Britain. After the Manner of Mr Bayle. Drawn from Original Writers and State-Papers* (2nd edn, London, 1772). In his fondness for fine clothes, King James forgot that Solomon in all his glory could hardly match a lily of the field. Sir John Harrington, in his gossipy *Nugae Antiquae* (ed. Park, 1804, II, 390ff.), quotes a 1611 letter from Lord Thomas Howard telling of James's firing eighteen servants because he did not like the way they were dressed. Again, when a nobleman presented a petition to James mounted on his roan jennet and was told to come back for an answer the next day, James refused it with these words: 'Shall a King give heed to a dirty paper, when a beggar noteth not his guilt stirrops?'

12 William Barlow, *The Summe and Substance* ... [1604], facs. ed. by W. T. Costello, S. J., and C. Keenan, S. J. (Gainsville, Fla., 1965).

13 J. Nicols, *The Progresses* ... *of King James the First* (London, 1828, II, p. 62.

14 ibid., IV, p. 1037.

15 At about the same time, 1608–9, Hall's early companion in patronage, John Donne, became interested in the writings of Solomon, possibly in hope of advancement under James I. Solomon is traditionally supposed to have written the Song of Songs in his youth, Proverbs in middle age, and Ecclesiastes towards the end of his life. Hall, already in favour at court and fairly free in his conscience, emphasizes the Proverbs. Donne, outcast at Mitcham as a result of an earlier profligacy culminating in a romantic but rash marriage, emphasizes Ecclesiastes. Donne's greatest sermon from Ecclesiates was preached at Whitehall before the king after he had at last gained royal favour. cf. Robert Bozanich, 'Donne and Ecclesiastes', *Publications of the Modern Language Association*, XC (March, 1975), pp. 270–75.

16 cf. William Whallon, 'Hebraic Synonymy in Sir Thomas Browne', *English Literary History*, XXVIII (1961), pp. 335–52.

17 Sir Sydney Lee, 'The Beginnings of French Translation from the English', *Transactions of the Bibliographical Society*, VIII, 97–106, quoted by Kirk, p. 55.

18 H. V. Routh, in *CHEL* (1928), IV, 385, says that 'Characters' are supposed to describe action and that Hall's are inferior because they often portray a state of mind. Perhaps the fact that many of Hall's *Characters* are psychological or inward shows that they are more Christian than Theophrastan: Müller-Schwefe (see note 4 above) notes Hall's description of his characters' bodily movements. In this, Hall's *Characters* and character-writing in general play a part in the development of the novel.

19 *The Overburian Characters*, ed. W. J. Taylor, Percy Reprints, No. 13 (Oxford, 1936), 'What a Character Is', p. 92.

20 The birth-dates of these children and subsequent details are given in George Lewis, *A Life of Joseph Hall* (London, 1886), pp. 426–7.

21 *The History of the Worthies in England* (London, 1662), 'Leicester', p. 130.

22 In the King James version of Proverbs and Ecclesiastes, the words 'wise' and 'wisdom' occur fifty-three times; and the words 'fool', 'foolish', and 'folly' occur fifty times, as many if not more times then they occur in all the other books of the Bible. Thus, since the terms are inseparable from Solomon's ethical philosophy, the sobriquet is inevitable for King James. It is superb. Did Sully invent it?

23 For facts and much of the interpretation here I rely on Per Palme, *Triumph of Peace: A Study of the Whitehall Banqueting-House, Figura*, VIII (Stockholm, 1965), kindly brought to my attention by Nathan Whitman, my colleague at Michigan.

5. *The* Epistles *and Early Controversies*

1 Logan Pearsall Smith (ed.), *The Life and Letters of Sir Henry Wotton*, 2 vols. (Oxford, 1907), I, p. iv.

2 Charles M. Coffin (ed.), *Complete Poetry and Selected Prose*, 'Everyman edition' (New York, 1952), p. 370.
3 Translation by R. M. Gummere, Loeb Classical Library (1952).
4 *English Literature in the Earlier Seventeenth Century, 1600–1660* (Oxford, 1962), p. 205.
5 *Ludus Literarius*, 1612, p. 165.
6 Joseph Jacobs (ed.), *Familiar Letters of James Howell*, 2 vols. (London, 1892), Introduction, 'Authenticity'. cf. the article by V. M. Hirst, *Modern Language Review*, LIV (1959).
7 For Drewrie and Kett, see *DNB*. Within four or five years of Hall's writing this letter, the barbarous executions came to an end. The last two 'heretics' to be burned at the stake, Bartholomew Legate and Edward Wightman, met their fate at Smithfield in 1612.
8 *The Collected Poems of Joseph Hall*, ed. A. Davenport (Liverpool, 1949), Introduction, p. xiv, n. 1.
9 Franklin B. Williams, Jr, 'An Introduction into Initials', *Studies in Bibliography* (Virginia), IX (1957), p. 167.

6. *The Art and Practice of Protestant Meditation*

1 Hall has given us further details of this trip in his epistle (published in 1608) to Sir Thomas Challoner, Chamberlain to Prince Henry (Wynter, VI, 138–43). He was made peculiarly aware of the providences of God by the fact that whenever he travelled abroad he usually arrived at his destination despite unfavourable winds, and always returned despite unconscionable delay or *diarrhoea biliosa*. At the conclusion of his journey with Sir Edmund Bacon, he left the party at Antwerp in order to visit an old friend at Middleburgh in Zealandt – probably the Reverend Jonas Reigesberg (see Hall's epistle to him in Wynter, VI, 303). Intending to rejoin his travelling companions at the appointed time in Flushing, he discovered to his horror that the captain of the vessel, to take advantage of the wind, had left the night before.
2 Text: 1605 [1606], A 4v. All my quotations will be from this text.
3 The year 1606, as the Gunpowder traitors were tried and executed, was the climax of anti-Jesuitism in England. cf. F. L. Huntley, '*Macbeth* and the Background of Jesuitical Equivocation', *Publications of the Modern Language Association*, LXXIX (1964), pp. 390–400.
4 A. Davenport (ed.), *The Collected Poems of Joseph Hall* (Liverpool, 1949), p. 123. As early as 1603 Hall had warned King James against the Jesuits, 'those swarmes of Locusts sent/Hell's cursed off-spring, hyred slaues of Spaine' ('The King's Prophecie', lines 67–8).
5 'Pharisaism and Christianity', Wynter, V, 21. In a marginal note Hall cites an experience he had in 1605 at Winnoxberg in Flanders near Dunkirk; there he witnessed a charitable lady's bequest to a hospital 'cunningly turned to the maintenance of the Jesuits'.
6 Louis L. Martz, *The Paradise Within: Studies in Vaughan, Traherne, and Milton* (New Haven and London, 1964), pp. 22–3. (Quoted by permission.)

7 For a comparison of Hall's *topoi* with those of Thomas Wilson's popular *Rhetoric*, see U. Milo Kaufmann, *The Pilgrim's Progress and Traditions in Puritan Meditation* (New Haven, 1966), pp. 122–4.

8 Louis L. Martz, *The Poetry of Meditation: A Study in English Literature of the Seventeenth Century* (New Haven, 1954, 1962), places Hall in an appendix entitled 'Mauburnus, Hall, and Crashaw: the "Scale of Meditation"'.

9 Hall was even called 'Bernard' by one admirer. The 1625 edition of Hall's *Works* contains a valuable 'Alphabetical Table' by one 'Ro. Lo.'. who promises 'that if God shall lend this Mellifluous Bernard of our Times the time of perfecting his Contemplations', he, 'Ro. Lo.', will continue his 'table'.

10 Étienne Gilson, *The Philosophy of St Bonaventura*, trans. Dom. Illtyd Trethowan and F. J. Sheed (New York, 1938), pp. 96–7. (Quoted by permission.)

11 cf. Anne Louis Masson, *Jean Gerson: sa vie, son temps, ses oeuvres* (Lyon, 1894); and James L. Connoly, *John Gerson: Reformer and Mystic* (Louvain, 1928).

12 Pierre Debongnie, *Jean Mombaer de Bruxelles . . .*, Universitaire de Louvain: Conferences d'Histoire et de Philologie, 2nd series (1928), No. 11, p. 207.

13 cf. Karl Ullmann, *Reformers before the Reformation*, trans. R. Menzies (Edinburgh, 1855), 'The Life of John Wessel', II, 263–615; an authoritative and briefer study is that by Jacques Huijben and Pierre Debongnie, *L'Auteur ou les auteurs de l'imitation* (Louvain, 1957), pp. 111–20.

14 Martz, *The Poetry of Meditation*, p. 331.

15 (Paris, 1932–), columns 1848–51; translation by Sister Emmanuel as *Meditations on the Life of Christ, attributed to St Bonaventura* (St Louis, 1934).

16 *The Poetry of Meditation*, p. 289.

17 I have not seen this book, and until further fascicles of the *Gesamtkatalog der Wiegendrucke* appear must be content with less detailed descriptions. One of the best is in J. E. G. De Montmorency, *Thomas à Kempis: His Age and Book* (London, 1906), p. 131. Hain describes as No. 9103 in *Reportorium Bibliographicum*, II, 121, a copy which he examined in the Hof-und Staatsbibliothek in Munich. Augustin de Backer, *Essai bibliographique sur le livre De Imitatione Christi* (Liège, 1864), No. 40, quotes Hain. The British Museum has a 1518 octavo edition of the same combination, an anonymous *De Imitatione Christi* with *De meditatione cordis ab I. de Gersonne*, printed, significantly enough, in Antwerp (by H. Eckert).

18 Translation by Leo Sherley-Price, (London, 1952, 1954), I, 20, p. 50. Hereafter quotations from this translation will be followed by reference within my text. As an introduction I have found useful Leonard A. Wheatley, *The Story of the 'Imitatio Christi'* (London, 1891).

19 Samuel Kettlewell, *Thomas à Kempis and the Brothers of Common Life* (London, 1887), I, p. 422.

20 While in Antwerp (in 1605), Hall tells us, he watched a procession celebrating St John the Baptist's Day. Since this day comes on 24 June, Hall must have received his inspiration for *The Arte of Divine Meditation* in

June 1605. Antwerp was famous for the largest Puritan-Anglican congregation abroad.

21 De Montmorency (see note 17 above).

22 Hall's *Poems*, ed. Davenport, p. 127.

23 *The Sermons of John Donne*, ed. Evelyn M. Simpson and George R. Potter (Berkeley, 1953–62), VIII, 220. cf. Winifred Schleiner, *The Imagery of John Donne's Sermons* (Providence, 1970), 'The Book of the World' (pp. 94–103) and 'The Eyes of the Soul' (pp. 137–56).

24 Text: *Occasional Meditations* (1631), pp. 266–7.

25 Most of these were gathered in one volume (VIII) by Peter Hall (ed.), *The Works of Bishop Hall* (Oxford, 1837). According to that editor they are 'Meditations and Vowes', 'Holy Observations', 'Holy Raptures', 'Select Thoughts', 'Supernumeraries', 'Breathings of the Devout Soul', 'Susurrium cum Deo', 'The Soul's Farewell to Earth', 'The Great Mystery of Godliness' and 'The Invisible World'.

26 The central position that the Bible held in Hall's theory and practice of meditation is shown by his fondness for the character of Enoch and by one of his strange titles, *Henochismus* ('The Way of Enoch'). Enoch 'walked with God' (Genesis 5:24), and in the fifth and last of his *Supernumeries* (Wynter, VII, 636ff.), Hall fills in the 'steps' of this walk as Enoch 'learned to reconcile the use of the creatures with the fruition of the Creator'. Of the ten 'steps', the first two – (1) 'pious thoughts' and (2) 'heavenly affections' – correspond to the major division of his *Arte*. But the next eight 'steps', all apparently coming under 'heavenly affections' (or will), are different both in substance and order from those in the *Arte*: (3) 'fervent love', (4) 'reverential fear', (5) 'spiritual joy', (6) 'holy desires', (7) 'divine ravishment', (8) 'strict obedience', (9) 'firm resolution', (10) 'endeavours for good'. At least the proportion of space given to heart as against mind is about the same. For the continental background of the Protestant devotions on the Bible, see Terence C. Cave, *Devotional Poetry in France* (Cambridge, 1969), ch. i.

27 *The Soules Farewell to Earth*, 1651, pp. 391–2 (Wynter, VIII, p. 107).

28 I received this idea long ago in a conversation with Father Walter J. Ong, S. J. Peter Ramus (Pierre de la Ramée, killed in the St Bartholomew Massacre in 1562) seems to have anticipated the 'method' of the computer. One is reminded of John Updike's 'Conclusion' of *Midpoint*:

> Praise IBM, that boils the brain's rich stores
> Down to a few electric either/or's.

29 For further evidence of Hall's fame in meditation and a comparison of Hall and other Puritan 'meditators' see Kaufmann (note 7 above), pp. 120–33.

30 Text: 1631, Epigram No. 78 of the 'Third Book'.

31 *The History of the Worthies of England*, ed. P. A. Nuttall (1840), I, p. 566.

32 *Susurrium cum Deo*, 1651, p. 58. My thanks go to Harriet Jameson of the Rare Book Room, University of Michigan Library. Some material from this chapter and the next appeared in F. L. Huntley, 'Bishop Hall and

Protestant Meditation,' *Studies in the Literary Imagination,* Atlanta: Georgia State Univ., X (1977), pp. 57–71.

7. *Hall's* Occasional Meditations *and Imaginative Literature*

1 A sentence like the following on the *Occasional Meditations* spells the general disappointment of the reader of T. F. Kinloch's *The Life and Works of Joseph Hall* (London and New York, 1951): 'We shall begin with them, for they are of no great importance' (p. 80). Ruth Wallerstein, however, bears witness to the rich background of such meditations in *Studies in Seventeenth Century Poetic* (Madison, Wis., 1950), ch. VIII.

2 Rosamund Tuve, *Elizabeth and Metaphysical Imagery* (Chicago, 1947), p. 159; J. A. Mazzeo, 'Metaphysical Poetry and the Poetic of Correspondence', *Journal of The History of Ideas,* XIV (1953), pp. 221–34.

3 Bodley's first librarian, Mr Thomas James, was well known to Hall; see Hall's epistle to him, published in 1608 (Decade IV, No. viii). Hall applauds the librarian's success in showing that 'Papists' falsify the church fathers. Mr James was also instrumental through his 1598 translation of du Vair's *La Philosophie Morale des Stoiques* in acquainting Englishmen with Christian Stoic philosophy, another link between the Bodleian's Mr James and 'the Christian Seneca'. Mr James in 1605 dedicated the first Bodleian Library catalogue to Prince Henry.

4 U. Milo Kaufmann, in *The Pilgrim's Progress and Traditions in Puritan Meditation* (New Haven, 1966), seizes upon this category as the most significant. He notes Bunyan's 'appreciation of a tradition of meditation that, because of its characteristic matter and manner, the Puritan writers uniformly handled under a separate heading. Known as occasional meditation, it was a method of redeeming the manifold occasions of immediate experience and was often concerned with the "creatures" of the natural order as they offered themselves to observation' (p. 175).

5 Kitty Scoular, *Natural Magic* (Oxford, 1965), p. 12; Miss Scoular gives credit, as I do, to H. Fisch's ground-breaking article, 'Bishop Hall's Meditations', *Review of English Studies,* XXV (1949), pp. 210–21. In this article, Fisch pointed out that the *Occasional Meditations* combine aphorism, conceit, exemplum and exegetical gloss in an original way (p. 217).

6 *The Poetical Works of Robert Herrick,* ed. L. C. Martin (Oxford, 1956), p. 64.

7 The Hon Robert Boyle, *Occasional Reflections upon Several Subjects, with a Discourse about such Kind of Thoughts* (Oxford, 1848), p. xiii; it is apparent that Boyle had read beforehand both the *Arte* and the *Occasional Meditations.* Well known is the anecdote of Swift's inserting his own satirical '[Occasional] Meditation upon a Broom-stick' into the volume by Boyle and solemnly reading it aloud to the ladies: 'A *Broomstick* ... is an Emblem of a Tree standing on its Head: and pray what is Man but a topsy-turvy creature?' (*A Tale of a Tub* ..., ed. Herbert Davis (Oxford, 1957), pp. 239–40).

8 Text: 1650, p. 705. Hereafter page references to this text of Baxter will be incorporated.

9 Baxter quotes (p. 809) eight lines from the second day of the first week beginning 'Th'Empyreal Pallace, where th'Eternal Treasures/Of *Nectar* flows', from p. 67 of the 1605 Sylvester. And on p. 815, Baxter quotes ten lines from the seventh day of the first week beginning 'With cloudy cares th'one's muffled up somewhiles', which appear on p. 246 of the 1605 Sylvester.

10 *The Works of George Herbert*, ed. F. E. Hutchinson (Oxford, 1945), p. 172.

11 ibid., p. 131.

12 ibid., pp. 107–9.

13 On the distinctly Protestant tradition of Grace and its impact upon devotional literature, particularly that praising the Creation, see William H. Halewood, *The Poetry of Grace* (New Haven and London, 1970). Although Henri Brémond was once a Jesuit, his exciting studies of prayer and poetry are closer to the spirit of Joseph Hall than to that of St Ignatius. See his massive *Histoire Littéraire du Sentiment Religieux en France*, and more specifically *Prayer and Poetry*, trans. by Algar Thorold (London, 1927).

14 Louis Martz, *The Paradise Within: Studies in Vaughan, Traherne, and Milton* (New Haven and London, 1964), p. 301.

8. *Royal Embassies Abroad, Further Controversy*

1 John Nichols, *The Progresses . . . of King James the First* (London, 1828), III, pp. 390, 421.

2 Since graduation from Emmanuel, Hall evidently had inherited wider pews. In 1605 in the Lowlands he was seen kneeling in church, a posture that a Jesuit took to be a sign that Hall had accepted transubstantiation.

3 A. Davenport (ed.), *The Collected Poems of Joseph Hall* (Liverpool, 1949), pp. 150–52.

4 cf. 'Dort' in Bayle's *Dictionary*. For Dort, the medal, and John Donne, cf. Paul R. Sellin, 'Daniel Heinsius and the Genesis of the Medal Commemorating the Synod of Dort, 1618–19,' *LIAS*, II (1975), pp. 177–185; and 'John Donne: The Poet as Diplomat and Divine,' *HLO*, XXXIX (1976), pp. 267–275.

5 At the 145th session on 20 April 1619. One of the best sources for the English activity at the Synod is the correspondence of Ambassador Sir Dudley Carleton in *The Letters of John Chamberlain*, ed. N. E. McClure, 2 vols. (Philadelphia, 1939). cf. also Thomas Fuller, *The Church History of Britain* ed. J. S. Brewer, 6 vols. (Oxford, 1895), V, pp. 462–79. Anglican polity and liturgy were not unadmired on the continent. Bancroft, then Bishop of London, at the 1604 Hampton Conference, had quoted Sully as saying that 'if the reformed churches in France had the same order, there would have been thousands of protestants more than there are' (Fuller, V, p. 281).

6 Instead of Wynter's edition of Hall's works, for this sermon I am using that of Peter Hall (12 vols., London, 1837–9), XI, 477–87. A note declares: 'Here, for the first time, [the sermon at the Synod of Dort is] included among the works of Bishop Hall. The translation is contributed by a

friend.' The original Latin and the English translation are printed on facing pages.

7 For the various interpretations of Romans 9 which have led to tremendous differences of opinion, see the chapter on 'A Short history of the Idea of Original Sin' in F. L. Huntley, *Jeremy Taylor and the Great Rebellion: A Study of His Mind and Temper in Controversy* (Ann Arbor, Mich., 1970). I believe Hall took Romans 9 : 21, on the potter and the clay, as a metaphor, but stricter Calvinists made it literal.

8 These five points are often simplistically recalled through the mnemonic device of T–U–L–I–P, the national flower of Holland: Total depravity, Unconditional election, Limited atonement, Irresistible grace, and Perseverance of the saints. To many a Christian outside strict Calvinism, the articles seem heavily anti-synergistic.

9 Herbert D. Foster, 'Liberal Calvinism; the Remonstrants at the Synod of Dort in 1618', *Harvard Theological Review*, XVI (1923), pp. 1–37.

10 John Jones, *Memoirs of Bishop Hall* (London, 1826), pp. 91–2. On English Arminianism, cf. Rosalie L. Colie, *Light and Enlightenment: A Study of the Cambridge Platonists and the Dutch Arminians* (Cambridge, 1957); G. R. Cragg, *From Puritanism to the Age of Reason: A Study of Changes in Religious Thought within the Church of England, 1660 to 1700* (Cambridge, 1950); A. W. Harrison, *The Beginnings of Arminianism* (London, 1926).

11 The original of Hall's will, dated 21 July 1654 and amended 28 April 1656, is in the Folger Library, Washington, D. C. Wynter prints it in Vol. I. According to an article in *Emmanuel College Magazine*, XXX (1935/6), pp. 13–18, the medal passed to Hall's daughter Ann Weld, whose granddaughter, Mary Starkey, became the mother of William Jermy of Corpus Christi College, Cambridge, and later of Bayfield, Norfolk. He bequeathed the medal to Emmanuel College at his death in 1752. My thanks go to Dr Graham Pollard, Curator of Coins and Medals at the Fitzwilliam Museum, and to his assistant, Dr Volk, for these references and for allowing me to examine the medal closely at first hand.

12 See the descriptions of the medal by the eighteenth-century numismatist George Vertue, *Notebooks*, Vol. IV (Oxford, 1936), p. 155; and in *Medallic Illustrations of British History* (London, 1885), I, p. 222.

13 Generally, seventeenth-century Anglican apologetics rested on (1) Scripture, shared with all Protestants; (2) tradition, shared with Roman Catholics; and (3) individual reason. Anglicans applied reason and tradition to Scripture *vis-à-vis* the sectarians; they used reason and Scripture when arguing about tradition with the Roman Catholics.

14 *Animadversions*, ed. Rudolf Kirk. [The Yale] *Complete Prose of John Milton* (New Haven, 1953), I, p. 734.

9. *The Bishop of Exeter, John Milton, and the 'Modest Confutant'*

1 W. G. Hoskins, 'Exeter in the Seventeenth Century: Tax and Rate Assessments, 1602–1699', *The Devon and Cornwall Record Society*, n.s., Vol. II (1957).
2 *A Catalogue of the Archiepiscopal Mss.* (London, 1812), p. 94, in the Lambeth Palace Library.
3 For Nansogge's bilingual lampoon on his bishop, see Davenport's edition of Hall's *Poems*, p. xxxiii, n. 2.
4 From Hall's will.
5 Ethel Lega-Weeks, 'Some Studies in the Topography of the Close, Exeter', *Devon and Cornwall Notes and Queries*, VII, pt ii (1915), p. 139.
6 Hall's own words in his will.
7 *Transactions of the Devonshire Association*, LXXVI (1944), pp. 35–6.
8 The dates come from J. Milton French, *The Life Records of John Milton* (New Brunswick, N.J., 1950), Vol. II.
9 All of Hall's pieces (Nos. 1, 2, 6 and 8) are available in Wynter's Vol. IX of Hall's *Complete Works*; and all of Milton's (Nos. 3, 4, 9 and 11) in Vol. I of the Yale edition of *Complete Prose Works of John Milton* (1953). Hereafter my quotations of Hall and Milton will be from these collections. respectively. The Smectymnuan papers (Nos. 5 and 7) are harder to come by, though the University of Michigan owns first editions (1641) of both works. The anonymous pamphlet defending Hall (No. 10) is reproduced in facsimile in W. R. Parker's *Milton's Contemporary Reputation* (1940), pp. 120ff. I am grateful, again, to John Huntley for his helpful criticism of this part of my chapter; and especially to Arthur Barker for conversations concerning it, both vocal and epistolary.
10 Arthur Barker, *Milton and the Puritan Dilemma, 1641–60* (1942); Audrey Chew, *Joseph Hall and John Milton* (1950); Emerson, *Prose Works of John Milton*, ed. Max Patrick (1967); Michael Fixler, *Milton and the Kingdoms of God* (1964); J. Milton French, *The Life Records of John Milton*, Vol. II (1950); J. H. Hanford, *A Milton Handbook* (1927); M. C. Jochums, *John Milton's 'Apology'* (1950); David Masson, *The Life of John Milton* (1875–94), Vol. II; W. R. Parker, *Milton: A Biography*, Vol. I (1968); F. L. Taft, [The Yale] *Prose Works of John Milton*, Vol. I (1953).
11 Edited by Michael Lieb and John T. Shawcross (Amherst, Mass., 1974). See esp. the first two essays, by J. A. Wittreich, Jr, and Michael Lieb, respectively.
12 The texts I use, incorporating references hereafter, are the facsimile of *A Modest Confutation* in W. R. Parker, *Milton's Contemporary Reputation* (Columbus, Ohio, 1940); the *Animadversions* ed Rudolf Kirk and William Baker, and the *Apology* ed. Frederick L. Taft, the two latter works in the Yale *Complete Prose Works of John Milton*, Vol. I (New Haven, 1953).
13 Parker suggests that by 'vomited out' the Confutant probably meant merely 'graduated', but that Milton was conscious of his own rustication.

14 Milton's phrase 'untempered cement' (I, p. 711) refers to Hall's sermon preached before the King at Whitehall on the second Sunday in Lent, 1641, in which Hall pleads for moderation and hopes to bind like the mortar between bricks (*Works*, ed. Wynter, (Oxford, 1863), V, p. 517.)

15 The page numbers are unaccountably off by one; otherwise the Confutant's quotations are accurate.

16 J. A. Wittreich, Jr (*Achievements of the Left Hand*, 1974) reads the same texts I do, but comes to directly opposite conclusions. I say the Confutant gets his tone and playhouse-image from Milton. Of the *Apology*, Wittreich says, 'Through abusive rhetoric adopted from *A Modest Confutation*, Milton exposes the misguided arguments and foul character of his opponent ... ' (p. 22). Again, 'In refutation (and this is essentially what *An Apology* ... is) the orator's style is not determined by him but is dictated by the one his opponent used ... hence he adopts a *persona* that matches the character of his opponent' (p. 23). It is Milton's original *persona* in the *Animadversions*.

17 The occasion was Hall's argument in 1619 in favour of clerical marriage; Hall twits the English priest on his 'virginity' (*Works*, ed. Wynter, VII, pp. 497ff.).

18 ibid., IX, p. 388.

19 Parker notes (*Milton's Contemporary Reputation*, p. 268): 'The much-discussed reference to Milton's seeking "a rich Widow" [the Confutant mentions her twice] was probably a blind thrust, although it may have been an indirect hit at Stephen Marshall [the SM of Smectymnuus], who had, in fact, married a rich widow.'

20 cf. the devastating review by Ernest Sirluck of Jochum's edition of the *Apology* (Urbana, Ill., 1950) in *Modern Philology*, L (1952–3), pp. 201–5.

21 In the *Second Defence* Milton summarized his quarrel of more than a decade before with two 'Bishops of particularly high repute': 'I replied to one of the bishops in two books [*Of Prelatical Episcopacy* and *The Reason of Church-Government* – this is Usher], while to the other bishop [Hall] I made reply in *Animadversions* and later in an *Apology*' (Yale *Complete Prose*, IV, part i, pp. 622–3).

22 Clement Boase and W. P. Courtney, *Bibliotheca Cornubiensis* (London, 1874–82), as far as I know, turned Walker's report of the assize sermon into a bibliographical ghost – '*An Assize Sermon at Launceston*, 1661, 4°.'

23 Yale *Milton's Prose*, I, pp. 108–9. Stanley Fish goes more deeply into some of the patterns and their effects in *Self-Consuming Artifacts* (Berkeley, Calif., 1972), pp. 265ff.

24 According to Rudolf Kirk, Yale *Milton's Prose*, I, p. 654.

25 ibid., p. 866. Again (ibid., p. 655) Professor Kirk states: 'We can scarcely condone the language he [Milton] initiated against a good man [Hall].'

26 'Puritanism and the Church of England' in *St Paul and Protestantism* (1887), *Works*, ed. R. H. Super (Ann Arbor, Mich., 1968), VI, pp. 74–5.

27 cf. W. R. Parker, *Milton: A Biography* (1968), I, pp. 151–2.

28 William Haller (ed.), *Prose Tracts in the Puritan Revolution, 1638–1647* App. (1961), Vol. I, pp. B, pp. 129–39; Parker, *Milton's Contemporary Reputation*, p. 12.

29 Matthew Sylvester, *Reliquae Baxterianae* (London, 1696), part ii, p. 149.

30 (London, 1663), p. 29.

31 cf. Godfrey Davies, *The Early Stuarts, 1603–1660* (2nd edn, Oxford, 1959), pp. 31–4.

32 R. W. Ketton-Cremer, in *Norfolk in the Civil War: A Portrait of a Society in Conflict* (London, 1969), has two chapters on Hall's temper and actions during the war.

10. *Norwich, Sequestration and Last Days*

1 Variety of sects, of course, is the key-note; some of these named came in earlier and some later than Hall's actual residence in Norfolk. The list could be extended from such works as *A Relation of Several Heresies* (1646), Thomas Edwards's *Gangraena* (1646), Alexander Ross's *A View of All Religions of the World* (1653), J. H. Blunt's *Dictionary of Sects, Heresies . . .* (1874), Robert Barclay's *The Inner Life of the Religious Societies of the Commonwealth* (3rd edn, 1879).

2 *The Rise of Puritanism* (New York, 1938), pp. 327–8.

3 Anonymous preface to Hall's *The Shaking of the Olive Tree*, 1660, A 3 v.

4 Simon Patrick, 'A Brief Account of My Life', *Works*, ed. A. Taylor (London, 1858), IX, pp. 5–6.

5 Casuistry is treated in W. K. Jordan, *The Development of Religious Toleration in England*, 4 vols. (1932–40); H. R. McAdoo, *The Structure of Caroline Moral Theology* (1949); Thomas Wood, *English Casuistical Divinity during the Seventeenth Century* (1952); and G. L. Mosse, *The Holy Pretence* (1957). I highly recommend two recent books: Elliott Rose, *Cases of Conscience: Alternatives open to Recusants and Puritans under Elizabeth I and James I* (Cambridge, 1975); and Dwight Cathcart, *Doubting Conscience: Donne and the Poetry of Moral Argument* (Ann Arbor, Mich., 1975).

6 Cited by Cathcart, *Doubting Conscience*, p. 58. Donne's 'The Flea' is one example of casuistry; under certain circumstances one can make an exception to the law forbidding fornication.

7 Rose (see note 5 above) treats the subject broadly from this very human point of view. Incidentally, Hall's book on casuistry was finished at Heigham, the author says, on '27 Mar. 1650', and is introduced fulsomely by John Downame. At the end, Hall repeats that he had been urged to continue it but that he defers to a much more compendious work by the late Ralph Cudworth which he hopes Cudworth's son, the great 'Cambridge Platonist' and antagonist of Hobbes's ethical theories, will publish. Both Dr Ralph Cudworths, father and son, had been Fellows at Emmanuel College.

8 Fortunately unaware of an event that took place a month later, on 24 October 1656. One James Naylor – looking by the shape of his beard and hair like the pictures of Jesus Christ; his women followers kneeling before him and kissing his feet; adherents singing hosannahs and crying, 'Holy,

Holy, Holy' – made his triumphal entry into Bristol in the rain. Parliament condemned him to be publicly flogged, branded on the forehead with "B" for blasphemy, and his tongue bored through. The sentence was carried out.

9 Ed. 1660, A 2 v.

10 "Reportorium', *The Works of Sir Thomas Browne*, ed. Sir Geoffrey Keynes (Chicago, 1964), III, p. 134.

11 Named as such in Hall's will.

12 This and a great deal of other information was kindly communicated to me by Mr Frank Sayer, County Local Studies Librarian in the City of Norwich. Descriptions of the tomb are also given in Blomefield's *History of Norfolk* (2nd edn, 1806), III, p. 580; W. Rye, *The Parish of Heigham* (1917); and Edmund Farrar, *Church Heraldry of Norfolk*, Vol. III (1893). An incompetently drawn picture of the tomb appeared on the cover of *Fisher's Norwich and Eastern Counties' Almanac for 1916*.

13 John Whitefoot, *Death's Alarum, or, the Passage of Approaching Death* (2nd edn, London, 1657), p. 61. Wynter reprints the sermon in Vol. I. The same preacher in the same church (St Peter Mancroft), twenty-six years later, preached the funeral sermon for Sir Thomas Browne.

Index

Bacon, Francis, Viscount St Albans (1561–1626), and identity of Hall's 'bad poet', 23; Yelverton succeeds, 58; titles of his essays, 64; and Hall's *Meditations and Vowes,* 71, 72; and biblical manna metaphor, 84; and Hall's essays, 94; Milton and, 125; Confutant familiar with, 126

Baker, William, 159

Balcanquel, Walter (*c.*1586–1645), 108

Baldwin, E. C., 48, 151

Bancroft, Richard, Archbishop (1544–1610), 5, 24, 151, 157

Barclay, Robert, 161

Barker, Arthur, 119, 159

Barlow, William, Bishop (d.1568), 51, 152

Barneveldt, Jan van Olden (1547–1619), 108

Bartas, Guillaume de Salluste de (1544–90), 18, 37, 91, 100, 133

Baxter, Richard (1615–91), 99–101, 131, 156, 157

Bayle, Pierre, 157

Bedell, William (1571–1642), Master of Trinity College, Dublin, 4; chaplain in Venice, 6, 27; gift to Emmanuel College, 7; rector of Bury St Edmunds, 44, 150; and Hall's letter to Mole, 65; Hall's letter to, 66; *A Protestant Memorial,* 73; a moderate, 133

Bellarmine, Robert, St., (1542–1621), 141

Bennett, J. A. W., 147

Bernard, St (1090–1153), 63, 75, 77, 80

Bible, Hampton Court Conference, 5; King James version, 51; style of poetic parts of Old Testament, 55; seventeenth century belief in, 56; influence on Hall's *Characters,* 56; and Hall's view of meditation, 73, 155; and *Arte of Divine Meditation,* 81; meditation and the Psalms, 82–3; its importance to Protestants, 85; its influence on Hall's style, 89, 91, 95; word incidence in Proverbs and Ecclesiastes, 152; interpretations of 9th chapter of Romans, 158

Blomefield, Francis, 162

Blunt, J. H., 161

Boase, Clement, 160

Bodenham, John (*fl.* 1600), 29

Bonaventure, St. (1221–74), 75, 77, 80

Bossuet, Jacques Bénigne (1627–1704), 132

Boyce, Benjamin, 151

Boyle, Robert (1627–91), 99

Bozanich, Robert, 152

Bradshaw, William (1571–1618), 3

Braithwaite, Richard (*c.*1588–1673), 48

Brémond, Henri, 157

Greville, Sir Fulke, 1st Baron Brooke (1554–1628), 58
Grosart, A. B., 33, 149
Grotius, Hugo (1583–1645), 108, 126
Guilpin, Edward, 18, 24, 25, 39
Gummere, R. M., 153
Gwynne, Owen, 42, 150

Hackett, John, Bishop, 151
Hain, 154
Hales, John (1584–1656), 108
Halewood, William H., 157
Hall, Ann, *later* Mrs Weld, *daughter*, 59, 110, 158
Hall, Edward, *son*, 126
Hall, Elizabeth, *née* Wynniff, *wife* (d.1652), 44, 143
Hall, George, *son* (1612–68), 59, 117
Hall, John, *father* (d.1608), 2, 3, 4, 66
Hall, Joseph, Bishop (1574–1656), *see also* Works of Joseph Hall; vii;
    Sterne on, viii; literary output, 1; childhood background, 1, 2; at-
    titude to religious belief, 2, 3; on his mother, 2–3; on Gilby, 3; his
    education, 3–4; and Wadsworth's 'perversion' to Rome, 6; and
    Order Book of Emmanuel library, 7; commemorative poem to
    Whitaker, 7; Fuller on, 7–8; rhetorician, 8, 70; receives degrees,
    8; preface to *Ludus Literarius*, 8; and Marston, 25, 26, 31, 33,
    35–41; and authorship of second *Return from Parnassus*, 31–3,
    35–43, 45; and 'Kinsayder' epigram, 33–4; his popularity at
    Cambridge, 42; at Hawstead, 44, 46, 47, 52, 71, 73, 110, 150; his
    meagre salary, 44, 46; rector of Waltham, 47, 58, 59, 60, 93, 150;
    chaplain to Prince Henry, 47–8, 52; and James I, 51–2, 57, 60,
    108–9, 132–3; his soubriquet, 57; his patrons, 58; laments mis-
    education of noblemen, 58–9; personal life, 59, 66; personal
    characteristics, 62, 66; with mission to Low Countries, 72, 153,
    154; Herrick's poem to, 99; sent to France, 102; ill-health, 102,
    105, 108, 109, 153; dean of Worcester, 102; and Scottish confor-
    mity with Church of England, 102–3; and Synod of Dort, 104,
    105–7, 109; Dort gold medal, 109–10, 145, 158; preacher, 110;
    and bishopric of Gloucester, 111; on schism with Rome, 112; and
    Rome as visible church, 113–14; Bishop of Exeter, 115, 117, 142;
    letter to Commons, 116; coat of arms, 116–17, 144, 145; and
    Laud, 117; Burton attacks, Cholmley defends, 118; and prelatical
    controversy, 118; and authorship of *A Modest Confutation*, 119,
    129; defended in *Confutation*, 119–24 *passim*; in Tower, 125, 129,
    135; and Milton, 130, 133, 143; established in reputation and
    profession, 131; on controversy, 131; Ken on, 132, 133; and Civil

War, 132; Bishop of Norwich, 133, 135, 137–9; 'modest Confuter' on, 133–4; impeached, 135; and Act of Sequestration, 137; on desecration of Norwich Cathedral, 138; in retirement, 140; and casuistry, 141, 142, 161; death of, 143; his tomb, 143–4, 145; and St. Bernard, 154

meditation: 'occasional', 72; interest stimulated by visit to Low Countries, 72–3; and 'Protestant' tradition, 73–4; defined, 74, 89; method, 74–5; sources of his theory of, 75–81; 'Book of the Creatures', 81–4, 91–3; 'Book of Scriptures', 81–4, 86, 87; 'Book of the Soul', 81–4, 85, 87; metaphors in 'reading' of God, 84; 'art' of, 88; his contribution to, 88; his belief in Christians' ability to learn, 89; his style, 89; his reputation as writer of, 89; his works on, 90; meditational writings in retirement, 141; Bible in his theory and practice of, 155

satirist: in English verse, 8; in Latin prose, 10, 26–8, 42; Warton's evaluation of, 10–11; his definition and philosophy of satire, 11–12; stylistic mannerisms, 12–13; neologisms, 13–14; paraphrased, 14, 15–16; heroic couplet, 17, 21; title for his satires, 17, 19; his purpose, 17, 19; willow metaphor, 18, 19; subjects of *Toothless Satires*, 19–20; subjects of *Byting Satires*, 20–21; differences between Volumes One and Two, 21–2; concealment of identity, 22–4; *Virgidemiarum* proscribed, 24–6; his stature as, 150

writer: dramatist, 29; to become a serious writer, 44–5; classical influences, 46; Christian philosophy, 46–7; character writing, 48; publishes his epistles, 61, 62–7; early controversies, 67–70; impact on seventeenth century literary minds, 99–101; autobiographer, 125

Hall, Joseph, *son* (1607–69), 59
Hall, Peter, 27, 147, 155, 157
Hall, Robert, *son* (1605–67), 59, 93, 94, 117, 125
Hall, Samuel, *son* (1616–74), 59, 117
Hall, Winifride, *mother*, 2–3
Haller, William, 131, 138, 161
Hammond, Henry (1605–60), 131
Hanford, J. H., 119, 159
Harbison, O. B., 146
Harington, Sir John (1561–1612), 51, 63, 67, 151
Harris, William (1720–70), 151
Harrison, A. W., 158
Harrison, G. B., 148
Harvard, John (1607–38), 5
Harvey, Gabriel (*c.*1550–1630), 23, 24, 33

Hutchinson, F. E., 157

Ignatius of Loyola, St (1491–1556), and Hall's view of meditation, 73, 74; writes down system of meditation, 76; *Spiritual Exercises*, 77, 87, 90; *Compositio loci*, 96; question of influence on Herbert, 101
Independents, 137, 139
Ingram, William, 18

Jacobs, Joseph, 65, 153
James I of England, VI of Scotland, King (1566–1625), vii; Hall and, 2, 51–2, 53, 57, 60, 89, 91, 110, 111, 132–3; Hampton Court Conference, 5; visits Emmanuel College, 5, 6, 146; *Essayes of a Prentice*, 37; Hudson's dedication to, 37; accession, 44; and Hay, 48; and character writing, 49; and Casaubon, 49; *Basilikon Doron*, 49–50, 53, 151; his identification with Solomon, 50, 51–2; his personality, 50, 104; funeral sermon for, 52; at meal-times, 53; translated into French, 57; and Earl, 58; his soubriquet, 60, 152; and Whitehall Palace, 60; his policy, 67; and Louis XIII, 102; his mission to Scotland, 102; and celebration of feast-days, 104; and Synod of Dort, 104–5, 107, 109; Hall on, 107, 108–9, 115; and Hall's *Via Media*, 111–12; death of, 115; and Hall's coat of arms, 117; and divine right, 132; and minority religions, 136; and *De Libertate Ecclesiastica*, 151; Archbishop Williams on, 151; his fondness of finery, 151; and Donne, 152
James, Thomas (c.1573–1629), 156
Jameson, Harriet, 155–6
Jebb, Sir Richard (1841–1905), 48
Jensen, Ejner, 147, 150
Jermy, William, *great-great-grandson*, 158
Jerome, St (c.342–420), 63
Jesus Christ, 91, 142
Jochums, M. C., 119, 126, 159, 160
John the Apostle, St, 46
Jones, John (c.1766–1827), 1, 150, 158
Jonson, Ben (1572–1637), and second *Return from Parnassus*, 42; and character writing, 48; and Hall, 101; and Drummond, 104; Confutant and, 126
Jordan, W. K., 161
Junius, Franciscus (François du Jon; 1589–1677), 126
Juvenal (c.55–c.140), 10, 11, 16, 22, 126

Kaufman, U. Milo, 154, 155, 156
Keenan, C., S.J., 152

Lupton, Donald (d.1676), 48
Luther, Martin (1483–1546), 68–9, 123

McAdoo, H. R., 161
McClure, N. E., 157
Machiavelli, Niccolò di Bernardo dei (1469–1527), 126
Mack, Jesse F., v
Macray, W. D., 30, 31–2, 148
Macrobius (5th century), 126
Markham, Gervase (1568–1637), 37
Marlowe, Christopher (1564–93), 24, 25
Marshal, Stephen (c.1594–1655), 160
Marston, John (1576–1634), 149; and Hall, 11, 12, 25, 26, 31, 33, 35–41, 43, 150; proscribed, 17, 24; 'Kinsayder' epigram, 22, 33–4, 39; and identity of Hall's characters, 23; his books burnt, 25; and *Return from Parnassus*, 31, 35; and Hall's satires, 34; lampooned in Parnassus plays, 34, 38; quotations from, 34–5; and authorship of second *Return from Parnassus*, 35–41; becomes more moderate, 45; his stature as satirist, 150
Martial (c.40–c.104), 22, 24, 116, 126
Martin, L. C., 156
Martz, Louis L., 73–4, 76, 77, 78, 81, 153, 154, 157
Mary, Queen of Scots (1542–87), 2
Mary I, Queen (1516–58), 135
Masson, Anne Louis, 154
Masson, David (1822–1907), 119, 125, 127, 159
Matthews, A. G., 127
Mauburnus, Johannes, 75, 76–7, 78, 89
Maurice, Prince of Orange (1567–1625), 108
Mazzeo, J. A., 156
Melville, Andrew (1545–c.1622), 5
Menzies, R., 154
Meres, Francis (1565–1647), 11, 12
Michigan University, Rackham School of Graduates, vii
Middleton, Thomas (c.1570–1627), 24, 25
Mildmay, Sir Henry (d.c.1664), 58
Mildmay, Sir Walter (c.1520–89), 4–5, 6
Miller, Edwin H., 148
Miller, Perry, 146
Milton, John (1608–74), and *Toothless Satires*, 19; and *Mundus*, 27, 43; and Hall, 43, 68, 114, 130, 160; and contemplation of creatures, 96; and corruption of Anglican bishops, 116; and prelatical controversy, 118, 119; *Animadversions*, 119–25 *passim*, 160; *Apology for*